VOLUME 676

MARCH 2018

THE ANNALS

of The American Academy of Political
and Social Science

Migrant Smuggling as a Collective Strategy and Insurance Policy: Views from the Margins

Special Editors:

SHELDON X. ZHANG
University of Massachusetts, Lowell

GABRIELLA E. SANCHEZ
European University Institute

LUIGI ACHILLI
European University Institute

Los Angeles | London | New Delhi
Singapore | Washington DC | Melbourne

Origin and Purpose. The Academy was organized December 14, 1889, to promote the progress of political and social science, especially through publications and meetings. The Academy does not take sides in controverted questions, but seeks to gather and present reliable information to assist the public in forming an intelligent and accurate judgment.

Meetings. The Academy occasionally holds a meeting in the spring extending over two days.

Publications. THE ANNALS of The American Academy of Political and Social Science is the bimonthly publication of the Academy. Each issue contains articles on some prominent social or political problem, written at the invitation of the editors. These volumes constitute important reference works on the topics with which they deal, and they are extensively cited by authorities throughout the United States and abroad.

Subscriptions. THE ANNALS of The American Academy of Political and Social Science (ISSN 0002-7162) (J295) is published bimonthly—in January, March, May, July, September, and November—by SAGE Publishing, 2455 Teller Road, Thousand Oaks, CA 91320. Periodicals postage paid at Thousand Oaks, California, and at additional mailing offices. POSTMASTER: Send address changes to The Annals of The American Academy of Political and Social Science, c/o SAGE Publishing, 2455 Teller Road, Thousand Oaks, CA 91320. Institutions may subscribe to THE ANNALS at the annual rate: $1129 (clothbound, $1275). Individuals may subscribe to the ANNALS at the annual rate: $126 (clothbound, $185). Single issues of THE ANNALS may be obtained by individuals for $39 each (clothbound, $54). Single issues of THE ANNALS have proven to be excellent supplementary texts for classroom use. Direct inquiries regarding adoptions to THE ANNALS c/o SAGE Publishing (address below).

All correspondence concerning membership in the Academy, dues renewals, inquiries about membership status, and/or purchase of single issues of THE ANNALS should be sent to THE ANNALS c/o SAGE Publishing, 2455 Teller Road, Thousand Oaks, CA 91320. Telephone: (800) 818-SAGE (7243) and (805) 499-0721; Fax/Order line: (805) 375-1700; e-mail: journals@sagepub.com. *Please note that orders under $30 must be prepaid.* For all customers outside the Americas, please visit http://www.sagepub.co.uk/customerCare.nav for information.

THE ANNALS

© 2018 by The American Academy of Political and Social Science

Editorial Office: 202 S. 36th Street, Philadelphia, PA 19104-3806
For information about individual and institutional subscriptions address:
SAGE Publishing
2455 Teller Road
Thousand Oaks, CA 91320

For SAGE Publishing: Peter Geraghty (Production) and Mimi Nguyen (Marketing)

From India and South Asia,
write to:
SAGE PUBLICATIONS INDIA Pvt Ltd
B-42 Panchsheel Enclave, P.O. Box 4109
New Delhi 110 017
INDIA

From Europe, the Middle East,
and Africa, write to:
SAGE PUBLICATIONS LTD
1 Oliver's Yard, 55 City Road
London EC1Y 1SP
UNITED KINGDOM

International Standard Serial Number ISSN 0002-7162
ISBN 978-1-5443-3821-7 (Vol. 676, 2018) paper
ISBN 978-1-5443-3820-0 (Vol. 676, 2018) cloth
First printing, March 2018

Information about membership rates, institutional subscriptions, and back issue prices may be found on the facing page.

Advertising. Current rates and specifications may be obtained by writing to The Annals Advertising and Promotion Manager at the Thousand Oaks office (address above). Acceptance of advertising in this journal in no way implies endorsement of the advertised product or service by SAGE or the journal's affiliated society(ies) or the journal editor(s). No endorsement is intended or implied. SAGE reserves the right to reject any advertising it deems as inappropriate for this journal.

Claims. Claims for undelivered copies must be made no later than six months following month of publication. The publisher will supply replacement issues when losses have been sustained in transit and when the reserve stock will permit.

Change of Address. Six weeks' advance notice must be given when notifying of change of address. Please send the old address label along with the new address to the SAGE office address above to ensure proper identification. Please specify the name of the journal.

THE ANNALS

OF THE AMERICAN ACADEMY OF POLITICAL AND SOCIAL SCIENCE

Volume 676   March 2018

IN THIS ISSUE:

Migrant Smuggling as a Collective Strategy and Insurance Policy:
Views from the Margins

Special Editors: SHELDON X. ZHANG, GABRIELLA E. SANCHEZ,
and LUIGI ACHILLI

FORTHCOMING

What Census Data Miss about American Diversity
Special Editors: KENNETH PREWITT and RICHARD ALBA

Evidence-Based Policy
Special Editor: RON HASKINS

Crimes of Solidarity in Mobility: Alternative Views on Migrant Smuggling

By
SHELDON X. ZHANG,
GABRIELLA E. SANCHEZ,
and
LUIGI ACHILLI

In this volume of *The ANNALS*, we present a collection of empirically based research projects on migrant smuggling, seeking to create a more nuanced understanding of the topic that supersedes perspectives that are often found in mainstream narratives of unscrupulous and ruthless criminal gangs preying on vulnerable and desperate migrants. The contributing authors rely on field data to reveal the complex and often symbiotic relationships between migrants and the people behind their journeys. Often misunderstood in juxtaposition to narratives of security and control, the lived experiences of migrants describe smuggling facilitators as relatives or close friends, acquaintances or distant operators—all members of a social network of varying relational proximity. Vulnerability in migration grows as the travel distance and transit points increase and the density of one's own community ties decreases. The procurement of smuggling services is always situated within the collective wisdom and lived experiences of the migrants and their communities, and the strategies to increase the odds of success and to reduce the hazards and uncertainty of traversing foreign terrains.

Keywords: migrant smuggling; irregular migration; organized crime; evidence-based policy

Illegal immigration generated much hyperbole in the most recent presidential election in the United States and remains a hot topic in public discourse, often tied to vital national interests such as security and employment. In the United States, the conversation on illegal

Sheldon X. Zhang is a professor at and chair of the School of Criminology and Justice Studies, University of Massachusetts, Lowell. His recent research primarily revolves around transnational organized crime and human trafficking issues.

Gabriella E. Sanchez is a senior research fellow at the Migration Policy Centre at the European University Institute. A sociocultural anthropologist, her focus has been on the social organization of migrant smuggling groups. She has conducted fieldwork on the U.S.-Mexico border, North Africa, the Middle East, Europe, and Australia.

Correspondence: sheldon_zhang@uml.edu

DOI: 10.1177/0002716217746908

immigrants or immigration in general continues to polarize politicians as well as the populace, despite that illegal entries into the United States have declined considerably in the past decade,[1] having now reached levels seen in the 1970s.[2] The United States is not alone. Recent migration flows to Europe are portrayed as constituted by economic migrants and refugees from war-torn and economically deprived regions from North Africa to the Middle East and from sub-Saharan Africa to Southeast Asia who have flooded refugee camps and stretched thin government resources in many European countries. Media images and political rhetoric have been effective at stoking anti-immigrant sentiment and prompting voters to favor regimes that seek to impose strict nation-state borders and controls and xenophobic immigration policies.

Illegal Migration and a "Crisis" in the (Western) World

The Western world has in recent years come under massive floods of migrants using unofficial channels (or illegal means) to enter their destination countries. By most government accounts, criminal gangs and illicit business networks are responsible for bringing these unfortunate migrants on precarious journeys and into risky circumstances replete with suffering and exploitation. Therefore, a dichotomous perspective has emerged in public discourse, dominated by government narratives on current irregular migration from the global South to the global North: (1) the brutality of the criminal smuggling networks and (2) the vulnerability of unfortunate migrants. For instance, according to Europol (2016), more than 1 million migrants reached European Union countries in 2015, and criminal networks as well as individual criminal entrepreneurs were responsible for assisting more than 90 percent of these migrants. These human smugglers "exploit the desperation and vulnerability of migrants" (Europol 2016, 1), while making off with enormous profits between 3 and 6 billion EUR. The United Nations, on the other hand, passed the Convention against Transnational Organized Crime and its supplementary protocols in 2000 that mandated all signatory member states (now numbering 184) to (1) combat the smuggling of migrants and (2) safeguard the rights of smuggled migrants.[3] The U.S. State Department (2017, 1) considers "people who are smuggled [to] be extremely vulnerable to human trafficking, abuse, and other crimes, as they are illegally present in the country of destination and often owe large debts to their smugglers."

Western governments largely consider combatting and eradicating migrant smuggling an important, if not the most important, aspect in stopping or reducing the influx of illegal migrants. For instance, in February 2016, Europol launched the European Migrant Smuggling Center to "proactively support EU Member States in dismantling criminal networks involved in organizing migrant smuggling."[4] The U.S.

Luigi Achilli is a Marie Curie Fellow at the European University Institute and San Diego State University. He is the author of Palestinian Refugees and Identity: Nationalism, Politics and the Everyday *(I.B. Tauris 2015). He is a social anthropologist with an extensive publication record on forced migration and refugee displacement.*

government practices the same response strategy—stepping up efforts to combat criminal smuggling organizations to reduce illegal entries by foreign nationals.[5] Along the same lines, major international organizations such as the United Nations also advocate positions that aim at improving legislative development and cooperation among member states to combat what is considered a multi-billion-dollar global criminal enterprise.[6]

The underlying logic for all these response strategies in the Western world seems remarkably similar—combatting smuggling organizations is key to reducing the influx of illegal immigrants. Such a belief and its concomitant policies are easy to translate into legislation and allocation of resources, against the backdrop of tragic images of capsized boats floating in the Mediterranean Sea, dead children washed ashore, and women and children in tattered clothes cramped in refugee camps in hopes of reaching Western countries. One such recent example is the San Antonio, Texas, tragedy of July 23, 2017, where ten migrants out of an estimated one hundred died after having travelled on the back of a truck with no refrigeration under the scorching summer sun; the act was labelled "sickening" and "demonstrating [of] kingpin smugglers' blatant disregard for human life" (Beavers 2017). The magnitude of these tragedies obscures the reasons behind migrants' use of smuggling services. Further, it reinforces the binary predator-victim position that saturates the official discourse on illegal migration and that has remained largely unchallenged in the West for decades: that migrant smugglers are major enablers to illegal transnational migration activities and the main cause of the human misery witnessed along migration routes worldwide. But is this the case?

Questions That Demand Answers

Migrants seeking to enter countries without proper, official papers continue to solicit and procure services along the migrant trail from human smugglers, despite the vilification of the latter in news media, law enforcement, and policy circles. It may also appear as if the demand for migrant smuggling services rises as Western countries continue to fortify their borders. The persistent demand for smuggling services in global irregular migration begs the question of why migrants fail to heed the warnings of government agencies around the world and continue to hire smugglers. Why do people continue to seek out smugglers, seemingly oblivious of the dangers awaiting them? Why do so many migrants continue to place their lives and nontrivial amounts of money into the hands of criminals? Are we missing something when we stick to a binary predator-victim perspective?

As with all forms of illicit enterprises, the rise of migrant smuggling requires a market environment where mutual vetting by buyers and sellers takes place, and sufficient trust must exist, at least superficially, before a transaction can occur. The binary predator-victim perspective rarely applies in a context where both migrants and smugglers actively engage in negotiating, vetting, and trading.

Researchers have found similar patterns in which smuggling merely presents an opportunity to sell or exchange one's resources (see Zhang 2007, 2008; Chin 1999; and Sanchez 2014). Even the roles of smugglers are often fluid, with migrants often taking the role of smuggling facilitators and vice versa, as Achilli, Gonzalez, Stone-Cadena, and Velasco describe in their contributions to this volume.

What then are the major considerations that influence migrants' decision to hire a smuggler? Since none of the transactions in this illicit market is legally enforceable, what insurance mechanism is available for migrants to ensure that the services will be delivered and for smugglers to get paid? As Kook, Sanchez, and Zhang argue in this volume, migrants are not passive actors in the process of transnational migration but active in vetting and procuring smuggling services, evaluating the reliability of smuggling facilitators, and learning through failed journeys which smugglers are worthy of trust and why. Based on their fieldwork, authors in this volume of *The ANNALS* present migrant smuggling as a complex and layered social process where kinship, friends and associates, overseas migrant communities, personal connections, money, and prior experiences coalesce to form the basis for protection, safety, and decision-making along the migration route (Maher, this volume).

Exploring Migrant Smuggling in the Field

At the onset of this project, authors were asked to explain why smugglers figure so prominently in transnational irregular migration narratives and draw so much attention from affected governments. Together these contributions set out to explore, in their respective corners of the world, not just the role and activities of smuggling facilitators, but their social lives. Our collective goal was to get as close as possible to the sources of the smuggling businesses and activities, and to collect data directly from the men and women who rely on smuggling as their livelihood. This goal emerged from our collective concern that existing literature on irregular migration has primarily drawn from the perspectives of government or law enforcement eager to contain migratory flows, or from migrants, refugees, and asylum seekers who are the unfortunate target of threats, scams, or violence during their clandestine journeys. The graphic images of migrant smuggling in the global news media also prevent views that contextualize smuggling amid the increasingly punitive migration regimes and the criminalization of migration. Irregular migration and its facilitation have long been viewed as a process deeply tied to the identities and livelihoods of entire communities, as Brachet, Stone-Cadena, and Velasco describe in the cases of the Sahara and indigenous Ecuador in this volume. Current public discourse that focuses on violence and exploitation has systematically silenced the insights of the vast majority of irregular migrants who successfully completed their journeys and the voices of those who played a role in that success, as Ayalew, Sanchez, and Zhang describe in their research in this volume on migrants travelling through the Horn of Africa into Libya and the U.S.-Mexico migration corridor.

Despite the current hypervisibility of irregular migration and condemnation of smugglers as its main enabler, empirical work on human smuggling and its facilitators has remained scant. By developing this special issue, we intend to energize a rather static field of study on irregular migration and provide an empirical challenge to the fragmented, often one-sided perspectives on the migratory journey, focusing instead on its sociocultural dynamics, the smuggling facilitator-traveler relationship, and its community dimensions, as described, for example, by Majidi in the experience of Afghan and Somali migrants.

Our field data suggest that most smuggling facilitators do not engage in violent acts, as most are subject to the control or influence of moral and social obligations toward the families and communities of those who rely on their services. Maher discusses this in the context of Senegal in this volume, and Achilli does so about Syrian refugees, smugglers, and the refugees who opt to become smugglers.

A main goal of this collective body of work is to raise a much larger question about the role of border control regimes prevalent in the global North in shaping transnational migrant smuggling practices. In other words, we seek to understand what and how individual as well as collective strategies toward mobility adapt and adjust under the increasing militarization of border control. As Spener (2009) argues, human migration from open to clandestine and from legal to illicit is not a mere reflection of migrants' preferences in travel but rather the manifestation of the obstacles created by border enforcement. The procurement of smuggling services is in this sense deeply intertwined with the implementation of border control regimes world over. As Brachet describes in this volume, migrant smuggling is manufactured not by criminal enterprises or obscure mafia organizations but by governments themselves. To echo the work of Spener, irregular migration is a form of resistance by people seeking to improve their life or to escape wars and conflicts, a universal desire that is often reserved for the privileged few in a world increasingly impacted by an economic apartheid.

Last, this volume of The ANNALS is unique not only in the collection and analysis of firsthand data on migrants' experiences in smuggling but also in the inclusion of the views of migrant smugglers themselves, to challenge the dominant narratives in public discourse (Sanchez 2014). In a time when open source and big data analysis are increasingly used to explain security-related phenomena, a distinctive element of this entire collection is its reliance on firsthand empirical data, collected by the authors themselves through extensive in-depth interviews and field observations along major migratory routes around the world. All contributors have spent considerable time in the field gathering data that have compelled them to rethink and reframe the very concept of smuggling, its actors, and its implications amid contemporary global migration control regimes. The richness of the empirical data included in this volume has given rise to unconventional perspectives, which contrast sharply with the dominant narrative of the migration control regime and policy discourse. Rarely do established researchers venture into restive regions and treacherous fields to talk to strangers and collect firsthand data. We hope this volume charts a new direction in research on irregular migration and that its contributions serve as an example of what fieldwork can do to challenge the status quo and counter dominant narratives.

The Purpose of This Volume

This volume of *The ANNALS* comes at a critical time in migration studies, given the current crisis on refugee and migrant protection systems worldwide. Compared to the abundance of research on the lives of migrants and refugees, empirical work on their journeys remains scant. Academics, law enforcement, and policy-makers are sorely in need of empirically based work about this much-maligned aspect of transnational migration. Our collection seeks to address this gap.

Empirical work and edited volumes or special issues on smuggling have been difficult to compile and find in existing literature. Kyle and Koslowski edited *Global Human Smuggling* in 2001 and a revised edition in 2013, both volumes standing as fundamental texts in smuggling scholarship, yet their geographical focus was the U.S.-Mexico border, and on China. While the second edition expanded to other regions, the majority of the articles continued to draw from secondary sources, or relied on government reports and archival records. In 2016, *Geopolitics* dedicated a special issue to clandestine migration journeys, coordinated by Mainwaring and Brigden, which addressed the myriad ways in which migrants engage with the geographies they cover in the context of their journeys. Their special issue sought to analyze how "geopolitics shape and animate the everyday experiences of clandestine migration journeys" and the ways migrants "negotiate and manoeuvre" their journeys from their marginalized positions (Mainwaring and Brigden 2016, 244).

This special issue focuses on the actual organization of the irregular journeys, and on the persona of the facilitator—not as members of transnational organized crime—but as guides, drivers, brokers, cooks, recruiters, and lookouts, the men and women behind migrants' journeys. We seek to establish smuggling first as a grounded social and cultural practice, while critically reframing its importance amid global border and immigration enforcement and controls. We hope our readers will find the articles in this volume different from much of the existing literature to date on political science or border criminology, which has focused on the experiences of migrants and their criminalization by the state. We are in no way minimizing the impact of border controls on migrants' lives nor condoning exploitative smuggling practices. Rather, we use this platform rich in ethnographic data from multiple locales around the world to question the utility of the dominant discourse on migrant smuggling, to challenge its concomitant policy ramifications, and to identify its intersections with criminal justice and migration controls. We present a series of empirically supported perspectives that portray human smuggling as a social process engaged in by irregular migrants who seek to mitigate the uncertainty and hazards inherent in their illicit journey and, in the process, build mechanisms of security from below (Ayalew, this volume). As our concluding piece from Triandafyllidou states, there is a need to dig deeper into realities on the ground, not least through qualitative empirical research and through comparative analysis, to understand the relationship between migrant smuggling and migration control policies. For policy-makers, we offer, unapologetically, a reality check against the rationale underlying the control regimes, and point out the culpability of current antitrafficking strategies in giving rise to criminal networks while causing human miseries along the smuggling routes. We seek to promote humanitarianism in our understanding of migrants aspiring to reach the global North, and to argue for the decriminalization of irregular migration and adoption of a harm-reduction approach toward undocumented migrants.

Diverse Voices from around the World

In this volume of *The ANNALS*, we have included eleven articles documenting smuggling practices in the Americas, Europe, the Middle East, Africa, and the Pacific. These articles were first presented at an international workshop on smuggling facilitation held at the European University Institute (EUI) in Florence, Italy, in April 2016 and organized by the Migration Policy Centre (EUI) and the University of Texas at El Paso. The contributions come from both sides of the Atlantic and beyond, and involve smuggling practices in Afghanistan, Senegal, Ecuador, Syria, Niger, Turkey, Pakistan, Ethiopia, Somalia, Korea, the Sahara, Central America, and Mexico, in addition to the more commonly analyzed U.S. and European contexts. These articles fall into three specific areas: (1) the political and moral economy of irregular migration facilitation, (2) the community understandings of and interactions with smuggling facilitators, and (3) the role and agency of migrants and refugees along their smuggling journeys.

While a complex and multilayered topic such as smuggling lends itself to qualitative research methods, we have also included conventional survey methods to illustrate efforts by researchers to systematically evaluate migrant-smuggler interactions. In this volume of *The ANNALS*, Slack and Martinez examine recent migrants' experiences with *coyotes* (i.e., human smugglers) along the U.S.-Mexico border, by drawing on data gathered through the Migrant Border Crossing Survey (MBCS). Using this unique dataset, consisting of more than one thousand postdeportation surveys, Slack and Martinez focus on migrants' satisfaction with the services that they were provided by their most recent smuggler, as well as whether they would be willing to put family or friends in contact with that person. No study to date has evaluated the qualities that migrants expect and desire in human smugglers. Slack and Martinez's quantitative findings are an ideal supplement to the qualitative portion of this collection, which, as a whole, points to the vast, complex set of perceptions that shape migrants' decision-making regarding their journeys and, in turn, their ability to exercise their agency from the margins.

Conclusion

In this volume of *The ANNALS*, we explore how human smuggling has evolved at the macro-level, amid the militarization, criminalization, and immigration controls of late modernity, as a practice historically grounded in solidarity and reciprocity among diasporas. At the same time, we also explore how smugglers and their clients adapt and develop specific strategies at the micro-level that are reflective of migrant communities and their collective traditions. The rich qualitative data in this special volume bring forth, to the broader society and nonacademic audiences, a perspective on smuggling's enterprising agents and their so-called criminal networks that is far more nuanced and easily accessible than the status quo offered by government reports and the news media. This special volume offers a rare but evidence-based portrayal of smuggling facilitators as otherwise ordinary citizens whose underground travel services are actively courted by people like themselves as an insurance policy or a protection scheme to reduce the uncertainty and hazards inherent in clandestine border crossings.

All authors of this volume identify the increased difficulties of border crossing as the primary force that is pushing migrants into the arms of enterprising agents. As border control regimes strain to erect migration barriers, people aspiring for mobility will continue to rely on their communities and kinship networks to find ways to migrate. It is therefore imperative to have a baseline from which to begin mapping the likely transformations of the smuggling industry, as recent geopolitical developments indicate the legal access to desired destinations will remain the purview of a privileged few (Gallagher 2015).

The empirical findings presented here run counter to the dominant narrative permeated in public discourse, which begs the question of why such a wide gap in conclusions exists between field research and the official position held by Western governments and their supported international organizations. We fully acknowledge the extensive evidence of abusive and exploitative smuggling practices, but identify their root causes in border and migration enforcement and control practices. We denounce the human cost of clandestine journeys, as reflected by the thousands of migrants who go missing or perish during their journeys.

Most authors in this volume come from or have resided in communities impacted by smuggling-related violence and witnessed its effect on migrants and ordinary citizens alike. It is in fact this awareness that has led us to problematize the simplistic predator-victim binary and to offer different views from the ground. We find the accounts of organized crime, mafias, and unlimited profits to be ineffective portrayals of the lived experiences of migrants and those behind their transits. We further consider the predator-victim binary used to designate the smuggler-migrant relationship a narrow portrayal of complex cooperation and mutually beneficial interactions. Because both smuggling facilitators and migrants are often members of the same social networks (e.g., relatives, friends, associates, or social acquaintances), they are subjected to the same informal control processes and therefore tend to engage in exchanges in ways similar to other social enterprises. Smuggling facilitators may break away from commonly accepted social mores and codes of conduct for profit and self-preservation, especially in the face of hostile social settings. Some may abandon their clients in the deserts or charge ransom-like fees. Yet the majority of their operations run uneventfully, with little fanfare.

We present this collection of articles not only to challenge the dominant narrative but also to make readers aware of the voices from the margins, scant in mainstream discourse yet abundantly supported by empirical evidence. At the minimum, we hope to start a discussion that questions the mainstream narrative of smuggling and forces policy-makers to confront the real causes of irregular migration. Together we hope to build an evidenced-based foundation for the development of rational and realistic, as opposed to knee-jerk, response strategies and national policies on irregular migration that focus on harm reduction while protecting the dignity of those swept up in migration flows worldwide.

Notes

1. According to the Pew Research Center (Krogstad, Passell, and Cohn 2017), illegal entries into the United States have been on the decline; non-Mexicans now outnumber Mexicans in border arrests; the majority of undocumented Mexicans living in the United States are long-term residents, which suggests fewer new arrivals.

2. Based on official statistics from the U.S. Border Patrol, arrests at U.S. borders have declined significantly from the height of more than 1.67 million to roughly 416,000 in 2016. Annual U.S. border apprehension statistics can be found at: https://www.cbp.gov.

3. The UN convention can be found at https://www.unodc.org/documents/human-trafficking/Migrant_Smuggling/09-81206_English_eBook.pdf.

4. Detailed information about this center can be found at https://www.europol.europa.eu/content/EMSC_launch.

5. The lead federal agency in charge of combatting migrant smuggling is the Immigration and Customs Enforcement (ICE) under the Homeland Security. For details of the U.S. official counter-smuggling strategies, see https://www.ice.gov/human-smuggling.

6. An example of the official assessment and counter measures advocated by the United Nations Office on Drug and Crime (UNODC) can be found at: https://www.unodc.org/toc/en/crimes/migrant-smuggling.html.

References

Beavers, Olivia. 23 July 2017. Texas lawmakers condemn San Antonio trafficking deaths. *The Hill.* Available from http://thehill.com.

Chin, Ko-lin. 1999. *Smuggled Chinese: Clandestine immigration to the United States.* Philadelphia, PA: Temple University Press.

Europol. 2016. *Migrant smuggling in the EU.* The Hague: Europol. Available from https://www.europol.europa.eu/.

Gallagher, Anne T. 2015. Exploitation in migration: Unacceptable but inevitable. *Journal of International Affairs* 68 (2): 55–74.

Kyle, David, and Rey Koslowski, eds. 2001/2013. *Global human smuggling.* Rev. ed. Baltimore, MD: Johns Hopkins University Press.

Krogstad, Jens Manuel, Jeffrey S. Passell, and D'Vera Cohn. 2017. 5 facts about illegal immigration in the U.S. *Fact Talk—News in the Numbers*. Washington DC: Pew Research Center. Available from http://www.pewresearch.org/fact-tank/2017/04/27/5-facts-about-illegal-immigration-in-the-u-s/.

Mainwaring, Cetta, and Noelle Brigden, eds. 2016. Beyond the border: Clandestine migration journeys. *Geopolitics* 21 (2): 243–62.

Sanchez, Gabriella. 2014. *Human smuggling and border crossings*. New York, NY: Routledge.

Spener, David. 2009. *Clandestine crossings: Migrants and coyotes on the Texas-Mexico border*. Ithaca, NY: Cornell University Press.

U.S. State Department. 2017. *Human trafficking & human smuggling: Understanding the difference*. Washington, DC: Office to Monitor and Combat Trafficking in Persons, U.S. State Department. Available from https://www.state.gov/.

Zhang, Sheldon X. 2007. *Smuggling and trafficking in human beings: All roads lead to America*. Westport, CT: Praeger/Greenwood.

Zhang, Sheldon X. 2008. *Chinese human smuggling organizations—Families, social networks, and cultural imperatives*. Palo Alto, CA: Stanford University Press.

Manufacturing Smugglers: From Irregular to Clandestine Mobility in the Sahara

By
JULIEN BRACHET

For decades, mobility between the Sahel and northern Africa was mostly irregular, but not clandestine. Most of the border crossings were supervised and (illegally) taxed by border police; everyone knew who did what with whom, and Saharan drivers were not thought of as smugglers of people. Starting in the early 2000s, European countries intervened, considering all trans-Saharan movements as a first step on a journey toward Europe, thus encouraging national authorities to stop them. This led to the tightening of border controls across northwest Africa. This article shows how the resulting criminalization of travel to and through the Sahara has led to the development of specialized passenger transport as a clandestine activity, resulting in an increase in the human and financial costs of those journeys. Thus, smugglers, as a particular category of actors, appear as directly manufactured by the migration policies that were drafted to control them.

Keywords: migration; smuggling; transport; irregularity; policies; Niger; Sahara

The city of Agadez … is now the infamous cradle of migrants' smugglers. (*Newsletter for the European Union* 2015)

Here in Agadez, people have always welcomed travellers, forever. And we have always travelled too, to Algeria, to Libya, like our fathers, our grand-fathers. Why is it a problem now?[1]

This crime [of smuggling] is not infamous in the public opinion. [It] is owing to the laws themselves. (Beccaria 1764/1872, 126–27)

The town of Agadez, situated at the edge of the Sahara in northern Niger, has recently been described by politicians and international

Julien Brachet is a research fellow at the French National Research Institute for Development (IRD – Sorbonne University), and currently Marie Skłodowska-Curie Individual Research Fellow at the University of Oxford. He has published on a wide range of issues concerning the Sahel and the Sahara.

Correspondence: julien.brachet@ird.fr

DOI: 10.1177/0002716217744529

media as a "hub for smugglers" (Damon, Swails, and Laine 2017), a "smugglers' paradise" (Politzer and Kassie 2016), the "smuggling capital of Africa" (Destrijcker 2016), or simply "one of the world's human smuggling capitals" (Sieff 2015). The "local underworld" is allegedly ruling the town, which has gone "from desert jewel to city of crime" (Agence France-Presse [AFP] 2015). Supposedly, corruption concerns "almost all military and police officials" (Flynn 2015), and sub-Saharan migrants who want to go farther north, across the desert, have no other choice than to deal with the famous "human smugglers of the Sahara" (Penney 2014), and make their "fortune" (BBC 2014).

On paper, Agadez and its 140,000 inhabitants are thus a perfect target for European migration policies. These policies aim to control and stop all irregular migration bound for the European Union (EU) as far upstream as possible, wrongly assuming that all (trans)Saharan migrations are nothing but the first step of irregular migration toward Europe (Brachet 2011; De Haas 2008).

In fact, though, the central Sahara has a long-standing history of migration, which forms part of local modes of livelihood (Boesen and Marfaing 2007; Bredeloup and Pliez 2005). Until the 1990s, there were few political concerns over those migrations. Since the 2000s, such irregular migration has become a growing issue in diplomatic relations among sub-Saharan, North African, and European governments. The region of Agadez has become in these last few years the one site where these policies are concretely implemented, much more so than elsewhere in Niger and probably than anywhere else in the Sahel and the Sahara. Henceforth, one can hardly find policy reports and projects on migration from Africa to Europe that do not explicitly mention Agadez as a key place to "secure" (see for instance Council of the European Union 2015; The Global Initiative against Transnational Organized Crime 2014; Organisation for Economic Co-operation and Development [OECD] 2015). Various international organizations (IOs) and nongovernmental organizations (NGOs) specializing in global migration management have opened up permanent local offices, including a transit and assistance center in 2014 and a migrant information office in 2016, both run by the International Organization for Migration (IOM). Meanwhile Nigerien migration policies have changed. Since 2016, people have started to be arrested in Agadez and the surrounding area, and sentenced to prison for years, accused of "human smuggling." This is the first time in Niger's history that people have been jailed for smuggling activities. Up to that point, smuggling was not criminalized in the country, and nobody was considered a smuggler within the national territory.

Indeed, in this town, which has been located on one of the main trans-Saharan migration routes since at least the mid-twentieth century, *smuggler/smuggling* in local languages (*d'an-sùmŏgàl* in Hausa, *afrod* in Tamasheq, *sahib al-frûd* in local Arabic) or even in French (*fraudeur*) refer to goods, not people. This does not mean that there were no people smugglers, but rather that most of them were first and foremost traders. Transporting migrants was a marginal activity for them, an adjunct to moving merchandise. Nonetheless, the idea of the existence of a clandestine Sahara-wide network of "unscrupulous smugglers who seek to benefit from the desperation of the vulnerable" (European Commission [EC]

2016b, 2) has informed most of the migration policies in the area over the last 15 years. Nowadays, many people in northern Niger have effectively specialized in the organization of the migrants' transport from Agadez to Algeria and Libya. They are sometimes in touch with each other upstream or downstream on the migratory routes.

This article investigates the relationship between human smuggling and smuggling policies in Niger, showing the ways in which policies that were supposed to fight human smuggling affected those who live in or travel through the area. Avoiding the semantic confusion between *clandestine* and *irregular* migration, this article highlights the diversity of mobility practices in the Sahara for a better understanding of the origins and the evolution of the networks that underpin them.

Research Methods

This article draws on information gathered between 2003 and 2016 in Niger. The total amount of time spent in the field was about three years. At first, I had no specific interest in migration issues and mostly lived and worked with nomads and herdsmen for a year, during which I participated in a caravan of camels between the Aïr Mountains and Kawar oases. This is where, by chance, I first met several trans-Saharan traders and so-called smugglers who were on their way to northern Africa. I already knew many of these people's relatives, who were involved in the pastoral economy of the area. When I then started to study trans-Saharan mobility, this background helped me to build trust with most of them; they became friends as much as informants. Data collection involved a combination of participant observations; informal conversations; and structured interviews with traders, transporters, guides, brokers, migrants, IO and NGO staff, policemen, custom officers, soldiers, and Nigerien and European state officials. Almost two hundred interviews were recorded, in French, English, and Tamasheq.[2] Much time was spent travelling and waiting with migrants and various facilitators, in several Saharan locations, including Ingal, Arlit, Assamakka, Iferwan, Dirkou, Bilma, Séguédine, and especially the key migration transit town of Agadez (these locations are shown in Figure 1).[3]

As part of a broader anthropological research project on Saharan mobility, most of my data analysis was a collaborative process involving informants and myself at the time of the interviews themselves.

A Brief History of (Trans)Saharan Migration in Niger

In the Sahel, migration to northern Africa is a long-standing phenomenon. Since the mid-twentieth century in French Algeria and then in Libya, North African governments have undertaken large-scale development projects in their Saharan regions (Blin 1990). This development created a demand for labor that could not

FIGURE 1
Agadez, Niger

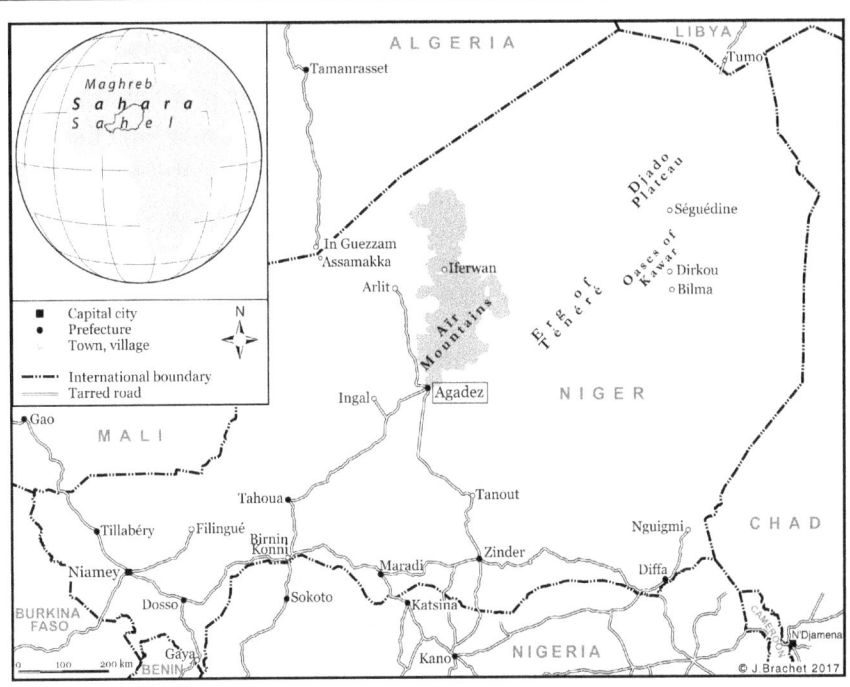

be met either locally or nationally, and so it drew on the workforce of neighboring countries.

Droughts in the Sahel in the 1970s and 1980s led to severe food shortages and intensified Sahelian and West African migration to the Algerian and Libyan Sahara (Copans 1975; Spittler 1993). Despite the need for labor, sub-Saharan immigrants remained mostly in an extralegal position. These irregular migrants were not considered as a problem by the national authorities, however, which did not really attempt to "manage" or "control" them. Although, several waves of expulsions were organized from the 1970s and 1980s.

In the early 1990s, various economic and political factors contributed to the increase in migration between sub-Saharan and northern Africa, mostly on the Nigerien route. By the end of the 1990s, roughly a hundred thousand migrants from sub-Saharan Africa travelled each year via Agadez to Libya and Algeria. Eighty to 90 percent returned home after a few months or years, and the other 10 to 20 percent tried to enter Europe (Brachet 2009).

For almost half a century, irregular migration of sub-Saharan nationals to Algeria and Libya was mostly tolerated by national authorities. People could travel relatively freely, most of the time. Whatever their situation, it was possible for all migrants to cross the borders on main roads, at official checkpoints. Migrants simply took advantage of the vitality of trans-Saharan trade to cross the desert. From Agadez, which is located at the end of a tarmacked road on the way to Libya (see Figure 1), migrants mainly travelled on desert-going freight trucks, on top of their loads, for low prices directly negotiated with the drivers. Migrants had no choice but to travel with these drivers, as they knew the desert well, and knew how to navigate it, physically and socially. These drivers were not risking anything because they were not considered smugglers of people by any border police, but simply traders carrying passengers; such mixed transport of goods and people has for a long time been the norm in the desert. At the checkpoints, migrants had to bribe officials (policemen, custom officers, and the military) with relatively small sums to be able to get into the country. In other words, migration through the Sahara was irregular but not clandestine. As a result, there was an unofficial social control of migrant transport, by transporters themselves, by their relatives who knew what they were doing, and by state officials, which blurred the boundaries between the legal and the illegal, and firmly rooted passenger transport within the licit economic sphere.

Professionalization in people transport from Agadez

Nigerien nationals accounted for half of all sub-Saharans who entered Algeria and Libya from Niger in the 1990s (Grégoire 1999, 227). Temporary labor migration to these countries had quite simply become an integral part of Nigerien's lives. The armed rebellion of 1990–1995 in Niger[4] marked the establishment of transport networks and the grassroots normalization of the involvement of Nigerien state agents in the Saharan migratory system. In a time of great instability for the state, members of the various security agencies routinely engaged in corruption without being called to order by their superiors (Tidjani Alou 2002), and the illegal taxation of migrants became the norm on the Saharan routes. Meanwhile, the growing number of migrants travelling via Agadez created a significant demand for transportation and related services, to which freight carriers in turn responded. However, such a vibrant commerce also aroused envy among many former rebels who returned to Agadez after the peace agreement in 1995. Unemployed and eager to make money, these former rebel soldiers enlisted four-by-four pick-ups and put their detailed knowledge of the central Sahara to use, knowledge that they had acquired as migrants, smugglers of goods, tour guides, or during the rebellion itself. They offered their services as drivers, guides, and escorts for migrant workers. Soon, the government and local politicians, to discourage them from further armed activity or banditry, allowed them to open the first official trans-Saharan travel agencies, locally called *agences de courtage*, specializing in carrying migrants to Algeria and Libya. As the mayor of Agadez told me: "The *agences de courtage* were legally created by the State, with legal authorization. … Those who did this activity at that time were only ex-rebels, those who were unemployed. … These transport activities were well organized at the bus station."[5]

Migration networks became locally structured and staffed, with a variety of agents involved in smuggling activities such as *coxeurs* (or recruiters),[6] drivers, intermediaries, travel agents, go-betweens, and other brokers. The same people could play several different roles if necessary. Some were professionals and permanently involved in these activities, others did it occasionally alongside another job. These *agences de courtage*, legally registered companies that used to pay taxes to the local authorities, were at the heart of these activities. Their small offices were located in the bus and bush taxis stations. Migrants who arrived in town were usually brought to one of them by a *coxeur*. They were offered a place (locally called *ghetto*) to stay according to their nationality or language, and different options of transport according to their destination, financial means, and schedule. In addition to trucks, which transported the bulk of migrants until the early 2000s, migrants could travel, at a slightly higher price, on board of a four-by-four pick-up. On both routes (to the Algerian border, four hundred kilometers [km]; or to the Libyan border, one thousand km), no effort was made to hide from the Nigerien police forces, who illegally taxed the migrants regardless of the migrants' own legality.

The journey from Agadez to southern Libya usually took between three and seven days, and sometimes longer because of mechanical problems or breakdowns. Migrants, who might be piled thirty high on the back of a pick-up, were checked and taxed a dozen times along the way by the Nigerien police and military. Each time, each migrant had to pay a few thousand CFA francs.[7] These illegal and arbitrary taxes placed a heavy burden on the migrants, and many times migrants found themselves stuck at some stage on the Nigerien migratory routes, lacking sufficient funds to continue (Brachet 2012b). Unable to go farther or to return home, these migrants stayed for weeks or months where their journey had temporarily been interrupted, either working or waiting for further money transfers from home. The money extorted from the migrants by the state officials represented a considerable proportion of these officials' income and circled, partially, back into the local economies, alongside the money that the migrants spent voluntarily on transport, housing, food, telecommunications, and money transfers. Migrants therefore became a source of income for many, and migration led to a blossoming of local service businesses.

Nigerien state agents did not try to apply any official legislation concerning the circulation of people in this region. They rarely stopped those who were travelling irregularly in Niger; but they also did not let the majority of travelers go freely, who, as Nigerien or West African nationals, were entitled to travel freely to the Algerian or Libyan border. In Northern Africa, meanwhile, sub-Saharan migration was still tolerated or even encouraged in Libya (Pliez 2004). Most migrants were able to cross the borders at the official checkpoints, bribing or paying illegal taxes to state officials. Their entry was nonetheless rarely acknowledged officially by the Algerian or Libyan authorities, whose attitude toward migration had long been ambiguous (see Bensaâd 2009). Thus, all the truck drivers and most of the four-by-four pick-up drivers could travel on main roads and between Niger and Northern Africa via official checkpoints. As Bachir, a bus station manager in Agadez, stated:

> Before we had a system of lists and roadmaps, and each truck driver gave us the number of passengers he carried and their names, their nationalities. … We knew that such and such trucks had left that day with this number of people.[8]

Everybody knew, in other words, who was carrying how many migrants, when, and to which places. This all changed when European governments became interested in trans-Saharan migration.

Europe Steps In: Toward Clandestine Migration

Beginning in the late 1990s, irregular migration from sub-Saharan Africa became an important issue in Europe, and North African governments found migration to be an important card to play in negotiations with the EU. Indeed, European governments declared in 2002 that they intended to "step up and make more efficient the fight against illegal migration, both in transit and in sending countries."[9] One way of doing this was by pushing North African states to tighten their border controls. First was their sea borders, in particular through the activities of Frontex (Papastavridis 2010);[10] then, gradually, their land borders, namely, the Saharan borders. The objective was to stop all trans-Saharan migration as far south as possible, because European policy-makers assumed that all trans-Saharan migrants intended to reach Europe, even though it is now widely known that only a small number of them want to go to Europe (Lessault and Beauchemin 2009).

Some North African officials felt that it was not their job to restrict migration to Europe, or that the intervention was useless. As the Consul of Algeria in Agadez stated, "They want to turn us into gendarmes. Migrants who arrive in Tamanrasset and want to continue to Europe are none of our business, but we are being asked to push them back. It is not normal."[11] The Consul of Libya in Agadez added, "You can shut your house, I can shut my house. But we live in a city, so we can't prevent everybody from coming in. It is the same with immigrants in the Sahara. You can control one place, but they still get through elsewhere. And moreover it is not good if you shut your house."[12] Nonetheless, in exchange for financial aid and economic cooperation, and for various internal economic and political reasons, Libya and Algeria agreed to implement most of the European demands to monitor, control, and impede migration.[13] This resulted in increased legal sanctions against migrants with no legal status, and against any third person who facilitated their entry, stay, or exit from the national territory. A similar tightening of legislation took place in Morocco and Tunisia (Perrin 2016). The EU had allocated considerable financial means for the surveillance and control of the Saharan borders to stop irregular migration through the desert.

One of the first programs implemented, called Aeneas, involved several European and African countries. It was funded from 2004 to 2013 by the EU, with a budget of more than 500 million euros. It aimed to "support third countries in their efforts to ensure better management of migratory flows," and advertized "the fight against illegal immigration" as one of its main objectives (EC 2007, 2). One part of the program was called the "Across Sahara project," and its "specific objective [was] to contribute to the enhancement of policies and practices to prevent and combat illegal migration, trafficking and smuggling of (transit) migrants in Libya and Niger" (EC 2007, 5). It was implemented in Niger by French police officers who equipped Saharan border posts with jeeps and night radar, computers, machines to detect fake identity papers and to take biometric finger prints, and Internet access to retrieve Interpol files. The technical support enabled local police officers to put on file in real time everybody who crossed the border, and to turn back those who had already been caught in an irregular situation elsewhere. Of course, in some border posts, like Assamaka, there was no electricity and no window panes at the little mud house that served as the police station. Nobody really seemed to mind. According to a French police officer based at the French embassy in Niamey, in 2010:

> We didn't do Assamaka because there is no electricity out there. … We install things where we can, and where we can't, never mind, we wait … as long as the Nigerien government doesn't do anything. … My main frustration after two years in Niger is that in fact we realize that our projects do not correspond at all to what they really need, but they always say yes, they always agree with everything. They don't make these projects their own. … Aid in security matters is such a waste. It's incredible.[14]

Numerous international, multilateral, and bilateral projects aiming to contain irregular migration have been implemented in Niger, by UN and EU agencies, IOs, European cooperation services, NGOs, and the Nigerien authorities. Although these projects were marked by their lack of coordination, they collectively hardened the borders in the Sahara, and criminalized trans-border movement of all kinds. Under the growing governmental pressure, Algerian border authorities, and even Libyan authorities, began to crack down on irregular entries, with or without bribes. As a result, drivers of large freight trucks stopped carrying irregular migrants through the borders on their way north, because it became too risky. At the same time, arrests and deportations became the norm in northern Africa, with the silent complicity of the EU and other organizations that collaborated in "Saharan migration management." The IOM, for instance, sometimes participated in the transport of sub-Saharan migrants from southern Libya and Algeria to Niger (Brachet 2016). This was the case even when migrants were arrested and deported, or repatriated, often in unacceptable physical conditions, as an IOM staff member in Niamey, the capital city of Niger, stated:

> We seek to ensure the highest quality standard in the transportation of repatriated migrants from Algeria, but transport is provided by the Algerian authorities. … The last time they brought us people, they were crowded by hundreds in cattle trucks, with metal gates, it was not a nice sight. … We don't have the right to publish photos, otherwise there would be too much criticism.[15]

The change in migration policies in the area resulted in the professionalization of passenger transport. Only fast and easily maneuverable four-by-four pick-ups were able to discretely bypass checkpoints and to reach the southern part of Algeria and Libya. Their activity remained legal in the Sahel (even though they were illegally taxed by the local police) but became clandestine as soon as they reached the Maghreb. These migrants became not only irregular but also systematically clandestine migrants in Northern Africa, and hence punishable by law.

In the late 2000s, the EU expanded its pressure to control migration from North Africa to the Sahelian states. In 2008, the 10th EDF (European Development Fund) mentioned for the first time issues of migration in its governance profiles.[16] The evaluation of migration control would determine the allocation of the EU's financial aid. The inclusion of this item appeared "to be informed mainly by concerns in the European Union about possible immigration" (Hout 2010, 8), and thus pushed the beneficiary countries, especially the African ones, to "better manage" their borders and the migration flows from and through their territories.

In January 2008, the heads of state of the Economic Community of West African States (ECOWAS) adopted a "common approach on migration" that aimed to improve their management of "intra-regional migration and migration to Europe" (ECOWAS 2008, 3). Largely influenced by European assumptions about West African migration, which are more ideological than based on facts, this objective reflected a change in the orientation of ECOWAS: from the facilitation of free movement of persons within the region[17] to measures of control of its external borders. This adoption of European security vocabulary suggested that West African elites no longer envisaged migration as a factor of development, but as a bargaining chip in their relations with the EU. Even the Nigerien police officers in charge of the implementation of these new policies realized that they were in a double bind, as the police chief in Agadez stated:

> The problem is that, with ECOWAS, we have to let these people travel in Niger. At least all those who are from ECOWAS countries. … We have to let them go until the Libyan or the Algerian border. … We don't have the right to stop them here.[18]

For the first time in history, irregular migration officially became a political issue in the Sahel, at the level of both the nation-states and ECOWAS (Kabbanji 2011). Migration policies, which until then had hardly existed, became a political necessity.

From an International Focus to Local Repression

Over the past few years, the EU has put Niger under pressure to crack down on "the business model of smugglers" (EC 2016b, 4), and applied a wide range of measures to achieve this goal. This is especially salient in Agadez, which is now more than ever considered by the EU as "the place where most of the flow [of irregular migrants] entering into Libya that enter Europe through the Central Mediterranean route is going through" (High Representative of the EU for Foreign Affairs and Security Policy 2016). For the EU, "Agadez is a very important laboratory, a test case for possible replication in other areas" (Maurice 2016).

A so-called capacity-building mission, EUCAP Sahel Niger, was launched in 2012 as one of the key tools of EU migration control in Niger. With eighty "international experts," mostly from European security forces, an annual budget that increased from less than €10 million in 2012 to €26 million in 2016 (European External Action Service [EEAS] 2015), and a permanent presence in Agadez, it aims to "assist the Nigerien central and local authorities as well as the security forces in developing policies, techniques and procedures to better control and fight irregular migration" (EEAS 2016c) and "associated criminal activity" (EEAS 2016b).

The international fight against migrant smuggling in the Sahel thus loomed large at the Valletta Summit on Migration that took place in November 2015, among African and European government representatives and numerous UN, IOs and intergovernmental organizations (IGOs). At the summit, the EC announced its decision to launch the "emergency trust fund for stability and addressing root causes of irregular migration and displaced persons in Africa," with an initial budget of €2.5 billion, taken mainly from the EU budget and the European Development Fund (EC 2016a). In its first year of activity, the trust fund committed more than €900 million to tackle "irregular migration and migrant smuggling" in the nine countries of the Sahel region and Lake Chad Basin. More than 20 percent of this budget was dedicated to Niger (EC 2016c), where the EU introduced a new "migration partnership framework" in June 2016. Again, the main aim of the partnership is "to reduce flows of illegal migration by disrupting the business model of smugglers" (EC 2016d)—a business model that stays unexplained. This is done in collaboration with the Nigerien authorities. In fact, the partnership was structured to support the implementation of the 2015 Nigerien law on migrant smuggling,[19] which had directly been "reviewed" by the EUCAP Sahel Niger Mission, "with the Mission's comments incorporated in the final draft" (EEAS 2016a, 17).

This law, whose stated aim is to "prevent and fight against all kind of illicit migrant smuggling" (Article 1), defines *migrant smuggling* as "the act of insuring, in order to make a [profit], the illegal entry in a country of a person who is neither a national nor a permanent resident of this country" (Article 3). *Smugglers* are defined as "everybody who insures the entry to or the *illegal exit* from Niger who is neither a national nor a permanent resident" (Article 10, emphasis added). Smugglers face a penalty of five to thirty years of incarceration, a fine of up to 30 million CFA francs, and the impounding of the vehicle used to transport the migrants (Articles 10, 17, 18).[20] Even "the attempt to commit the abovementioned offenses is liable to the same punishments" (Article 13). As Victor Hugo (1869/1886, 428) stated one and a half centuries ago, it seems that sometimes "law almost ignores right."

This law raises many legal issues and is the target of much local criticism. Because it mentions the "illegal exit" from the national territory,[21] and considers the attempt to illegally migrate as the act itself, this law is a legal aberration that allows individuals to be arrested and sentenced solely on the grounds of presumed intentions, rather than for what they have done. It goes against the UN's universal declaration of human rights that stipulates that "everyone has the right to leave any country, including his own" (Article 13.2), and that "everyone charged with a penal offense has the right to be presumed innocent" (Article

11.1), a principle also fundamental to Roman law, Islamic law, and the common law. That this principle is suspended in this case indicates that, increasingly, migration is being dealt with through a legal and institutional apparatus derived from war, as today, similar a priori suspensions of fundamental rights are mostly found in legislation addressing the "global war on terror" (Sanders 2011).

As a result of this law, so-called smugglers, judged for their supposed intentions or alleged past activities, face serious jail time. By the end of 2015, fourteen individuals, alongside a dozen managers of transit houses (*ghettos*) and a handful of officials, were arrested in Agadez, and about fifty police officials in the region were replaced. This was not the first time that people were accused of migrant smuggling in Niger, but this was the first time that such accusations led to jail sentences. In 2016, more than one hundred smugglers were sent to court and found guilty, and as many vehicles were seized (EC 2016a). While the Nigerien and European authorities considered these enforcement activities a success, feelings were quite different in the streets of Agadez. As one local recruiter stated: "at home … everybody can be arrested, just because somebody will tell the police that one day you have carried migrants, or because you've hosted a few *exodants*. It's nonsense."[22] Another recruiter added: "Now they can come to your home and take you like that, pop, and send you to prison. Or when you are ready to go with the migrants, the police come and pop, they take them, and they keep the vehicle too."[23] Another local driver said: "The police take advantage of the situation. There are more than 300 Hilux [Toyota pick-ups] at the gendarmerie, and who is going to keep them? Some have already disappeared."[24]

Moreover, many feel that the law is only targeting Agadez and its surrounding area in the north of the country, where feelings of stigmatization and marginalization by the national authorities are commonplace and often a reason for rebellion (Deycard 2007; Bourgeot 1996). As one recruiter stated: "If they want to arrest all those who carry migrants, then they must also arrest the drivers in Niamey, Dosso and Zinder. Why is it only us in Agadez who are arrested? The law is the same across the country, isn't it?"[25]

Currently the arrests are only taking place in Agadez. As the new law suggests, one need not even cross the border to be considered a smuggler. Even local authorities have asked the national government to "temper" its application because the law is too "brutal" (Diallo 2016). Many people in the town are involved in the transport or housing of migrants; they are worried about rising unemployment and shrinking revenue if "the town's main business" is stopped without offering alternatives, explained the president of the regional council of Agadez, (Olivier 2015). This concern is shared by many in town:

> Soon the army will close the gold mines in the Djado and the Aïr mountains, and there may be 20,000 men who will return to Agadez. They all have weapons. If there are no more passengers, if there is no more gold, and no more tourism, what will they do? Start another rebellion, for sure![26]

The first casualty of this new law was the *agences de courtage*. Too visible to keep operating, with or without police protection, staff removed all the timetables and price lists for travel, and officially changed the name of their agencies. Thus, one of the most important agencies is now supposedly operating to "help expelled migrants to go back home," and to "contribute to the fight against malaria, AIDS, and tuberculosis; combat drug use; and contribute to the education of girls" (Association d'Appui aux Migrants et Refoulés 2016, 1). Behind the facade, though, staff wait for calmer times. These people used to be quite wealthy by local standards, giving money to their families and friends. Now they have one meal a day and worry about what kind of job awaits them. As one local recruiter said: "Now the migrants leave from 200 km south of Agadez, straight through to Libya. And us, what do we gain? Nothing anymore. There is nothing left in Agadez now."[27]

Yet corruption has not disappeared. Some smugglers still bribe policemen to let them leave the town or pass through their checkpoints. "It's more difficult, we have to be more careful, pay more, but sometimes, when we know them well, we can still come to an arrangement," affirmed one local recruiter.[28] Policemen are not the only ones who turn a blind eye. On their way to Libya, some smugglers tag along with military vehicles that are going to Dirkou, without being bothered. Even if most of the smugglers and policemen, afraid of punishment, are less likely to accept bribes, they know that the recent arrests might merely be a one-off attempt to show determination to the European partners. As a French diplomat put it: "Issoufou [the Nigerien president] doesn't care about migration, he just wants to get the money from the EU and the training for his presidential guard."[29] In Niger, everybody knows that controlling the desert is even more difficult than controlling the sea, and that no police program can keep people from adapting to the new conditions.

Aggiornamento of the "smugglers of humanity"[30]

The smugglers who cannot or do not want to bribe for police or army protection continue to invent new ways of doing their job. "They bypass [the new checkpoints], they take more difficult routes" explained the president of the regional council of Agadez (Olivier 2015). Those who still operate from Agadez keep their migrants in closed compounds, behind walls, until departure, which always takes place at night. Others pick up migrants in their car in the south of the country and take them straight through to North Africa, without stopping in any town or village. This means that migrants do not have to come to Agadez anymore to reach northern Africa. The internationally famous "smuggling entrepot" (*The Economist* 2014) is thus being bypassed. Smugglers open new routes, more discreet, more arduous, and often more dangerous than the usual ones, because of the risk of breakdowns on remote tracks with no hope of rescue, or of being attacked by armed bandits. For instance, in northern Niger, forty-eight bodies were found in the desert in June 2015 (Radio France Internationale [RFI] 2015), thirty-four in June 2016 (*Le Monde* 2016), forty-four in May 2017 (Al Jazeera 2017), and fifty-two in June 2017 (BBC 2017). There have been numerous migrant deaths in the Sahara, but few are reported or counted. When bodies are found, it is usually by chance and often months or years after the deaths. The military patrols that encounter the bodies do not always report the discovery, perhaps to reduce the official paperwork or avoid negative publicity about their job. In most cases, deaths are caused by accidents, or because migrants become stranded after breakdowns or running out of fuel. In some cases, migrant deaths occur because smugglers abandon them in the middle of nowhere because they do not want to risk being arrested. According to many observers, notably the IOM Director General, "the Sahara may be as deadly as the Mediterranean" (IOM 2015); or "even more [so]" (Danish Refugee Council 2016). The recorded deaths may represent only the tip of the iceberg.

Stories of people being abandoned in the desert by unscrupulous drivers have long circulated in the region. As long as migrant transport is part of larger socio-economic networks that span the Sahara, it will be visible to all; and such stories of suffering and death are significant not only for the reality that they describe, but for what they stand for: they underline the subhuman nature of treacherous transporters (and sometimes of those transported), and serve to mark and reinforce the boundaries between acceptable and unacceptable behavior. Although irregular, migrant transport was, at one point, recognized as a normal and legitimate economic enterprise, which had to follow established social norms. The current criminalization of all forms of transport has literally pushed migrant transport out of the public gaze, sometimes beyond the geographic bounds of "humanity," making the unspeakable possible.

From an international point of view, these tragic deaths are not interpreted as the unfortunate product of border control and restriction of free movement of the continent's population, but instead as compelling proof of the need to keep fighting the "infamous" smuggling networks that take advantage of the misery of others (EC 2016b, 2). Ironically, humanitarian efforts are sometimes quite opportunistic (Brachet 2016), and few choose to acknowledge the limits or even counterproductivity of some security policies (Andersson 2016; Cornelius 2001). Still, deaths are always appalling and for many legitimize the criminalization of all those who participate in migrant transit through the desert. It is a tiny step from here to the obliteration of the distinction between smugglers and traffickers. These terms, however, refer to very different realities, practices, and legal issues (Pierce 2014; Iselin and Adams 2003). Yet reports from the news media, the UN, international agencies, and government agencies continue to blur the boundaries between smuggling and trafficking, referring indistinctly to the people involved in migrant housing and transportation with one term or the other, or talking about "human trafficking and migrant smuggling" at the same time, and thereby obliterating the migrants' choice and agency, that is, the fact that people smuggled go voluntarily.[31] Even though very few people are involved in human trafficking through the Sahara, European officials do not hesitate to brand baseless figures with authority to justify their actions, as one high-ranking French diplomat did in Agadez:

> Emigration from Zinder [Niger] to Algeria … is still 90% for prostitution. … They take people from Africa to shoot them in the foot, to chain them up, to make them work for free, to prostitute their wives and children … the European Union must fight against this. … This is our moral duty towards Africa.[32]

While in external rhetoric, the distinction between smuggling and trafficking is generally not emphasized; from the inside, it is the distinction between the legal and the illegal that seems to have little salience. Locally, the terms used to designate those who organize migrants' journeys and border crossings do not always make it easy to determine the legality of the activities, as other distinctions seem to have more cultural and linguistic salience. In Hausa, *dirēbà* refers to professional drivers who operate on main roads; and *edraga*, more commonly used in Agadez, designates drivers who cross the Sahara, legally or not.[33] In both cases, the emphasis is on the fact that they are drivers, a respectable activity. Similarly, the Hausa expression *yan tchaga* refers generally to economic operators, and is used in Agadez to refer to all intermediaries that migrants encounter, most notably the recruiters (*d'an-kamicho*), but sometimes also the hosts or transporters. Of all the words that refer to smugglers of goods in the local languages, all derived from French and English, none translates specifically into "human smugglers."

While policy-makers and the media tend to stress the involvement of large-scale criminal networks of smugglers and traffickers in irregular migration from Africa to Europe, in Niger, these so-called transnational networks are in fact rather fragmented and uncoordinated chains of actors. In the Agadez area, they are neither centralized nor possess any hierarchy. With just a few local contacts, everyone can take advantage of the opportunities created by the tightening of the migration policies. The networks and institutions drawn on by transporters of migrants mirror those in other Saharan economic sectors, some of which come from a long history of trans-Saharan activities (Marfaing and Wippel 2004). There are no transnational criminal networks in Agadez but rather small-scale, low-investment activities. In such a context, transnational networks are mostly the monopoly of the state, and it is international state involvement that, by criminalizing ordinary activities, may put people in a situation where they feel compelled to put themselves under the protection of "criminal networks" and pay the extra price—financially, and in terms of their own independence—that comes with this. At the time of writing, in northern Niger, the harm caused by the international criminalization of transregional mobility, both to local economic agents and to migrants who pay increasingly dearly for their passage, is very real and deeply felt.

Conclusion

Research literature on migration in northwest Africa and the Mediterranean suggests that migration from sub-Saharan Africa to Europe through the Sahara is very limited in absolute and relative numbers (Lessault and Beauchemin 2009), and that the vast majority of sub-Saharan migrants in North Africa have no intention of leaving the continent (see Bensaâd 2009). However, in Europe, the fear of migrant invasion has been used to legitimize ever-growing restrictions on the freedom of movement of certain peoples.

Like their North Africa neighbors, Sahelian states are now involved in the European fight against "illegal" migration. In Niger, people accused of migrant smuggling risk arrest. Migrants are forced—or strongly encouraged—to turn back if they are caught in the Sahel. As a result, the wide array of transport options that used to be offered to would-be migrants in the southern Sahara has shrunk. Irregular but socially regulated options are replaced by means of transport that are both irregular *and* clandestine. These clandestine operations tend to be more difficult, expensive, and risky, not only because they are using more dangerous roads, but also because they are less liable to internal social control by peers, friends, and families. Nevertheless, the tiny proportion of sub-Saharans who have, for several generations now, attempted to migrate to North Africa continue to do so. The overall conditions of travel, life, and survival in the desert are worsening. So are relations between state agents, transport agents, and their clients. Meanwhile, the number of deaths at the Saharan frontier of Europe continues to rise, and is met by even greater indifference than that afforded to those who have perished in the Mediterranean.

That people cross borders illegally or rather extralegally does not imply the existence of "human smugglers," who are identified as such, by migrants or by local authorities. The recent appearance in the media and in political rhetoric of "human smugglers" is, in Niger at least, the result of an external and highly politicized interpretation of long-standing local and regional practices, rather than of the emergence of a new phenomenon. The end of local tolerance toward irregular border crossing and the implementation of policies aimed at suppressing both irregular migratory practices and those who facilitate them have created a legal and social category of actors defined as beyond the law and thus punishable by law: human smugglers. Yet to arrest and condemn a few people to impede the mobility of others means forgetting the historical dimension of human mobility in this part of Africa.

Indeed, the Sahara is not merely a desert crossed but also an area shaped by migrants, merchants, and transporters who have contributed and are still contributing to the urbanization of the area and to its economic vitality (Pliez 2003; Brachet 2009; Scheele 2012). Moreover, none of the national and international policies implemented in the area has ever led to a real and sustainable decrease in the number of trans-Saharan migrants. Migration practices change accordingly, but migration does not disappear. Clandestine movement is always an option. What international intervention has achieved is to disturb a long-standing trans-border migration system that affects North Africa and the Sahel, and is beneficial for those who take part in it. It has thereby contributed to a worsening of the conditions for travel and for the overall economic and social conditions in the area over the last 15 years.

The case of the central Sahara illustrates how smugglers, as a category of actors playing a specific part in the global migration process, are directly manufactured by the migration policies put in place to stop them.[34] The degree of illegality and secrecy of the transport provided depends directly on the harshness of migration policies and on the ways in which they are implemented. In Niger, the laws on migration have effectively created "people smugglers" within the country, while repression has forced them into secrecy. Such is the performative dimension of the "fight against criminal networks of smugglers" (Council of the European Union 2016). Yet this blatant failure of migration policies implemented since the early 2000s at great cost (financial, material, and human) in the Sahara might be a matter of perspective.

For the last 20 years, the politicization of the issue of irregular migration through the Sahara has caused a sharp increase in the budget allocated to hire staff and buy equipment for the "control" and "securitization" of borders. In fact, the management of international migration has become an industry in and of itself, generating immense profits for a variety of actors from the manufacturers of military equipment for migrant surveillance, consulting gigs for independent experts, civil servants, and subcontractors, to institutions such as the UN, IOs and NGOs, all funded to intervene in this domain (see Andersson 2014; Gammeltoft-Hansen and Sorensen 2012).[35] Meanwhile, more border control means that more resources are necessary to bypass borders. As the fight against irregular migration and smuggler networks is strengthened, illegal transport of migrants becomes increasingly professionalized and clandestine. In response, politicians and officials are asking the international community for even more money to fight against ever more sophisticated smuggling. This is a vicious circle. Inherently, border control policy, in the Sahara and elsewhere, is self-sustaining: it has directly fostered the clandestine transport of migrants, which in turn gives rise to a state-mounted response. In short, if all industries tend to ensure the reproduction of the conditions for their existence, then the global failure of the industry of migration management appears as its greatest success.

Notes

1. Personal interview in Agadez on December 15, 2016.

2. Tamasheq is the language of the Tuareg, who live in the Central Sahara, mostly in Mali, Niger, and Algeria, and also in Libya and Burkina Faso.

3. For more detail on the methodology adopted, see Brachet (2012a).

4. This rebellion (mostly organized by Tuareg groups) play out a conflicted pattern of reaction to state power, with the aim of achieving autonomy or even independence of northern Niger.

5. Personal interview with the mayor on December 13, 2016.

6. In many African cities, *coxeurs* constitute a category of informal actors in the transport sector whose role is to put potential clients in touch with a transport agent (see for instance Okpara 1988). In Agadez, which is a relatively small town, touts work only with foreign migrants. Numerous and often idle, they compete to collect the maximum number of customers for the agency with which they work. Immobile, because they are attached to the people and places in the city in which they work, *coxeurs* live by the mobility of others.

7. CFA franc have a fixed exchange rate to the euro: 1,000 CFA francs = 1.5 €.

8. Personal interview on October 15, 2009.

9. Ministerial Conference on Migration in the Western Mediterranean, Tunis, October 16–17, 2002. See also Boswell (2003) and Migreurop (2011).

10. Frontex is the European Agency for the Management of Operational Cooperation at the External Borders of the EU.

11. Personal interview on October 15, 2009.

12. Personal interview on October 16, 2009.

13. Even if, until the 2011 war in Libya, Libyan migration policy has always been ambiguous. Indeed, while, in the 2000s, Qaddafi agreed to be turned by the EU into one of its most important partners in its fight against illegal immigration, he nonetheless remained at the forefront of pan-Africanism and kept encouraging sub-Saharan immigration to Libya. On the ways in which Qaddafi used migration as a foreign policy tool, see for instance Paoletti (2011) and Perrin (2016).

14. Personal interview in Niamey on December 21, 2010.

15. Personal interview in Niamey on December 12, 2014.

16. EC's allocation policy "reward[s] countries according to their governance performance." Under the 10th EDF (2008–2013), more than €1.5 billion was spent in the Sahel. The budget of the 11th EDF (2014–2020) foresees almost €4 billion for the Sahel countries.

17. The one and only on migration among the ECOWAS members, the 1979 Dakar Protocol on Free Movement of Persons, allows for 90 days of visa-free stay for nationals of all Member States.

18. Personal interview on October 12, 2009.

19. Loi n° 2015-36 du 26 mai 2015 relative au trafic illicite de migrants, Republic of Niger. This law is directly inspired by the UN protocol against the smuggling of migrants.

20. Any other person who lodges or transports irregular migrants on national territory can also be condemned (Articles 11 and 12).

21. The notion of "illegal emigration" was first adopted by the EU to legitimize the arrests of migrants on the Atlantic and Mediterranean coasts of Africa (Morice 2009).

22. Personal interview with Mr. M. in Agadez on December 14, 2016.

23. Personal interview with Mr. A. in Agadez on December 13, 2016.

24. Personal interview with Mr. I., a driver, in Agadez on December 14, 2016.

25. Personal interview with Mr. A. in Agadez on December 11, 2016.

26. Personal interview with Mr. A.K., a trader, in Agadez on December 16, 2016.

27. Personal interview with Mr. H., recruiter in Agadez on December 14, 2016.

28. Personal interview with Mr. M. in Agadez on December 16, 2016.

29. Personal interview with a French diplomat in Agadez on December 13, 2016.

30. Kresevic (2016).

31. See for instance Hinshaw and Parkinson (2015), Nossiter (2015), various reports of the Anti-Human Trafficking and Migrant Smuggling Unit of the UNODC, McQuade (2015), and several newsletters of the European embassies in Niger.

32. Public allocution of the Minister-Counselor at the French Embassy in Niger, in Agadez on December 13, 2016.

33. In Tamasheq, *edderbé* refers to all kind of drivers. In French, *fraudeurs*, which is mostly used for smugglers of goods, can also be used for migrant smugglers, as well as *passeurs*, which is more specific.

34. The term "manufacturing" is taken here as a metaphor to underline how smuggling activities in the Sahara have been actively created and shaped by various policies. For similar use, see for instance Barkey (1994, 141–75) on banditry, and Herman and Chomsky (1988) on public opinion.

35. The budget of Frontex went up from less than €20 million in 2004 to more than €140 million in 2015; the budget of the IOM went from $240 million in 1998 to more than $1.3 billion in 2014; in 2007 to 2013, 60 percent of the EU budget for Home Affairs was earmarked for the "management of migratory flows"; since 2000, 11 billion Euros have been spent in Europe on repatriations. It is unfortunately difficult to obtain overall figures of money spent in Niger, but these are probably proportionally similar.

References

Agence France-Presse (AFP). 15 June 2015. Agadez in Niger has gone from desert jewel to city of crime. *AFP*. Available from www.afp.com.

Al Jazeera. 1 June 2017. More than 40 migrants "die of thirst" in Niger. *Al Jazeera*. Available from www.aljazeera.com.

Andersson, Ruben. 2014. *Illegality, Inc.: Clandestine migration and the business of bordering Europe.* Berkeley, CA: University of California Press.

Andersson, Ruben. 2016. Europe's failed "fight" against irregular migration: Ethnographic notes on a counterproductive industry. *Journal of Ethnic and Migration Studies* 42 (7): 1055–75.

Association d'Appui aux Migrants et Refoulés (AAMR). July 2016. Objectifs spécifiques. Agadez, Niger.

Barkey, Karen. 1994. *Bandits and bureaucrats: The Ottoman route to state centralization*. Ithaca, NY: Cornell University Press.

BBC. 6 May 2014. Migrant dreams turn into Sahara sex work. BBC. Available from www.bbc.com.

BBC. 26 June 2017. Niger migrants: 52 die during desert crossing. BBC. Available from www.bbc.com.

Beccaria, Cesare Bonesana di. 1764/1872. *An essay on crimes and punishments. By the Marquis Beccaria of Milan. With a commentary by M. de Voltaire*. Albany, NY: W. C. Little & Co.

Bensaâd, Ali, ed. 2009. *Le Maghreb à l'épreuve des migrations subsahariennes. Immigration sur émigration*. Paris: Karthala.

Blin, Louis. 1990. *L'Algérie du Sahara au Sahel*. Paris: L'Harmattan.

Boesen, Elisabeth, and Laurence Marfaing, eds. 2007. *Les nouveaux urbains dans l'espace Sahara-Sahel*. Paris: Karthala.

Boswell, Christina. 2003. The "external dimension" of EU immigration and asylum policy. *International Affairs* 79 (3): 619–38.

Bourgeot, André. 1996. Les rébellions touarègues: une cause perdue? *Afrique contemporaine* 100:99–115.

Brachet, Julien. 2009. *Migrations transsahariennes. Vers un désert cosmopolite et morcelé (Niger)*. Paris: Le Croquant.

Brachet, Julien. 2011. The blind spot of repression: Migration policies and human survival in the central Sahara. In *Transnational migration and human security. The migration- development-security nexus*, eds. Thanh-Dam Truong and Des Gasper, 57–66. New York, NY: Springer.

Brachet, Julien. 2012a. Geography of movement, and geography in movement: Mobility as a dimension of fieldwork in migration research. *Annales de géographie* 687–688:543–60.

Brachet, Julien. 2012b. Stuck in the desert. Hampered mobility among transit migrants in northern Niger. In *The challenge of the threshold. Border closures and migration movements in Africa*, eds. Jocelyne Streiff-Fénart and Aurélia Wa Kabwe Segatti, 73–88. Lanham, MD: Lexington Books.

Brachet, Julien. 2016. Policing the desert: The IOM in Libya beyond war and peace. *Antipode* 48 (2): 272–92.

Bredeloup, Sylvie, and Olivier Pliez, eds. 2005. Migrations entre les deux rives du Sahara. *Autrepart* 36.

Copans, Jean, ed. 1975. *Sécheresses et famines au Sahel*. Paris: Maspero.

Cornelius, Wayne A. 2001. Death at the border: Efficacy and unintended consequences of U.S. immigration control policy. *Population and Development Review* 27 (4): 661–85.

Council of the European Union. 2015. *Council conclusions on the Sahel regional action plan 2015–2020*. Note 7823/15. Brussels: Council of the European Union.

Council of the European Union. 2016. *Council conclusion on migrant smuggling*. Brussels: Council of the European Union.

Damon, Arwa, Brent Swails, and Brice Laine. 21 July 2017. This city is a tinderbox, and the U.S. is building a drone base next door. CNN. Available from http://edition.cnn.com.

Danish Refugee Council. 2016. *Forgotten fatalities: The number of migrants deaths before reaching the Mediterranean*. Mixed Migration Monitoring Mechanism Initiative. Nairobi: DRC-IGAD.

De Haas, Hein. 2008. The myth of invasion. The inconvenient realities of African migration to Europe. *Third World Quarterly* 29 (7): 1305–22.

Destrijcker, Lucas. 17 October 2016. Welcome to Agadez, smuggling capital of Africa. Politico. Available from www.politico.eu.

Deycard Frédéric. 2007. Le Niger entre deux feux. La nouvelle rébellion touarègue face à Niamey. *Politique africaine* 108:127–44.

Diallo, Ibrahim Manzo. 13 December 2016. Migration à Agadez: Autopsie d'un phénomène. NigerInter. Available from www.nigerinter.com.

The Economist. 31 May 2014. No wonder they still try. *The Economist*. Available from www.economist.com.

Economic Community of West African States (ECOWAS). 2008. ECOWAS common approach on migration, 33rd ordinary Session of the Head of State and Government, Ouagadougou, 18 January 2008. Ouagadougou: ECOWAS Commission.

European Commission (EC). 2007. *Aeneas programme: Overview of projects funded 2004–2006*. Brussels: EC.

European Commission (EC). 2016a. Commission reports on first deliverables under the partnership framework on migration with third countries. Press release, Brussels.

European Commission (EC). 2016b. *Communication on establishing a new partnership framework with third countries under the European agenda on migration*. Strasbourg: EC.

European Commission (EC). 2016c. *Fact Sheet: EUR 381 million to tackle the root causes of irregular migration in the Sahel and the Lake Chad Basin*. Brussels: EC.

European Commission (EC). 2016d. *Partnership framework on migration yields first results*. Brussels: EC.

European External Action Service (EEAS). 2015. EUCAP Sahel Niger: Council nearly doubles mission's annual budget. Press release, Brussels.

European External Action Service (EEAS). 2016a. *Common security and defence policy of the European Union*. Missions and operations annual report 2016. Brussels: EEAS.

European External Action Service (EEAS). 2016b. *Common security and defence policy. The EUCAP Sahel Niger civilian mission*. Brussels: European External Action Service.

European External Action Service (EEAS). 2016c. EUCAP Sahel Niger: Mission extended, budget agreed, mandate amended. Press release, Brussels.

Flynn, Daniel. 19 June 2015. Insight—Graft stalls Niger's bid to end migrant route to Europe. *Reuters*. Available from https://af.reuters.com.

Gammeltoft-Hansen, Thomas, and Ninna Nyberg Sorensen, eds. 2012. *The migration industry and the commercialization of international migration*. Oxford: Routledge.

The Global Initiative against Transnational Organized Crime. 2014. *Smuggled futures: The dangerous path of the migrant from Africa to Europe*. Geneva: The Global Initiative against Transnational Organized Crime.

Grégoire, Emmanuel. 1999. *Touaregs du Niger, le destin d'un mythe*. Paris: Karthala.

Herman, Edward S., and Noam Chomsky. 1988. *Manufacturing consent: The political economy of the mass media*. New York, NY: Pantheon Books.

High Representative of the EU for Foreign Affairs and Security Policy/Vice-President Federica Mogherini. 2016. Press conference on the progress under the migration partnership framework, Brussels.

Hinshaw, Drew, and Joe Parkinson. 19 July 2015. Agadez traffickers profit from movement through Niger to Libya. *Wall Street Journal*. Available from www.wsj.com.

Hout, Wil. 2010. Governance and development: Changing EU policies. *Third World Quarterly* 31 (1): 1–12.

Hugo, Victor. 1869/1886. *L'homme qui rit*. Paris: Eugène Hugues.

International Organization for Migration (IOM). 2015. IOM cites discovery of more victims in Sahara among migrants bound for Libya. Press release.

Iselin, Brian, and Melanie Adams. 2003. *Distinguishing between human trafficking and people smuggling*. Geneva: UN Office on Drugs and Crime.

Kabbanji, Lama. 2011. Vers une reconfiguration de l'agenda politique migratoire en Afrique de l'Ouest. *Études internationales* 42 (1): 47–71.

Kresevic, Kieren. 20 January 2016. The African refugee crisis and smugglers of humanity. *Harvard Political Review*. Available from http://harvardpolitics.com.

Le Monde. 16 June 2016. Niger : trente-quatre migrants retrouvés morts dans le désert. *Le Monde*. Available from www.lemonde.fr.

Lessault, David, and Cris Beauchemin. 2009. Ni invasion, ni exode. Regards statistiques sur les migrations d'Afrique subsaharienne. *Revue Européenne des Migrations Internationales*. 25 (1): 163–94.

Marfaing, Laurence, and Steffen Wippel, eds. 2004. *Les relations transsahariennes à l'époque contemporaine. Un espace en constante mutation*. Paris: Karthala-ZMO.

Maurice, Eric. 18 October 2016. EU hails first result in Africa migration deals. *EUobserver*. Available from https://euobserver.com.

McQuade, Aidan. 22 April 2015. Migrant crisis: Smuggling or trafficking? Politicians don't seem to know. *The Guardian*. Available from www.theguardian.com.

Migreurop. 2011. *At the margins of Europe. The externalisation of migration controls. 2010– 2011 report.* Paris: Migreurop.

Morice, Alain. 2009. Conceptualisation des migrations et marchandages internationaux. In *Le Maghreb à l'épreuve des migrations subsahariennes. Immigration sur émigration*, ed. Ali Bensaâd, 193–212. Paris: Karthala.

Newsletter for the European Union. 29 June 2015. EU commits to boost border capacities of African countries. *Newsletter for the European Union.* Available from http://www.newslettereuropean.eu.

Nossiter, Adam. 20 August 2015. Crackdown in Niger fails to deter migrant smugglers. *New York Times.* Available from www.nytimes.com.

Okpara, Enoch E. 1988. The role of touts in passenger transport in Nigeria. *Journal of Modern African Studies* 26 (2): 327–35.

Olivier, Mathieu. 23 October 2015. Niger: à Agadez, la chasse aux passeurs est ouverte. *Jeune Afrique.* Available from www.jeuneafrique.com.

Organisation for Economic Co-operation and Development (OECD). 2015. Can we put an end to human smuggling? *Migration Policy Debates* 9.

Paoletti, Emanuela. 2011. Migration and foreign policy: The case of Libya. *Journal of North African Studies* 16 (2): 215–31.

Papastavridis, Efthymios. 2010. "Fortress Europe" and Frontex: Within or without international law? *Nordic Journal of International Law* 79 (1): 75–111.

Penney, Joe. 25 May 2014. Human smugglers of the Sahara. Reuters. Available from https://widerimage .reuters.com.

Perrin Delphine. 2016. Regulating migration and asylum in the Maghreb: What inspirations for an acceler- ated legal development? In *Migration in the Mediterranean*, eds. Seline Trevisanut and Francesca Ippolito, 192–214. Cambridge: Cambridge University Press.

Pierce, Sarah. 12 November 2014. The vital difference between human trafficking and migrant smuggling. *Open Democracy.*

Pliez, Olivier. 2003. *Villes du Sahara. Urbanisation et urbanité dans le Fezzan libyen.* Paris: CNRS.

Pliez, Olivier. 2004. De l'immigration au transit? La Libye dans l'espace migratoire euro- africain. In *La nouvelle Libye. Sociétés, espaces et géopolitique au lendemain de l'embargo*, ed. Olivier Pliez, 138–55. Paris: Karthala-Ireman.

Politzer, Malia, and Emily Kassie. 21 December 2016. The 21st century gold rush—How the refugee crisis is changing the world economy. The Huffington Post. Available from http://highline.huffington post.com.

Radio France Internationale (RFI). 16 June 2015. Migrants morts dans le Sahara: des drames difficiles à chiffrer. RFI. Available from www.rfi.fr.

Sanders, Rebecca. 2011. (Im)plausible legality: The rationalisation of human rights abuses in the American "global war on terror." *International Journal of Human Rights* 15 (4): 605–26.

Scheele, Judith. 2012. *Smugglers and saints of the Sahara: Regional connectivity in the twentieth century.* New York, NY: Cambridge University Press.

Sieff, Kevin. 25 July 2015. Inside Niger's boom in people smuggling: Sneaking people across the Sahara to Libya and eventually Europe is big business in Agadez. *The Independent.* Available from www.inde- pendent.co.uk.

Spittler, Gerd. 1993. *Les Touaregs face aux sécheresses et aux famines.* Paris: Karthala.

Tidjani Alou, Mahaman. 2002. La petite corruption au Niger. *Études et Travaux du Lasdel* 3:1–55.

Out of West Africa: Human Smuggling as a Social Enterprise

By
STEPHANIE MAHER

Drawing on 18 months of ethnographic research in Senegal, this article focuses on the sociality of migrant facilitation. Although it has become relatively common in media and policy reports to suggest that irregular migrants are manipulated by greedy and unscrupulous human smugglers, this article shows how migrants in Senegal are often familiar with their handlers and are more likely to call them a friend (*ami*) than a criminal. Also, most migrants do not see themselves as "smuggled," which implies victimhood. Rather, they see themselves as making calculated choices to migrate based on a host of social factors. By exploring the relationships between handlers and migrants, this article reveals the social worlds of negotiation, assistance, and protection that feature prominently in West African migrant narratives and practices.

Keywords: migration facilitation; social proximity; migrant smuggling; Senegal

T he year 2016 was another banner year for clandestine migration across the Mediterranean. Though not as dramatic as 2015, when nearly 1 million people reached Europe by sea (International Organisation for Migration [IOM] 2015), the past 12 months as of this writing have seen more than 350,000 people enter Europe through maritime routes.[1] Faced with a seemingly endless "wave" of migrants and refugees landing on its southern shores, the European Union has mobilized military interventions and discursive strategies to authorize and expand border control operations. One axis of intervention is to combat human smuggling networks, which are commonly characterized as transnationally syndicated (European Commission 2015, 49),

Stephanie Maher has conducted ethnographic research on clandestine migration, religious aspirations, and forced repatriation in Senegal. She is currently a postdoctoral fellow at the African Centre for Migration and Society (ACMS) at the University of the Witwatersrand.

Correspondence: stephanie.maher@wits.ac.za

DOI: 10.1177/0002716217743935

ANNALS, *AAPSS*, 676, March 2018

hierarchically organized (United Nations Office on Drugs and Crime [UNODC] 2011b, 10) mafia-like cartels (Bhabha 2005, 8) that truck in human desperation (Europol 2016). Underwriting such interventions, media outlets and policy reports routinely feature stories of smugglers abusing and abandoning people in the Sahara Desert or the Mediterranean (BBC 2015; Chonghaile 2015; Kingsley 2015; Searcey and Barry 2017; UNODC 2011a).

Such stories overlook the degree to which militarized borders produce riskier and thus more lethal forms of migration (Andersson 2015a; Cross 2013; Mainwaring and Bridgen 2016).[2] They also collapse the nuanced social relations between migrants and their facilitators under the umbrella of coercion and criminality and, instead, advocate a paternalistic agenda to "protect" migrants by shutting down smuggling operations. Though migrants on the move can and do face dangers along the way to Europe, abuse at the hands of facilitators is the exception rather than the norm. Moreover, empirical work reveals that rather than being hierarchically organized, many, if not most, facilitation practices are small-scale and oriented around personal and communal connections, which involve notions of protection and even solidarity between handlers and their human cargo.

Disrupting the persistent image of smugglers as hardened criminals, and the corollary image of migrants as consummate victims, this article shows how migrant facilitation in Senegal often operates through preexisting economies of social proximity. I explore boat migration out of Senegal between 2006 and 2008, when tens of thousands of young men reached the Canary Islands via wooden fishing pirogue. In 2006 alone, thirty thousand to forty thousand successfully arrived,[3] with untold numbers perishing in the crossing.[4] Like other "irregular" travelers, Senegalese migrants relied on a variety of facilitators to access passage across unknown and dangerous territories. Their relationships with their *passeurs* (or handlers) formed part of a larger social landscape of value that was far from constant and was continually shaped by shifting degrees of social proximity.

Drawing on Jane Guyer's ethnographic work on economic transactions in West Africa, this article underlines how securing the assistance of a handler is contingent on relational economies of social proximity, which informed how exchanges were conducted. I use the term *social proximity* to index the extent to which migrant-handler relations were informed by how well people knew each other through interpersonal relations, which often determined the services and protections that were provided for migrants along their journeys. In economic geography, "relational" theorists argue that markets are structured not merely on the inherent stability of laws and historically established patterns but also on the extent to which collaboration and "social interaction between economic agents ... [shapes] economic performance" in emergent ways (Boggs and Rantisi 2003, 109). In social network theory, proximity mechanisms regulate interpersonal relations based on reciprocity and shared interests (Rivera, Soderstrom, and Uzzi 2010), even when actors are separated by physical distance (Torre and Rallet 2005). Working from these two general premises, I theorize relational economies of social proximity as determining and attaching value to goods and services based on spheres of relation rather than material equivalences, institutional efficiencies, or physical location. This analytic approach runs contrary to the rationalist underpinning of the "smuggling as business" literature. I also use the term *relational cosmology* to describe how migrants understand and construct their social universe based on their location within a field of personal interconnections, whose contours of distance and nearness are ever changing.

In Senegal, objects such as cars or tracts of land are often sold or exchanged to pay for passage, but these material liquidations are neither the only nor even the most important transfers. Rather, a kind of alternative economy is at play, whereby the value of a pirogue fare is not strictly linked to fixed currency indices, but is translated into and accrued through social relations of obligation and reciprocity. As such, migration strategies form part of a larger landscape of fungibility and risk that remains in a constant state of flux. Understanding human smuggling practices in West Africa as shaped by notions of socio-spatial proximity and distance reveals how clandestine migration is a fundamentally social enterprise. In this way, the smuggler-as-criminal trope is neither accurate nor useful when it comes to understanding how people move within and out of Africa today.

Background, Methods, and Theoretical Contributions

Since the end of the twentieth century, a wide range of scholars and policy-makers have defined human smuggling in different ways.[5] Some have articulated smuggling as part of a global "migration business" or "industry" (Gammeltoft-Hansen and Sørensen 2013; Hernández-León 2005; Salt and Stein 1997; Zhang 2007). Echoing the language of commerce, some have defined smugglers as "migration merchants" who attempt to profit "legally or illegally, from the commodification of the international migration process" (Kyle 2000, 67). The business of smuggling has frequently been articulated as hierarchical and organized (Kyle and Koslowski 2001; Salt and Stein 1997; Schloenhardt 2003). Policy-makers and media outlets continue to frame smuggling operations as fundamentally exploitative and criminal (Europol 2016), even though empirical research suggests that migration facilitation is based, to some degree, on relations of trust and reciprocity (Kyle and Liang 2001). Others have argued that focusing too heavily on the business model of smuggling ignores the internal social dynamics within family and community networks that participate in the movement of people across borders (Herman 2006). Moreover, some suggest that defining the human smuggler as distinct from the migrant may be inaccurate, as "many 'smugglers' are in fact migrants who facilitate illegal travel" (Baird and van Liempt 2016, 402; see also Ahmad 2011; Lucht 2012). Though the human smuggler in media and policy discourses often calls on tropes of the unscrupulous criminal (Pastore, Monzini, and Sciortino 2006), many of my participants saw their handlers as people with the connections and expertise to help them access a sure path out of Senegal. As Ilse van Liempt argues, "Migrants may have fewer stigmas attached to the smuggling business and more positive views on smugglers than the media and policy-makers" (van Liempt 2007, 128).[6]

I use the word *handler* to refer to a broad category of actors whose identities often overlapped. These include recruiters, intermediaries, middlemen, boat captains, boat crew, and, at times, boat owners. I translate the word *passeur* as *handler* instead of *smuggler* for several reasons. First, *smuggler* carries strong overtones of impersonal organized crime, a feature I did not find in migrants' accounts. Instead, journeys were frequently negotiated within close-knit communities among people who already knew each other. Most migrants were familiar with their handlers and were more likely to call them *sama guy* (my friend) rather than criminal. Also, the young men I met would not see themselves as smuggled, which implies victimhood. Rather, they saw themselves as actively staking claims to reciprocity and obligation from people they knew to access passage out of Senegal.

Additionally, migration intermediaries in West Africa in the mid-2000s did in fact "handle" everything from the purchasing of essential provisions to arranging transport to protecting passengers while at sea. Frequently, such preparations and protections were described as part of a moral obligation to ensure safe arrival. Using *handler* thus disrupts the popular "one-dimensional portraits of human behaviour [as] dictated by narrow agendas of economic utility" (Ahmad 2011, 7). Perhaps more importantly, uncritically adopting the legalistic definition of *human smuggler* risks reifying the socio-legal system that produced it, and the people within its definitional scope, without interrogating its inherent assumptions. As Theodore Baird has argued, "The growth of the category of human smuggling [is] a device of social control of undesirable populations and extra-state markets" (Baird 2016, 6–7). Using the trope of smuggler is thus neither neutral nor apolitical. Central to the goal of this article, then, is to disrupt such stereotypes and offer a nuanced picture of migration facilitation.

This article is based on an ethnographic study of the social and political lives of forcibly returned migrants in Senegal who attempted to reach the Canary Islands via pirogue between 2006 and 2008 but were repatriated by the state. Fieldwork was conducted over 18 months between 2011 and 2014 in multiple sites across Senegal, which yielded interviews with 170 repatriated migrants, as well as their families, *marabouts* (spiritual guides), and community members. Principal respondents were located through snowball sampling, and initial interviews typically consisted of collecting basic demographic data, such as age, marital status, family size, migration attempts and costs, and dates of deportation. Follow-up interviews were semistructured or unstructured and, in several cases, entailed multiple meetings over the course of many months. Focus groups were conducted with larger groups, with later follow-up interviews taking place with particular individuals. I also interviewed twenty state officials, local activists, and nongovernmental organization (NGO) workers operating in the domain of migration management in Senegal. It is important to note that of the 170 repatriated migrants I interviewed, 87 percent reported personally knowing their handler before 2006 when the exodus began. The remaining 13 percent accessed their handlers through other intermediaries such as friends or relatives.

Using this ethnographic data, and drawing on the economic anthropology of Jane Guyer (2004), this article proposes using a theoretical model based on economies of proximity rather than business or social network models to describe the relationship between migrants and their handlers. For one, commercial models are fundamentally Eurocentric and do not account for how exchange, risk, and speculation may work in other cultural contexts. In other words, such approaches do not always account for how "the economic weaves together social relations" (Mbow 2008, 17). In the words of Ibrahima, who attempted passage in 2006, "Money buys more than rice."[7] It creates and sustains social worlds of reciprocity and obligation. Seeing migration facilitation as primarily an economic, or business, enterprise privileges profit as the prime motivator of smuggling and thus ignores the possibility that social relations could be embedded within economies of proximity.

Additionally, social network models often do not adequately accommodate actors outside the family unit. Using a social proximity approach underlines how the value of a handler is contingent, manifold, and flexible. Modern liberal notions of value, or what Guyer calls "progressive monetary reductionism" (2004, 171), see quantitative value as a linear progression beginning at zero and numerically increasing to infinity. And yet, as Georg Simmel elaborated in *The Philosophy of Money* (1978/2011), "Value is never a 'quality' of the objects, but a judgment upon them which remains inherent in the subject" (p. 65). Thus, migrants and handlers actively and dialectically generate value through their interactions. Understanding how value is negotiated, both in terms of pricing and protection, reveals how migration facilitation is not always a simple predatory or even purely monetary transaction but is embedded in socio-spatial economies. Such economies are not without tension and conflict; nor are they purely based on ideal and normative notions of solidarity. Rather, they are the modality through which particular claims are lodged and subsequently negotiated depending on degrees of proximity. As the following will reveal, most prices, either for boat fare or other assistance, were negotiated, sometimes uneasily. Handler fees and services were often evaluated based on spatial, proportional, and relational scales rather than strictly tied to standardized indices of equivalence. In other words, a migrant may ask a handler for something he technically cannot "afford"; but because the handler is his cousin's wife's brother, or because they grew up in the same village, the migrant may make a claim based on their social proximity to one another. As one migrant, Mas, explains below, he was able to negotiate a reduced fare because he and his handler followed the same religious fraternity. Such a scenario challenges the idea that "smuggler networks" are hierarchically organized criminal consortiums based on profit-seeking business models.

This article begins with an examination of migrant-handler relations through the lens of *waxhaalé*. In Wolof, the most widely spoken language in Senegal, *waxhaalé* means to bargain or negotiate. Most prices, either for boat fare or other assistance, such as transportation to the departure point or accommodations prior to setting out, were negotiated rather than fixed. I argue that this flexibility in price reflects a larger convertibility of value in West Africa and maps onto speculations of investment and return that surround the unpredictable nature of life. While the notion of bargaining has long been studied by sociologists, economists, and political scientists as a game of competition and self-interest (Brams 2003; Bacharach and Lawler 1981; Nash 1950), it has been less explored in relation to migration facilitation. This article redirects our attention to the ways that bargaining and negotiation are inherent to clandestine migration out of West Africa. Using *waxhaalé* as an analytical lens to examine notions of value highlights how relations and negotiations between handlers and migrants are not always structured by exploitation and coercion, but are also shaped by notions of social proximity. The spheres of exchange that govern handler prices and services are spatial, proportional, and relational rather than strictly tied to notions of equivalence. As such smuggling itself calls on relationships that are, frequently, already in place, or are part of larger social, ethical, and religious constellations, which is at least one reason why many of my participants referred to their handlers as friends or kin.

Although migration facilitation from Africa to Europe is widely regarded as a criminal enterprise populated by a host of unscrupulous human smugglers whose disregard for the people they are presumably hired to help is surpassed only by their appetite for quick profits, the handlers and boat captains who I interviewed in Senegal considered it a moral and religious duty to ensure that their passengers arrived *sain et sauf* (safe and sound). Rather than being hardened criminals, handlers are often bound by moral and ethical norms to protect the people in their charge. The second section of this article explores precisely the ways in which handlers conceived of and ensured protection during transit across the Atlantic.

Far from being the neutral result of simple misinformation or overly dramatic journalistic fervor, discourses on the criminality of human smugglers produce a particular view of "irregular" migration and legitimize increasingly militarized border enforcement strategies. Ironically, such strategies and interventions only make migration more difficult and thus the need for facilitators more acute (Maher 2017). The case of Senegal is exemplary. With the implementation of Frontex-led joint patrols off the Senegalese coast in 2005 and 2006, Atlantic migration routes were effectively crippled, leading migrants to redirect their journeys across the Sahara to departure points in North Africa.[8] Such trajectories are not only longer, more expensive, and more dangerous, they are also more socially remote. Language barriers, foreign territories, and unfamiliar cultural hierarchies all further necessitate the need for migration facilitation. In this way, European border securitization has effectively rendered African borders more insecure to cross (Lemberg-Pedersen 2017). As the final section of this article reveals, military operations in the mid-2000s both reshaped clandestine migration across the Atlantic and inspired new patterns of migration across the Mediterranean that we see today.

Negotiated Beginnings

The journey begins with a price—a price that is not fixed, but is subject to debate and concession. Migrants frequently used the verb *waxhaalé* to describe the process of deciding on a fare. To *waxhaalé* is to bargain—a performance that governs nearly every sphere of exchange in Senegal. Most goods and services are subject to *waxhaalé*: taxi fares, food, textiles, bride wealth, land. *Waxhaalé* informs and reflects the sociality of consumption and exchange. Unlike Western notions of pricing that are linked to regulated or standardized indices of valuation, in Senegal value depends on, and is measured by, social proximity and distance. Such proximities and distances are displayed and performed through *waxhaalé*.

Jane Guyer has argued that in contrast to the West, where markets are presumably disciplined by state institutions such as federal reserves and exchange commissions, in West Africa, exchange has historically been mediated through "popular conventions rather than formal regulation" (Guyer 2004, 4). For Guyer, value in West Africa is ordered not by a fixed currency but instead by *relational* indices and performative transactions that allow people to respond flexibly to persistent volatility. When economies are formally regulated, the cost of a good or service is pegged to a currency; when economies are based on relational transactions, the cost of a good or service depends on who is asking (e.g., where they come from, who they know, where their family lives). A price is the result of *calculative flexibilities*, which require both the consumer and producer to be fluent in "orders of magnitude [and] possible thresholds of relative value" (Guyer 2004, 92). If value is not monetized in any strictly formal way, it becomes open to flexibility. Such flexibilities weigh consumer goods and services based not on currency and labor power, but on spatial and relational spheres. Being able to improvise in response to unpredictable situations calls on shared logics that govern exchange in volatile circumstances. As such, bargaining is social labor because it relies on a consensus of value and thus brings the volatile market, where prices fluctuate too wildly for people to control, into the domestic realm.

Because value in transactions of goods and services is spatially and relationally determined in West Africa, it should not be surprising that prices for boat passage fluctuate. Even within the same vessel, there were differences in what passengers were charged. Handlers and boat owners quickly and efficiently sized up candidates, depreciating costs for friends and charging more from those who seemed to possess the means and less from those who did not. For migrants, knowing someone was crucial. Khadim, a migrant from 2006, described how his failed first attempt bought him the sympathy of a boat captain who let him try a second time for free. "When the handler knows you, he has sympathy for you. He can trust you, so he will give you another chance," he said.

If a migrant knew the handler, he could petition for a reduced fare. Migrants could, and often did, try to claim social proximity by referring to common origins, distant relations, or religious fraternity. Making successful *waxhaalé* meant summoning all the connections at one's disposal no matter how remote. Some described how they were able to negotiate lower fares because their handlers were from the same or neighboring villages. Others described how their handlers were distantly related, often by several degrees of separation. When no direct connection to a handler could be found, an intermediary was used. Mas explained his consultations this way:

> I asked my friend how much the fare was and he told me I needed at least one million CFA [$2,000]. But we both follow the same *marabout* [spiritual guide], so I said, "That's

too much! He is my brother [belonging to the same Sufi brotherhood], and so there is solidarity between us. … Afterwards, he said, "If you have 500,000CFA [$1,000], I could negotiate for you with the handler." I told him okay. And later, he arranged everything.

In some cases, migrants were able to address the boat owner directly, though this was less common. Typically, arrangements were negotiated through a handler or other intermediary. In this case, Mas made *waxhaalé* with his "spiritual brother," a middleman who had a personal connection to the handler. This linked Mas to the handler through a kind of "social vouching."

In Senegal, as in much of West Africa, strangers—people who cannot be linked to a particular community—are potentially dangerous. Without friends or family members, strangers float outside the normal order of things; they are fundamentally *a*social because they occupy no space in the relational cosmology. Social vouching fixes the problem of strangeness by locating a person in a moral universe that binds them together with others, thus providing a value-indexed social proximity and its concomitant benefits. As Guyer makes clear, vouching stabilizes a potentially unpredictable social field by calling on "particular logics already in place and shared at the cognitive level" (Guyer 2004, 114). In this way, some migrants managed the "turbulence" of not personally knowing their handlers by using other intermediaries and facilitators as bridges or social connectors across thresholds of remoteness.

Knowing what a voyage is worth is of critical importance in a world where the price is not set in stone but instead shifts across a spectrum of value. As Guyer observes with respect to volatile West African markets, where fakes, authentic fakes, counterfeits, and originals are pegged to various gradients of quality, "Access to a helper who can provide sound advice … is a valuable resource" (Guyer 2004, 92). What is important to note is that even if these "helpers" were friends, they still attempted to make a small profit from their connections. For Iran, his helper could not be blamed for trying to seize an opportunity. "Like me," he said, "my friend was struggling to get by."

He told me there was a boat leaving for Spain. I asked how much, and he said 500,000CFA. I told him, "I don't have 500,000CFA. I have only 300,000CFA." Because he was attaching himself to me, you see? He is my friend, but he wanted to earn something [from the transaction]. … Still I only proposed 300,000CFA, and he said, "Okay."

As Iran recounted the interaction to me, I was left with the distinct feeling that the negotiations were in themselves valuable as performances. Echoing Simmel above, Michael Ralph argues that value is not merely inhered in objects but can "assume the shape of a public performance" (Ralph 2008, 17). If Iran's performative *waxahaalé* was good enough, this helper could bridge the gap between Iran and the boat owner. As such, Iran's degree of social proximity, and his understanding of how local spheres of exchange operated, were key to his access.

In addition, notions of friendship neither prohibit nor exist outside spheres of economic exchange. It was understandable, even expected, that Iran's friend would attempt to turn a profit from a chance encounter. Most migrants described the negotiation process as one that required caution, even if the people guiding and mediating on their behalf were trusted allies. "Everyone must make an effort in life," Iran explained. "But it's God who sets the price." For Iran, bargaining for pirogue fare was part and parcel of the larger struggle of life whose architecture was divinely ordered. As other scholars have pointed out, people can and often do interpret empirical evidence through religious idioms, whereby God is seen as a "primary actor" in the unfolding of events (Heiß 2003). To make his case for entry into a pirogue was, for Iran, not to usurp this divine ordering, but to work within in it. The recognition that ultimately the final price was not up to him endowed Iran with spiritual maturity. *Waxhaalé* was thus nested in a broader constellation of social forces, wherein travel, piety, and adulthood were consubstantial. *Waxhaalé* not only signified the variability of value, it was also a performance of pious labor.

A paid fare did not necessarily mean an expedited departure. For many migrants, waiting was inherent in the act of transit (Brigden and Mainwaring 2016; Hagen-Zanker and Mallett 2016, 19–21; Vogt 2016). No longer at home but not yet at sea, migrants were frequently housed in remote villages while awaiting departure. Domestic compounds in rural villages were transformed into warehouses where as many as "ninety clandestine candidates waited in one room," Youssoupha said. Other times, groups were partitioned off to various compounds, suggesting that organizing clandestine journeys was something of a village undertaking in some cases. The longer it took to amass enough passengers, the lower the price fell. Frequently, boats only left when all the "seats" had been filled, which could sometimes take weeks.

Other passengers, such as captains and crew, were not required to pay at all. Moustapha, a captain from 2006, explained that normally he would be compensated for conducting a pirogue to the Canary Islands. Instead, he declined payment and brought his brothers as crewmates to help him because, as he said, "The journey is long, and no one knows what can happen in the ocean. I needed them to maintain the security." As a longtime fisherman, Moustapha understood that the journey could present serious challenges.

Protective Transits

In contrast to depictions of smugglers who routinely abuse and abandon their passengers, the handlers and captains I met were committed to protecting people from the vagaries of passage. Many of them linked their professional obligations as handlers to their religious obligations as Muslims to ensure that passengers arrived *sain et sauf* (safe and sound) (Hagan 2011; Sarat 2013). If the condition of the boat was sound and the weather remained calm, the journey would take roughly eight days. According to Abdoulaye, a boat captain in 2006, it was exactly 1,647 kilometers from Kayar, in Senegal, to Tenerife, the largest of the Canary Islands. "Good boats" were the ones where the captain had purchased plenty of rice, cooking oil, and bottled water. Many also brought vitamins and medication for those too seasick to eat.

Like other captains I met, Abdoulaye undertook several additional protective measures before departing. He consulted with his *marabout* who gave him special ablutions to use on the day of departure, several prayers to recite before stepping in the boat, and *gris-gris* (protective amulets) to wear during the journey. As Abdoulaye described it, these devices would ultimately protect both him and the passengers under his watch. Because his relationship with his *marabout* was one of spiritual education and enlightenment it was also necessarily centered on managing risk and insecurity. As he described it, though the journey was indeed dangerous, not going to see his spiritual elder beforehand would have been unthinkable, and could have provoked risks "worse than any ocean," he said.

Like Abdoulaye, other captains and handlers used their own money to protect their boats before setting out. Ouseynou, a captain in 2007, described how his *marabout* recommended killing a sheep and donating the meat to the poor families in his village. "This protects your journey and your passengers because God will see that you have sacrificed something of yourself. Yes, 100 lives may be worth more than a single sheep, but God makes calculations you cannot understand. The point is to bring your soul close to Him. That way he will recognize you." As Simmel argues, value is a judgment that "we experience [as] a sentiment … [which] demands recognition" (Simmel 1978/2011, 70–71). Reflecting the notion that value is not necessarily tied to standard equivalence, Ouseynou's comment reveals how one's social proximity to God determines what the sheep is "worth."

Several of the handlers I met also traveled to Mauritania to purchase the correct "programs" to input into their GPS devices, which would then guide their pirogues on a sure path to the Canaries. That migration facilitators invested their own time and resources into such preparations counteracts the image of "human smugglers" as nefarious criminals, and underscores the degree to which facilitators felt responsible for the lives on board. For Abdoulaye, it was "no small thing to be charged with ensuring the safe arrival of roughly 100 souls across a dangerous ocean."

In an effort to avoid crossing paths with maritime patrols, the *grande pirogue* would frequently wait offshore, while smaller pirogues would go back and forth, hauling goods and loading passengers in groups. The threat of exposure was always present, whether by local police or border control vessels patrolling offshore. Another captain, Mamadou, recounted his departure in 2006 this way:

> I left Mbour around 4 PM and took the pirogue to Kayar. When I arrived, I told the boat owner that I wouldn't wait around given the fact that the patrols were everywhere. I could see their boats morning and night going back and forth along the coast hoping to catch migrants. So I told the owner we needed to leave no later than 2 AM because otherwise it wasn't safe; otherwise, I would leave and go back home if it got too late. So, we started loading the bags around 8PM until midnight. And then we loaded the passengers until 1 AM, and cast off at 2 in the morning.

Even experienced boat captains knew that unexpected circumstances could arise. Maritime patrols could catch them before they even embarked on their trip. Storms could come out of nowhere and immobilize the pirogue at best or sink it at worst. People could "lose their head" and create destabilizing disturbances on the boat. Abdoulaye's pirogue was incapacitated for two days during a violent squall. Being a man of the sea, Abdoulaye knew how to read the ocean itself as a fluid landscape of risk. His fluency in managing this risk required positioning the pirogue to avoid oncoming waves while not exhausting the limited fuel supplies.

Many captains quickly realized that their passengers were ultimately ignorant of what it would mean to sit in a boat for seven to eight days. Moustapha described how it was his job to teach the passengers how to behave while aboard the pirogue.

> We are fishermen. We've been out there [at sea] for a long time. We figure things out as we go because we're habituated to it. For example, if we need to use the bathroom, we know what to do. But for many *clandestins*, they had no sense. Some would sit there in their own filth and then fights would break out with their neighbors. We had to give them a bucket and show them how to empty it when they were done.

Directing the passengers in proper comportment, Moustapha and his crewmates were ultimately able to keep the peace. Moustapha delegated different social tasks on board, such as bailing water, cooking, and looking after sick passengers. "I made sure the passengers participated in the functioning of the pirogue. That way, they would cooperate and we could arrive safely," he said. Meals were taken together, in classic Senegalese style, with groups of people kneeling around stainless-steel bowls of cooked rice. The image of communal meals and "teams," each performing their tasks, paints a portrait of transit that was, at least in part, a convivial experience.

At the same time, arguments among the passengers would often break out, and handlers and captains had to step in to quell the fighting. "There were nights when no one slept because of all the quarrels," Abdoulaye said. He described how the canvas tent that his crew had constructed for cooking during inclement weather became a zone of contention as people jostled and shoved each other for shelter during the cold nights. Other times, people simply "lost their head" after several days at sea.

> Sometimes we had to tie them up because you had to protect them. Listen, the ocean is deep. *Géeg, dafa dé war* [The ocean is mystical]. As fishermen, we understand that there are things in the water, things like *djinns* who try to trick you. In my boat, people would scream at night because they had visions. Sometimes, people would go crazy and try to jump overboard. Me, on my boat? I couldn't afford to have anyone drown in the ocean. A death like that would follow me to my own grave.

Other captains reported the same circumstances. As Djibril recounted to me, "Sometimes restraining passengers was the only way to make sure they wouldn't disturb the boat." Such disturbances could be lethal, as vessels filled with people could easily capsize.

As a fisherman who had spent his life in a boat, Abdoulaye had more personal knowledge of the vagaries of the sea than many of his passengers. He knew the journey would be long and dangerous. Conducting a pirogue across the open Atlantic would not be easy no matter what the circumstances. But with so many souls aboard, it would be an especially serious, and potentially grave, challenge. As Abdoulaye said, "We were like brothers because we all had the same goal in mind: to arrive safely in Spain.[9] I had to make sure we arrived safely. I was the captain, and if anything happened to the pirogue I would have suffered the consequences [in the afterlife]." Being the captain meant that Abdoulaye was responsible for the passengers arriving unharmed, so much so that his own existential fate was hanging in the balance. Safe arrival was thus both a spiritual and a practical imperative.

Uneasy Futures

In 2006, media coverage of clandestine migration to Europe exploded in the press and filled the pages of the BBC, *The New York Times*, and *The Guardian*. Images of overcrowded pirogues descending on Spanish shores were frequently accompanied by descriptive metaphors, such as a "wave" or "flood," which suggested that Europe was indeed being "invaded" by African migrants. Such media representations effectively summoned an atmosphere of panic (Andersson 2015b), and a consequent call to immediate action on the part of European nations (Erjavec 2003; Horsti 2012; Maher 2015).[10]

The European Union and individual Member States swiftly adopted and expanded several strategic responses. One of these responses was border management. Beginning with Operation Hera in 2005, Frontex, the external border management arm of the European Union, began coordinating operations with African states to expand maritime patrols and surveillance systems in the Mediterranean and off the Senegalese coast. Such operations played a major role in crippling clandestine naval routes to Europe by stopping journeys before they began in Senegal and by policing the North African coast.[11] Like Frontex, Spain's Sistema Integrado de Vigilancia Exterior (SIVE) was another effective border control mechanism. By positioning highly sophisticated infrared technologies off the Spanish coast, boats were detected and intercepted earlier and thus fewer pirogues were able to make it to European shores (Carling 2007).[12]

A second strategy focused on developmental diplomacy. Bilateral and multilateral partnership agreements with African states such as Senegal, Mauritania, and Morocco required African nations to police European borders from the other side of the Mediterranean in exchange for foreign aid. Such a policy transfer dynamic has been described as "border externalization" by some scholars (Lavenex 2006). The 2007 Country Strategy Paper (CSP) and National Indicative Programme (NIP) signed by the EU and Senegal are cases in point. Citing the "unprecedented wave of clandestine emigration coming from Senegal [which] descended on the Canary Islands" in 2006 (Senegal-European Commission 2008, Part I, 19), the NIP provided significant "financial instruments" for, among other things, the control of clandestine migration (Senegal-European Commission 2008, Part II, 2).[13]

The mobilization of both Frontex and SIVE contributed to a significant drop in irregular migration from West Africa. Whereas approximately forty thousand migrants arrived in 2006, a little more than two thousand arrived in 2009. While significant, these numbers obscure how clandestine migration has not disappeared, but has shifted in response to the militarization of border controls in the Atlantic. The dismantling of the trans-Atlantic route meant that clandestine journeys out of Senegal would necessitate travel over the Sahara Desert and embarking from points along the North African coast. Consequently, migration from Africa to Europe is becoming longer, more fragmented, and more dangerous (Collyer 2007). Past routes that took weeks now sometimes extend to months or years, with migrants spending significant periods in one of the several "transit nodes" trying to earn money for the next leg of the journey (Gnisci and Trémolières 2006, 9). Intended to reduce clandestine migration, militarized controls instead often make such travel riskier and more protracted.

One consequence of this increased militarization is that migrants and handlers are sometimes several degrees removed in social proximity, which can lead to increased risk. As Moustapha put it, "It used to be that we put everyone in a boat. Passengers were with us from start to finish. Now there are so many other handlers involved. It can become dangerous." As travelers move across the Sahara, handlers with high degrees of social proximity are less involved in getting people to their final destination. Instead, handlers may transfer their passengers to a colleague at the next point of transit, usually at a border, or simply leave migrants to negotiate the next leg on their own. As such, the "chain of trust" degrades (van Liempt 2007, 171). Whereas friends may have helped to organize journeys off the coast of Senegal in 2006, today migrants may "experience more exploitation … as they are less able to rely on personal networks" (Baird and van Liempt 2016, 407). That said, Senegalese migrants continue to call on social and religious communities in North Africa to access passage through dangerous spaces. Moustapha explained, "There are Senegalese in Morocco, in Libya, all along the route. Though it's not easy, they will help if you send someone to them."

Not only are journeys longer and more insecure, the cost of smuggling services or other migrant assistance has also increased as a response to the escalating risk. According to my respondents, passage to the Canary Islands in 2006 cost between $400 and $800; today Senegalese migrants must pay from $300 to $1,000 to get to Libya and then an additional $300 to $2,000 to cross the Mediterranean (Darme and Benattia 2017; United Nations High Commissioner for Refugees [UNHCR] 2013, 57). These small fortunes are often earned incrementally en route or allocated by family members back home. With greater kin investments, family debt escalates and migrants become less likely to turn back (Collyer 2007).

Rather than stopping migration facilitation, patrols and surveillance systems have simply redirected it. "With Frontex, migration just moves elsewhere," Moustapha said. The result is a cycle in which border controls, meant to inhibit migration, provoke it (Bensaâd 2005, 19; Castles 2004). Moreover, as borders become harder to cross, migrants and refugees must increasingly rely on handlers and facilitators for assistance. In 2006, Europol reported that 80 percent of irregular migration from Africa to Europe was facilitated. A decade later, that number has increased to 90 percent (Europol 2016, 13). Such figures are often mobilized to license military campaigns that seek to combat human smuggling while ignoring the extent to which border controls have created the necessary conditions for the rise in facilitation practices. As scholars have routinely pointed out, the rise of border militarization only increases the need for smugglers' services. "For would-be migrants, what used to be a relatively low-cost, informal affair ... now requires greater risks and resources and is less likely to be attempted without some type of professional smuggler" (Kyle and Dale 2001, 30). David Kyle and Zai Liang argue that "human smuggling ... is a trade positively correlated with *greater* border controls" (Kyle and Liang 2001, 3). And according to Hein de Haas, "There's no point in blaming the smugglers, when in fact the border restrictions have created this phenomenon in the first place" (Osman and Pinault 2016).

Another consequence of border militarization is that migration across the Mediterranean has become more dangerous than ever. As a way to evade detection, Libyan facilitators increasingly employ smaller inflatable rafts, as opposed to larger wooden vessels, placing more people at risk. Whereas in 2015, just over thirty-seven hundred went missing or died in the Central Mediterranean route, more than five thousand faced the same fate in 2016. According to a 2017 report, average death rates in the Mediterranean increased from 1.2 per 100 arrivals in 2016 to 2.1 per 100 in 2017 (Black et al. 2017, 6).[14] What this means is that death to arrival ratios have steadily risen since 2014. As the Office of the United Nations High Commissioner for Refugees recently reported, a migrant's chances of dying in the Mediterranean rose from one death per 269 arrivals in 2015 to one death in 88 arrivals in 2016. The ratio is even more dramatic in the Central Mediterranean context, where one in forty-seven arrivals perished (UNHCR 2016).

In a troubling development, the language of humanitarian intervention is increasingly used to justify military response. Contemporary narratives, which tend to paint smugglers as part of regional mafia-like criminal organizations, are strikingly similar to those circulated 10 years ago. News stories of smugglers abusing or abandoning their human cargo in unseaworthy boats in the middle of the Mediterranean have become commonplace, generating ire and moral repulsion in the public sphere. Such repulsion has authorized military interventions, such as European Union Naval Force Mediterranean (EUNAVFOR MED) Operation Sophia, whose mission is to combat smuggling operations in the Mediterranean and thus "protect" vulnerable migrants and refugees from their nefarious handlers. As stated on the EUNAVFOR MED website, a central target is to "disrupt the business model of human smuggling and trafficking in the Southern Central Mediterranean and prevent further loss of life at sea."[15] More recently, Europol launched the European Migrant Smuggling Center,[16] in an effort to "[tackle] the sophisticated international ... smuggling networks ... that exploit the desperation and vulnerability of migrants" (Europol 2016, 2). For both agencies, the mission is vast.

Tracking down and immobilizing the "40,000 individuals suspected of being involved in migrant smuggling" (Europol 2016, 7) is not only practically ambitious; like Operation Sophia, it also frames intervention as a humanitarian response. Playing on the "care and control duality of humanitarianism" (Pallister-Wilkins 2015, 54), police interventions "control" the national borders while "caring" for the vulnerable migrant who is presumably exploited by criminal thugs. As Polly Pallister-Wilkins has pointed out, "[The] increased use of humanitarianism in *both* the discourse and practice of European border policing over the past decade … fram[es] and legitimiz[es] interventions at sea, promoting certain technologies and shaping operational responses" (Pallister-Wilkins 2015, 54). Such discourses do not merely license restriction; they *produce* truths about the way migration works. Stopping the smuggler presumably stops the migrant from heading down a dangerous path filled with thieves, extortionists, rapists, drug lords, prostitution kingpins, and violent murderers. Increased military patrols, then, are mobilized in the migrant's best interest. And yet, as this article has shown, facilitators often provide protective services to clandestine migrants.

Ironically, the logical conclusion of migration management discourses and policy interventions has been to curtail migration because of the number of lives presumably placed at risk rather than establishing safer channels for legal mobility. In a neat, if too convenient, calculus, migration management has been operationalized to police borders in a kind of "paradox of protection" (Pallister-Wilkins 2015, 54), whereby hapless victimized migrants are saved through humanitarian intervention and, at the same time, Europe's borders are protected from the criminalized invasion of the "illegal" other. In this way, caring for the migrant and controlling his or her movements become part and parcel of the same unproblematized conflation that frames institutional ethics and responses to clandestine migration.

Conclusion

Though migration facilitation is increasingly used in today's climate of global migration, we still understand very little about how it works, and how people on the move use facilitators to negotiate dangerous spaces. While violence along the clandestine migrant route does exist, this article has shown that captains and other facilitators are more often protectors and guides who serve a necessary role in helping people to transit unknown territories. By pointing out the nuances of the persistent image of the smuggler as criminal, this article shows the ways in which migration is a fundamentally human undertaking. I suggest that risk itself is not generated by the migration facilitator or handler per se, but by the political conditions along the migration routes, and highlight the degree to which immigration policy has resulted in journeys that are long and dangerous for Senegalese migrants and refugees.

Although it has become relatively common in media and policy reports to suggest that irregular migrants the world over are lured by greedy and unscrupulous human smugglers who do not fully disclose the dangers of passage, and who take advantage of passive or gullible migrants, this article emphasizes the sociality of migrant facilitation, arguing that that smuggling is embedded in social processes of exchange that are not universally exploitative but are often based on spatial economies that are culturally sanctioned and sustained. Contrary to alarmist reports of internationally syndicated human smuggling networks operating in Africa, I demonstrate that facilitation practices are mostly small-scale operations oriented around economies of social proximity. The majority (87 percent) of repatriated migrants who I interviewed in Senegal knew their handlers personally and relied on them to facilitate transit through unknown and dangerous spaces. Journeys were frequently negotiated within close-knit communities among people who already knew each other.

Future research on migration facilitation would do well to combine disparate theoretical approaches—for example, social networks and world systems approaches—which would help researchers to understand how migrants navigate the multisited landscape of socially remote migration facilitators. Such a hybrid approach would also contextualize migration facilitation within a larger political economy and global governance regime that creates the conditions necessary for "human smuggling" to flourish. As Baird points out, "critical research on migrant smuggling is to turn the focus from supporting states in their efforts to police and prohibit migration, towards a focus on ending harms and reducing suffering of those who have felt the most brutal effects of the regimes of prohibition" (Baird 2016, 8). More than trying to define *who* the migration facilitator is in terms of marked identity, critical research should focus on trying to understand such actors as "embedded in the complex interplay of systemic forces that lead to migration" (Baird and van Liempt 2016, 409). Further, as Line Richter has pointed out, rather than defining smugglers as ideal types (i.e., criminals, extortionists, blackmailers, and so on), migration facilitators and brokers can be better understood as "assemblages of practices," which underlines the relational, heterogeneous, and productive aspects of migration facilitation (Richter 2016).

Though migration patterns out of West Africa have shifted, the social landscape of clandestine migration remains largely the same. Prices for boat fares are persistently variable, as smugglers calculate what to charge from which passenger. In other words, access is still socially organized. The act of making *waxhaalé* for facilitation and protection between handlers and migrants was, and continues to be, governed not so much by fixed notions of value, but rather by social and spatial proximities that function, in some way, to domesticate volatile conditions. Such negotiations are "as routine in general as they are extraordinary in each instance, in an economic life lived under volatile conditions" (Guyer 2004, 114). Such negotiations form part of a preexisting paradigm wherein people use distance and proximity to gauge and negotiate value. As Jane Guyer makes clear, African systems of value are conditioned by a "multiplicity of scales" that are reflexively and mutually referential (Guyer 2004, 172). In much the same way, the spheres of exchange that govern facilitation prices and services are spatial, proportional, and relational. Who you know, and how remote or close they are in terms of kinship or community, influences the migrant-handler relationship in specific ways.

Understanding the economies of migration facilitation as social rather than strictly monetary renders facilitation itself as something more complex than a profit-seeking industry. It also disrupts the notion of handlers as criminals and migrants as victims, and instead accommodates the possibility that the handler-migrant relationship, including negotiating prices and providing security, might be shaped by the social variability of value. By taking a more socio-spatialized approach to migration facilitation, we can see that clandestine migration itself is not a static institution but rather one that operates according to local conceptions of fungibility and proximity, which shape how social and material exchanges are conducted and how migrant pathways are facilitated.

Notes

1. See UNHCR's most recent figures at http://data.unhcr.org/mediterranean/regional.php.

2. As a recent report from the House of Lords reveals, Operation Sophia, which is tasked with patrolling the Mediterranean and disrupting "the business model of human smuggling," has actually led to "a tragic increase in deaths" in the Central Mediterranean (2017, 2). Even the EU's Joint Commission found that one consequence of Operation Sophia has been "journeys [becoming] increasingly dangerous and to the rise in the number of deaths" (JOIN 2017, 6).

3. Like many data associated with Senegal, arrival estimates are notoriously inconsistent. According to Papa Demba Fall, professor of geography and long-time scholar of Senegalese migration at the Institut Fondamentale de l'Afrique Noire (IFAN), 41,000 arrived on the Canary Islands in 2006 (Fall 2010, 31). By contrast, *The New York Times* reported that 39,180 arrived that year (Minder and Yardley 2013). A 2011 country report on Senegal's changing demography estimated that between 2006 and 2007, "a little more than 40,000 individuals" (of Senegalese and other nationalities) reached the Canary Islands," the majority of whom (30,000) arrived in 2006 (ANSD 2013, 55–56). And according to a 2009 report commissioned by the IOM, 901 vessels landed on the Canary Islands in 2006 with 35,488 migrants on board (Some 2009, 103).

4. It is impossible to know how many migrants perished in the Atlantic crossing. Most estimates suggest that roughly six thousand people died en route in 2006 (Ifekwunigwe 2013, 226). However, these figures are likely underestimated by a significant margin because migrant remains are often unfound or unidentified.

5. For critical reviews of the literature, see Baird (2016), Baird and van Liempt (2016), and Sanchez (2017).

6. Kyle and Liang also find that "smugglers are often quite open about their activities in the sending communities" (2001, 21), and are even regarded as "freedom fighters" (2001, 2).

7. All names have been changed to protect the identity of my participants.

8. With budgetary autonomy and legal personality, Frontex, the external border management agency of the EU, does not operate independent policing units, but rather manages border control initiatives conducted with Member States and third countries.

9. Caroline Melly's Senegalese respondents also confirmed that clandestine migrants "battled risk and worked together as brothers" (2011, 370).

10. Other more measured voices have argued that the discourse of invasion is an outright myth, and that in fact intra-continental migration within Africa is far more pronounced (De Haas 2007).

11. Though it has been highly effective, Frontex's methods came under scrutiny by NGOs, such as CARITAS Europe, which accused the agency of abuse, neglect, and not complying with the standards of non-refoulement (Gaydazhieva 2012).

12. SIVE became operational in 1999 across the Strait of Gibraltar. Since then, highly advanced surveillance stations have spread along the entire Andalusian coast, and are now equipped with infrared sensors that can detect vessels 25 kilometers from shore.

13. In the amount of 288 million Euros between 2008 and 2013.

14. Mortality estimates should be approached cautiously, as the real death toll is likely much higher. As Tara Brian and Frank Laczko point out, "Some experts have suggested that for every dead body discovered, there are at least two others that are never recovered" (Brian and Laczko 2014, 15).

15. See https://eeas.europa.eu/csdp-missions-operations/eunavfor-med/36/about-eunavfor-med-operation-sophia_en.

16. See https://www.europol.europa.eu/content/EMSC_launch.

References

Ahmad, Ali Nobil. 2011. *Masculinity, sexuality and illegal migration: Human smuggling from Pakistan to Europe*. Burlington, VT: Ashgate.

Andersson, Ruben. 26 October 2015 (2015a). The illegality industry: Notes on Europe's dangerous border experiment. *Border Criminologies*. Available from https://www.law.ox.ac.uk/ research-subject-groups/centre-criminology/centreborder-criminologies/blog/2015/10/ illegality.

Andersson, Ruben. 8 October 2015 (2015b). REDUX: Fear by numbers: On the rise of Europe's "illegality industry" #Borders. *Allegra*. Available from http://allegralaboratory.net/fear- by-numbers-on-the-rise-of-europes-illegality-industry/.

ANSD (Agence Nationale de la Statistique et de la Démographie). 2013. *Situation économique et sociale du Sénégal en 2011*. Dakar: Ministère de l'Economie et des Finances, République du Sénégal.

Bacharach, Samuel B., and Edward J. Lawler. 1981. *Bargaining: Power, tactics, and outcomes*. San Francisco, CA: Jossey Bass.

Baird, Theodore. 2016. Defining human smuggling in migration research: An appraisal and critique. European University Institute, Robert Schuman Centre for Advanced Studies, Working Paper 2016/30, Fiesole.

Baird, Theodore, and Ilse van Liempt. 2016. Scrutinising the double disadvantage: Knowledge production in the messy field of migrant smuggling. *Journal of Ethnic and Migration Studies* 42 (3): 400–17.

BBC. 23 April 2015. Migrant crisis: Who are Africa's people smugglers? Available from http://www.bbc.com/news/world-europe-32381101.

Bensaâd, Ali. 2005. Les migrations transsahariennes: Une modialisation par la marge. *Maghreb-Machrek* 185:13–36.

Bhabha, Jacqueline. 2005. Human smuggling, migration and human rights. Paper prepared for The International Council on Human Rights Policy Review Meeting, 25–26 July, Geneva.

Black, Julia, Kate Dearden, Ann Singleton, and Frank Laczko. 2017. Global overview of the available data on migrant deaths and disappearances. In *Fatal journeys*, vol. 3, *Improving data on missing migrants*, eds. Frank Laczko, Ann Singleton, and Julia Black, 1–24. Geneva: International Organization for Migration.

Boggs, Jeffrey S., and Norma M. Rantisi. 2003. The "relational" turn in economic geography. *Journal of Economic Geography* 3:109–16.

Brams, Steven J. 2003. *Negotiation games: Applying game theory to bargaining and arbitration*. New York, NY: Routledge.

Brian, Tara, and Frank Laczko. 2014. Counting migrant deaths: An international overview. In *Fatal journeys: Tracking lives lost during migration*, eds. Tara Brian and Frank Laczko, 15–43. Geneva: International Organisation for Migration.

Brigden, Noelle, and Ðetta Mainwaring. 2016. Matryoshka journeys: Im/mobility during migration. *Geopolitics* 21 (2): 407–34.

Carling, Jørgen. 7 June 2007. The merits and limitations of Spain's high-tech border control. *Migration Information Source*. Available from http://www.migrationpolicy.org/articles/merits-and-limitations-spains-high-tech-border-control.

Castles, Stephen. 2004. Why migration policies fail. *Ethnic and Racial Studies* 27 (2): 205–27.

Chonghaile, Clár Ní. 31 July 2015. People smuggling: How it works, who benefits and how it can be stopped. *The Guardian*.

Collyer, Michael. 2007. In-between places: Trans-Saharan transit migrants in Morocco and the fragmented journey to Europe. *Antipode* 39 (4): 668–90.

Cross, Hannah. 2013. *Migrants, borders and global capitalism: West African labour mobility and EU borders*. New York, NY: Routledge.

Darme, Marie-Cecile, and Tahar Benattia. 2017. *Mixed migration trends in Libya: Changing dynamics and protection challenges*. Tripoli: UNHCR-Libya.

De Haas, Hein. 2007. The myth of invasion: Irregular migration from West Africa to the Maghreb and the European Union. International Migration Institute, Research Paper, Oxford.

Erjavec, Karmen. 2003. Media construction of identity through moral panics: Discourses of immigration in Slovenia. *Journal of Ethnic and Migration Studies* 29 (1): 83–101.

European Commission. 2015. *A study on smuggling of migrants: Characteristics, responses and cooperation with third countries*. Brussels: European Commission. Available from http://www.emn.lv/wpcontent/uploads/study_on_smuggling_of_migrants_final_report_master_091115_final_pdf.pdf.

Europol. 2016. Migrant smuggling in the EU. *Europol Public Information*. Available from www.europol.europa.eu.

Fall, Papa Demba. 2010. Sénégal: Migration, marché de travail et développement. Organisation Internationale du Travail, Working Paper, Geneva.

Gaydazhieva, Stanislava. 18 September 2012. EU ombudsman asked to look closer at FRONTEX. *New Europe*. Available from http://neurope.eu.

Gammeltoft-Hansen, Thomas, and Ninna Nyberg Sørensen, eds. 2013. *The migration industry and the commercialization of international migration*. New York, NY: Routledge.

Gnisci, Donata, and Marie Trémolières. 2006. *Atlas on regional integration in West Africa: Population series, migration*. Paris: OECD Publications.

Guyer, Jane. 2004. *Marginal gains: Monetary transactions in Atlantic Africa*. Chicago, IL: University of Chicago Press.

Hagan, Jacqueline Maria. 2011. *Migration miracle: Faith, hope and meaning on the undocumented journey*. Cambridge, MA: Harvard University Press.

Hagen-Zanker, Jessica, and Richard Mallett. 2016. *Journeys to Europe: The role of policy in migrant decision-making*. London: Overseas Development Institute.

Heiß, Jan Patrick. 2003. Imbrication du modèle religieux et des connaissances empiriques dans les travaux agricoles des paysans manga. In *Le travail en Afrique noire: Représentations et pratiques à l'époque contemporaine*, eds. Hélène d'Almeida-Topor, Monique Lakroum, and Gerd Spittler, 81–92. Paris: Karthala.

Herman, Emma. 2006. Migration as a family business: The role of personal networks in the mobility phase of migration. *International Migration* 44 (4): 191–230.

Hernández-León, Rubén. 2005. The migration industry in the Mexico-U.S. migratory system. University of California, California Center for Population Research, Working Paper CCPR 049-05, Los Angeles, CA.

Horsti, Karina. 2012. Humanitarian discourse legitimating migration control: FRONTEX public communication. In *Migrations: Interdisciplinary perspectives*, eds. Michi Messer, Renée Schroeder, and Ruth Wodak, 297–308. New York, NY: Springer.

House of Lords. 2017. Operation Sophia: A failed mission. House of Lords Paper 5. London: European Union Committee.

Ifekwunigwe, Jayne O. 2013 "Voting with their feet": Senegalese youth, clandestine boat migration, and the gendered politics of protest. *African and Black Diaspora: An International Journal* 6 (2): 218–35.

International Organisation for Migration. 22 December 2015. *Irregular migrant, refugee arrivals in Europe top one million in 2015*. Geneva: International Organisation for Migration. Available from https://www.iom.int/news/irregular-migrant-refugee-arrivals-europe-top- one-million-2015-iom.

JOIN. 2017. *Migration on the Central Mediterranean route: Managing flows, saving lives*. Brussels: European Commission.

Kingsley, Patrick. 24 April 2015. Libya's people smugglers: Inside the trade that sells refugees hopes for a better life. *The Guardian*.

Kyle, David. 2000. *Transnational peasants: Migrations, networks, and ethnicity in Andean Ecuador*. Baltimore, MD: Johns Hopkins University Press.

Kyle, David, and John Dale. 2001. Smuggling the state back in: Agents of human smuggling reconsidered. In *Global human smuggling: Comparative perspectives*, eds. David Kyle and Rey Koslowski, 29–57. Baltimore, MD: Johns Hopkins University Press.

Kyle, David, and Rey Koslowski, eds. 2001. *Global human smuggling: Comparative perspectives*. Baltimore, MD: Johns Hopkins University Press.

Kyle, David, and Zai Liang. 2001. Migration merchants: Human smuggling from Ecuador and China. University of California, Center for Comparative Immigration Studies, Working Paper, San Diego, CA.

Lavenex, Sandra. 2006. Shifting up and out: The foreign policy of European immigration control. *West European Politics* 29 (2): 329–50.

Lemberg-Pedersen, Martin. 2017. Effective protection or effective combat? EU border control and North Africa. In *EurAfrican borders and migration management: Political cultures, contested spaces, and ordinary lives*, eds. Paolo Gaibazzi, Alice Bellagamba, and Stephen Dünnwald, 29–61. New York, NY: Palgrave Macmillan.

Lucht, Hans. 2012. *Darkness before daybreak: African migrants living on the margins in southern Italy*. Berkeley, CA: University of California Press.

Maher, Stephanie. 10 February 2015. Interrogating the wave: Media representations of African migrant youth. *Youth Circulations*. Available from http://www.youthcirculations.com/blog/2015/2/10/interrogating-the-wave-media-representations-of-african-migrant-youth.

Maher, Stephanie. 2017. Historicising "irregular" migration from Senegal to Europe. *Anti-Trafficking Review* 9:77–91.

Mainwaring, Ćetta, and Noelle Bridgen. 2016. Beyond the border: Clandestine migration journeys. *Geopolitics* 21 (2): 243–62.

Mbow, Penda. 2008. L'émigration clandestine: Le profil des candidats. Paper presented at the Forum CARITAS meeting, 26–28 November, Savana Saly, Senegal.

Melly, Caroline. 2011. Titanic tales of missing men: Reconfigurations of national identity and gendered presence in Dakar, Senegal. *American Ethnologist* 38 (2): 261–376.

Minder, Raphael, and Jim Yardley. 4 October 2013. Desperation fuels trips of migrants to Spain. *New York Times*.

Nash, John F. 1950. The bargaining problem. *Econometrica* 18 (2): 155–62.

Osman, Abdulaziz, and Nicolas Pinault. February 2016. Adrift: The invisible African diaspora. *Voice of America News*. Available from: http://projects.voanews.com/adrift-african-diaspora/.

Pallister-Wilkins, Polly. 2015. The humanitarian politics of European border policing: Frontex and border police in Evros. *International Political Sociology* 9:53–69.

Pastore, Ferruccio, Paola Monzini, and Giuseppe Sciortino. 2006. Schengen's soft underbelly: Irregular migration and human smuggling across land and sea borders to Italy. *International Migration* 44 (4): 95–119.

Ralph, Michael. 2008. Killing time. *Social Text 97* 26 (4): 1–29.

Richter, Line 2016. Strange adventures: Brokering in the borderlands. Paper presented at the Duke University-Africa Initiative conference on African Refugees and Migrants at Europe's Doorstep, 7–9 March, Durham, NC.

Rivera, Mark T., Sara B. Soderstrom, and Brian Uzzi. 2010. Dynamics of dyads in social networks: Assortative, relational, and proximity mechanisms. *Annual Review of Sociology* 36:91–115.

Salt, John, and Jeremy Stein. 1997. Migration as business: The case of trafficking. *International Migration* 35 (4): 467–94.

Sanchez, Gabriella. 2017. Critical perspectives on clandestine migration facilitation: An overview of migrant smuggling research. *Journal on Migration and Human Security* 5 (1): 9–27.

Sarat, Leah. 2013. *Fire in the canyon: Religion, migration, and the Mexican dream*. New York, NY: New York University Press.

Schloenhardt, Andreas. 2003. *Migrant smuggling: Illegal migration and organised crime in Australia and the Asia Pacific region*. Leiden: Brill Publishers.

Searcey, Dionne, and Jaime Yaya Barry. 22 June 2017. Why migrants keep risking all on the "deadliest route." *New York Times*.

Senegal-European Commission. 2008. Country Strategy Paper and National Indicative Programme, 10th EDF (2008–2013). Brussels: Senegal-European Commission.

Simmel, Georg. 1978/2011. *The philosophy of money*. New York, NY: Routledge.

Some, Aymar Narodar. 2009. *Migration au Sénégal: Profil national 2009*. Geneva: International Organisation for Migration.

Torre, Andre, and Alain Rallet. 2005. Proximity and localization. *Regional Studies* 39 (1): 47–59.

United Nations High Commissioner for Refugees (UNHCR). 2013. *Mixed migration: Libya at the crossroads, mapping of migration routes from Africa to Europe and the drivers of migration in post-revolution Libya*. Tripoli: United Nations High Commissioner for Refugees. Available from http://www.refworld.org.

United Nations High Commissioner for Refugees (UNHCR). 25 October 2016. *Mediterranean death toll soars to all-time high*. Tripoli: United Nations High Commissioner for Refugees. Available from http://www.unhcr.org/news/briefing/2016/10/580f1d044/mediterranean-death-toll-soars-2016-deadliest-year.html.

United Nations Office on Drugs and Crime (UNODC). 2011a. *The role of organized crime in the smuggling of migrants from West Africa to Europe*. New York, NY: United Nations.

United Nations Office on Drugs and Crime (UNODC). 2011b. *Smuggling of migrants*. New York, NY: United Nations.

van Liempt, Ilse. 2007. *Navigating borders: Inside perspectives on the process of human smuggling into the Netherlands*. Amsterdam: Amsterdam University Press.

Vogt, Wendy. 2016. Stuck in the middle with you: The intimate labours of mobility and smuggling along the Mexican migrant route. *Geopolitics* 21 (2): 366–86.

Zhang, Sheldon X. 2007. *Smuggling and trafficking in human beings: All roads lead to America*. London: Praeger.

Refugee Protections from Below: Smuggling in the Eritrea-Ethiopia Context

By
TEKALIGN AYALEW
MENGISTE

This article is an analysis of the role of human smuggling practices and of the transnational social relations of Eritrean refugees exiting and transitioning through Ethiopia. Based on two years of multisited ethnographic fieldwork, I explore how smugglers, aspiring migrants, and former migrants, settled en route and in diasporic spaces, try to minimize the risk of violence through communities of support and knowhow. In so doing, I argue that smuggling is a socially embedded collective practice that strives to facilitate safe exit and transitions of Eritrean refugees despite the criminalization of migration, the militarization of borders, and the potential and existing criminal activity along Eritrean, Sudanese, and Ethiopian migratory corridors. The facilitation of irregular transits by migrants themselves reproduces a collective system of migratory knowledge that aims to bring refugees to safety—a community of knowledge—in which smuggling emerges as a system of refugee protection from below.

Keywords: community of knowledge; migrant smuggling; *delaloch*; Eritrea; youth

Eritrea has become one of the largest refugee-generating nations in the world. Between 2013 and 2015, Eritreans constituted about 20 percent of migrants and refugees entering Italy by sea (Belloni 2016; Frouws 2017). The so-called Eritrean Exodus, particularly as it relates to clandestine departures, has attracted media, political, and academic attention in Europe and beyond. The mainstream narratives depict Eritrean refugees desperately running away from poverty, political repression, and dictatorship; their long, dramatic journeys at the hands of violent criminal ransom kidnappers in the Sinai and the Sahara deserts; and their tragic drownings on boat in the

Tekalign Ayalew Mengiste is a researcher in the Department of Social Anthropology at Stockholm University. His research interests include diaspora, refugees, smuggling, and high-risk migration.

Correspondence: tekalign.ayalew@socant.su.se

DOI: 10.1177/0002716217743944

Mediterranean Sea. In line with these claims, smugglers are assumed to be part of criminal organizations that exploit fleeing refugees physically, economically, and sexually (see Van Reisen, Estefanos, and Rijken 2012; Frouws, Phillips, and Horwood 2014; Albahari 2015), taking advantage of the gap between increasing repression and decreasing possibilities of mobility. Particularly disturbing are the graphic depictions of torture, extortion, sexual exploitation, and enslavement, or refugees left to die after their organs are taken by criminals in the Sinai desert (Belloni 2015). While not underestimating refugees' suffering during their precarious journeys, official accounts rarely contextualize the violence amid (or rather, as a result of) restrictive migration regimes or unequal access to formal and safe means of mobility—in particular, to refugees' inability to file asylum claims in Europe. Moreover, the focus on victimization and suffering at the hands of allegedly organized criminals often silences the perspectives of the refugees who travelled irregularly and settled successfully in Europe and the voices of those who played a role in that success. Furthermore, criminological and security perspectives of migration (see Gerard 2014) fail to include in their analysis the social formations and community dimensions of migrant smuggling—namely, how collective practices such as reciprocity, solidarity, and the sharing of resources and knowhow (how to survive violence and appropriate effective smuggling services) are generated among fellow travelers and former migrants settled en route or in the diaspora.

Accounts of Eritrean refugees collected in African and European countries reveal a multifaceted migratory landscape: while thousands of Eritreans attempt to reach Europe, many other thousands remain in the immediately surrounding countries of the Sudan and Ethiopia while mapping their journeys. Indeed, rather than sudden journeys into the unknown, refugee departures and journeys are fragmented, slow, and gradual processes that involve prolonged and careful planning, while generating material and financial resources and knowhow through connections with social networks.

But journeys also tell the story of the role that local and transnational smuggling networks play. Based on the research I present in this article, I show how the journeys of these migrants are organized by facilitators (many times migrants themselves) who work and live in transit lands, and who provide services to migrants for a fee, while also remaining vested in their survival. Smuggling facilitators (individuals known as "pilots" and *delaloch*), guide Eritrean refugees to safe routes across borders and out of refugee camps, secure employment options for them or set up payment plans that allow them to earn money to eventually pay for their journeys to a destination abroad, or house them while in transit and provide other mechanisms for their survival while they transition to other destinations. The process of mobility facilitated by smugglers is, then, contrary to mainstream narratives of exploitation and crime, and far from perceived as exploitative by migrants. Rather, smugglers and refugees conceptualize the facilitation of irregular migration as a mechanism that allows those in transit to be guarded from criminal organizations, environmental challenges, and restrictive migration regimes, but also from the trap that asylum conditions—including refugee camps—have become.

Using ethnographic data collected between 2013 and 2015 through anthropological fieldwork in countries located along the Eritrean overland migration routes toward Europe (Ethiopia, the Sudan, Italy) and in destination countries (Sweden and the UK), this article maps the practical and social organization of Eritrean smuggling into Ethiopia. It examines, in particular, how the service of smuggling thrives amid transnational social relations, diasporic practices, and knowledge production, elements of what I refer to as community of knowledge. Often disregarded as simply advice or commonsense information, migration knowledge is generated by and embedded in the everyday dynamics of refugee communities and transmitted during their migration journeys, creating a transnational protective sphere.

The incorporation of the community of knowledge into the analyses of irregular migration increases our understanding of how human smuggling emerges and operates in the context of previous migrations, translocal and transnational social relations, and the circulation of information and economic resources. Most importantly, I argue that in the context of postcolonial conflict, dictatorship, and economic stagnation that deprive the life chances of young people in places such as Eritrea—compounded by contemporary structural violence manifested through unequal access to safe and formal mobility rights between people in the Global South and North—entanglements with human smuggling and diasporic transnational practices become an alternative form of social protection. I argue that smuggling constitutes a form of protection from below for refugees seeking to leave their countries of origin or those who get stranded while en route. I will tease out how community relations and smuggling practices—using Hannam, Sheller, and Urry's terms (2006, 3)—become the "spatial, infrastructural and institutional moorings" that configure and facilitate informal but often successful departures, journeys, and transitions of Eritrean refugees into Ethiopia. Through this approach, I go beyond simplistic narratives of victimized refugees or heinous smugglers responsible for the so-called refugee crisis in Eritrean-Sudanese borderlands, the Mediterranean region, and beyond, and call for a framework that contextualizes smuggling facilitation as an element of diasporic knowledge in the translocal community space.

Context of Eritrean Refugee Flights

Eritreans' migration to international destinations is related in part to Eritrea becoming a nation-state, which generated conflict that in turn induced migratory waves. The first phase of Eritrean refugee migration took place during the 30-year-long war of independence, which took place from the 1960s to 1991 and was compounded by recurrent drought and famine. The conflict generated an estimated 1 million Eritrean refugees and created the foundation for Eritrea's conflict-induced diaspora, mainly to the West and the Middle East (Bariagaber 2006, 52; Arnone 2008; Tecle and Goldring 2013). Many Eritrean refugees also settled in countries along contemporary Eritrean migration routes to Europe, such as Ethiopia, the Sudan, Libya, and Italy. These settled Eritrean communities became the source of support and information for newly arriving Eritrean refugees and provided them with shelter, informal employment opportunities, and contacts with reputable smugglers who could organize the next stage of their journey. It was also this time that traders and local people in border areas began to engage in small-scale smuggling services to help Eritrean refugees fleeing to neighboring countries (Kibreab 2009).

The second phase of refugee migration from Eritrea began in 1992 and continues as of the time of this writing. The war between Ethiopia and Eritrea ended in 1991, and in 1993 Eritrea became an independent nation-state (Bariagaber 2006). After the brief slowdown of refugee flight between 1991 and 1998 (as the country experienced relative peace following the end of the war of independence in 1991 until the border war with Ethiopia broke out in in 1998), another round of mass exodus began (Kibreab 2013), when, as a result of the 1998–2000 Eritrean-Ethiopian border wars, many youths fled Eritrea to escape the conflict (Arnone 2008). In 1998, the Ethiopian government also expelled Eritreans living and working in Ethiopia. These Eritreans found themselves back in Eritrea with nothing, and so decided to leave their country in search of security and opportunity.

The National Service (NS) by the Peoples' Front for Democracy and Justice (PFDJ) presented another challenge for society in general and for youth in particular in Eritrea (Treiber 2013d, 2013a). Kibreab (2009, 2013) states that after independence, many expected that the Eritrean regime would use the sense of heroism that had grown during the war and unite for the postconflict reconstruction of the country and the economy. Capitalizing on this rhetoric, the Eritrean regime instead introduced the NS in 2002, which imposed upon every citizen between 18 and 41 years old enrollment in compulsory and indefinite military service (with the exception of the disabled or those with special cases). The unpaid "open-ended national service in the military enabled the government to keep thousands of Eritreans in a state of perpetual control and exploitation" (Kibreab 2013, 636). The Eritrean government also used the so-called no-war no-peace situation against Ethiopia, accusing the country of not accepting border resolutions dictated by the Boundary Commission after the peace agreement in Algiers, and using the ongoing tension to disseminate fear that a war with Ethiopia was imminent, thereby justifying the recruitment of citizens into an army.

Everyday life in Eritrea and Ethiopia is difficult. Eritrea has become a highly militarized state defined by war and run by soldiers and veterans—the *tegadelay* (Treiber 2013a, 2013b). Authoritarianism and harsh political repression have isolated Eritrea from the international community, while environmental disasters and related economic stagnations have made Eritreans increasingly desperate to leave their country (Kibreab 2009, 2013; Treiber 2013d, 2013c, 2013b; Belloni 2015).

These conditions have rendered Eritreans, but particularly young people, unable to pursue their life plans, meet social expectations, or fulfil responsibilities (Treiber 2013a, 2013b). Those who attempt to escape Eritrea are tortured; people detected at the borders who refuse to surrender also risk being killed because of the government's "shoot-to-kill policy" (Belloni 2015).

The exodus of young and educated Eritreans gave rise to considerable criticism of the Eritrean regime by the international community. In response, the regime began to regulate movement out of the country and to control exit visas. Mobility within the country also became difficult because of checkpoints along highways. Emigration became illegal as no one could desert the NS and leave the country (Belloni 2015). The regime also detained and penalized the families of refugees who had stayed behind. The Eritrean response to migration coincided with the implementation of stricter immigration controls in and by Europe, and on the insistence of the European Union of shutting down of external borders. Libya, the Sudan, and Ethiopia often accept development aid in exchange for intercepting clandestine refugees before they reach European territory (Andersson 2014; Albahari 2015).

Combined, these policies have been partially responsible for the birth of complex human smuggling practices. Eritreans began to devise different and new ways to cross the border into Ethiopia; from there, they could journey to other countries abroad. It was not long before the practice of smuggling extended to the Sahel, Saharan, and Sinai deserts, with human smugglers facilitating passages to African, Middle Eastern, and European destinations via Libya or Egypt (Kibreab 2009; Treiber 2013c).

Starting in 2000, thousands of Eritreans began to flee the country to seek asylum first in the Sudan and Ethiopia, and then, from there, to migrate to the rest of the world. While Eritreans have migrated to countries around the world, the Sudan and Ethiopia have historically been the leading destinations and transit locations for Eritrean refugees. Since the 1980s, Eritrean refugees have been joining their friends, relatives, and neighbors residing in cities such as Kassala, Port Sudan, Gedaref, Addis Ababa, and Khartoum (Hassanen 2007; Kibreab 2013). Since 2003, an estimated sixteen hundred Eritrean refugees have crossed the border and entered Ethiopia every month; and in 2011 alone, about 106,362 Eritreans fled to the Sudan, mainly through Ethiopia (Kibreab 2013). Using Khartoum as a steppingstone, some migrants move toward Europe, preferably Northern Europe (Belloni 2016).

In the context of state failure, the absence of formal mobility channels, and the challenges the young face, organizing clandestine overland departures has become an everyday practice, which has emerged from Eritreans' personal and familial hopes to survive and thrive amid uncertain socioeconomic and political environments. However, mainstream narratives of irregular migration often articulate clandestine migration facilitation and its practices solely through the frameworks of violence, organized crime, and exploitation in a largely ahistorical fashion. There is also a tendency to individualize and reduce Eritrean refugee flights to narratives of trafficking victimhood (Tesfagiorgis 2013; Van Reisen, Estefanos and Rijken 2012; Belloni 2016). This approach often neglects the underlying structural factors fueling migration, the social and cultural configurations of clandestine migratory mobility, and migrants' collective agency in the face of their exchanges with smugglers. Eritreans do not escape the dictatorial regime and the precarious political and economic conditions they face overnight. Rather, their clandestine exit and mobility are gradual and processual, and involve a range of actors and networks of help and knowhow, which are generated by translocal and transnational social relations and diasporic practices. Refugees view smugglers as helpers who facilitate safe journeys amid state persecutions and risks of clandestine mobility. In the section that follows, I conceptualize this type of facilitation of irregular migration using the notion of community of knowledge.

Smuggling as a Community of Knowledge

Networks of support and migration knowledge are critical amid the increasing difficulties and risks involved in clandestine, long, and fragmented journeys from places such as Eritrea. The practice of human smuggling and organizing overland clandestine migration thrive on being embedded in diasporic transnational engagements, material practices, and the circulation of migration-specific knowledge. To capture these complex relations and collective practices that facilitate the clandestine migration process, I use the concept of community of knowledge (Ayalew 2016). Before I define the concept, I elaborate on the community dimensions of knowledge, taking up perspectives from the sociology of knowledge and linking these to contemporary refugee mobility.

In the tradition of sociology of knowledge, scholars point out that individuals acquire and incorporate knowledge in the course of social interactions, and manage their behavior and everyday actions within a certain social setting (Schütz 1944/1964; Schütz and Luckmann 1973). Sociological perspectives "consider knowledge as a dynamic process constituting human and therefore meaningful action" (Treiber 2013d, 188). In everyday life, human beings draw on a "collective stock of knowledge, which is produced and reproduced during interactions" (Soeffner and Zifonun 2008, 5). Clandestine departures and overland journeys—for instance, those occurring from Africa to Europe—require multiple plans, improvisation, and adaptability in the face of risk. Together these tactics constitute a learning process that involves the appropriating and sharing of information in new conditions and encounters during the migration process (Collyer 2007; Treiber 2013d, 189).

Treiber stated that "knowledge is acquired and transformed through communication within the fluid and geographically dispersed transnational milieu of migrants ... continuous comparison of success and failures, gives migrants meaning and orientation for their action and life-worlds" (2013d, 209). Migration knowledge is generated and circulated within a transnational social space, which reflects long-term transnational migration patterns, dynamics, and sustained cross-border social relations (Faist 2000).

Alpes (2012) introduced the notion of "economy of migratory knowledge," referring to "cultural and societal factors that structure flows of information and influence constructions of meaning." She pointed out that there is "a system of symbolic transactions within which information is handled, created, exchanged, and transformed in transnational settings" (2012, 93). Earlier studies on migration introduced related concepts such as "migration industry" (Gammeltoft-Hansen and Sørensen 2013) and "migration infrastructure" (Xiang and Lindquist 2014) to explain actors and processes involved in border controls and those facilitating or mediating contemporary clandestine labor and refugee mobility, particularly from the Global South to North.

However, the reliance on terms like industry, infrastructure, and economy conceives clandestine migratory mobility largely as an entrepreneurial, business venture. It gives less attention to migrants' subjective energy and agency in mobilizing migration knowledge and resources as well as the social and family obligations that complement the organization of migratory trajectories, in addition to the interactions between migrants and smugglers (Herman 2006, 217; Collyer 2007).

Baird and Liempt, after highlighting the limitations of existing theories in human smuggling, have called for critical, empirically grounded, and socially embedded understandings of human smuggling (2016, 403–13). Following their claim, contemporary irregular migratory journeys are possible because of cross-border social networks and smuggling practices. Hence, we must take into account the community dimensions and knowledge productions in facilitating irregular migratory journeys when studying human smuggling. For example, Sanchez and Natividad (2017) have demonstrated how migrant smuggling on the U.S.-Mexico border constitutes a form of knowledge. They state that by providing material support and information on contacts, specific details regarding smuggling routes, and so on, friends and families knit the web of social protection for prospective migrants. They have argued persuasively that because mobility is difficult and there are risks involved in clandestine journeys, migrant smuggling becomes part of community-oriented forms of protection designed to reduce vulnerability in clandestine journeys—"a form of human security from below that carries deep epistemological roots" (2017, 69). Sanchez and Natividad call for the recognition of past migration memories and "narratives of migration as constituting a system of knowledge, that when transmitted allows for the survival and protection of those traveling clandestinely" by way of constructing and maintaining social relations (2017, 79). "Extra-legal journeys build upon collective, accumulated, and also improvised forms of knowledge acquired, developed and shared by those in transit and their communities" (2017, 80). To capture the complex processes and collective practices of generating and using knowledge in smuggling and irregular refugee mobility, and to recognize the role of diaspora, I coined the term *community of knowledge*.

By *communities of knowledge*, I refer to the diverse and dynamic strategies collectively devised and mobilized by migrants, their cotravelers, families and friends settled en route and in the diaspora, and friendly strangers and diverse facilitators to reduce risks in clandestine journeys and who allow for successful transits, while not discounting the violence and suffering encountered by migrants and refugees on their paths. The accumulated body of information pertaining to and allowing for past, ongoing, and future experiences of migration to be transmitted constitutes a collective system of knowledge, in which communities are vital in guiding migrants in the negotiation and performance required at various stages of the migration process (cf. Vogt 2016). Through these processes, migrants and refugees on the move "cultivate and multiply individual and collective agencies" (Wheatley and Gomberg-Muñoz 2016, 406) to survive risks and accomplish migration projects. Migration knowledge of routes, timing of departure, how to behave during interactions with border authorities and other actors, accessing shelters and temporary jobs in transit lands, and so on are channeled through smuggling and social networks. The practice and facilitation of migratory journeys reproduce transnational social relations and vice versa. These relationships, information sharing, and previous experiences construct knowledge. While trust, a culture of sharing, and networks make such relationships possible, social and family obligations and mutual benefits generate the necessary financial and material resources for mobility.

Refugees' knowledge creation along the migration trail is inherently connected to actions taken in fast changing conditions. Migrants and refugees must constantly reshape, update, and improvise their knowledge depending on context-specific challenges and available opportunities during migration. In the sections that follow I empirically demonstrate how Eritrean refugees generate and employ knowledge in the specific case of smuggling into Ethiopia, organizing their clandestine exits, transcending the vulnerabilities of their journeys, and eventually managing irregular transitions into and out of Ethiopia.

Research Methods

Primary data for this study was collected through multisite ethnographic fieldwork in Stockholm (Sweden), Rome (Italy), Khartoum (the Sudan), and Addis Ababa (Ethiopia). I chose these cities because they are both main destinations and transition nodes of Eritrean migration, and they are located along the overland migration routes that link Eritrea with main European destination countries such as Sweden and the UK (see Belloni 2016).

I conducted interviews, group discussions, and participant observations between 2013 and 2015. I carried out ninety-five in-depth interviews with key informants, both men (fifty) and women (forty-five), aged 19 to 65. I contacted them through different actors involved in the migration process, namely, refugees, smugglers, nongovernmental and government personnel (twenty), and former migrants settled en route and in diaspora. Of these in-depth interviews, forty-five were detailed individual migration biographies of Eritrean refugees. Fifteen were conducted in Stockholm, fifteen in Addis Ababa, ten in Khartoum, and five in Rome. I also interviewed five male smugglers: one (aged 35) in Addis Ababa, two in Khartoum (aged 30 and 35), and two in Rome (aged 39 and 27).

I relied on a list of key themes and questions to conduct the interviews, including questions on exit management from Eritrea, the roles of smugglers and other actors who supported migrants during their border crossing, and the challenges actors faced and how they overcame them. These questions were helpful to learn the processes, practices, and actors involved in organizing smuggling, Eritrean refugee departures, transitions, and mobility (cf. Zhang 2008). Respondents were also allowed to present issues and events that they considered important in the process of practicing and facilitating migration. The interviews were conducted in migrants' homes; and sitting, standing, walking, and eating with respondents in public places like cafes.

I embarked on this project largely as the result of happenstance. Upon my arrival to Sweden for my PhD studies in 2012, I relied on my own community networks to get accommodations, and I shared a flat for 12 months with Eritrean refugees. During this time, I was introduced to the refugees and brokers who had shaped their journeys. These personal contacts helped me to systematically establish contacts among Eritreans in Europe, eventually building trust with those involved in smuggling organizations, and to learn how the practice of smuggling was embedded in complex transnational social relations (cf. Zaitch 2002). From Stockholm, relying on these interactions, connections, and contacts, I traveled to Italy, the Sudan, and Ethiopia to conduct multisited ethnography (Marcus 1995) and collect data from smugglers and refugees en route to Europe. I spent three months at each location. I carried out participant observations, including extensive casual conversations with refugees, brokers, and smugglers in reception camps, homes, churches, neighborhoods, squats, restaurants, workplaces, and a variety of other settings in Addis Ababa, Khartoum, and Rome. Informal conversations opened up opportunities to recruit key participants willing to describe the organization of migratory journeys from Eritrea to Europe.

Life history narrative techniques (Levitt and Glick Schiller 2004) were employed to generate data on practices and roles of various actors and stages of migration. Narrative data were triangulated for validity by asking people the same question at different times and by collecting more testimonies from a diverse group of people (men and women, young and elderly, new arrivals and established migrants). Primary data were also supplemented through reviewing research, policy, and critical media reports on contemporary refugee mobility from the Horn of Africa and practices of human smuggling across Euro-African borderlands and beyond. These helped me to attain a broader picture of the nature and operation of the human smuggling industry (Zhang 2008; Andersson 2014). Above all, I took advantage of my partial insider position: I speak the language my informants spoke; lived migrants' daily lives in destination countries; and experienced the same borders where they were stopped, interrogated, or denied visas as they travelled in Europe. These events helped me to collect in-depth, corroborated data.

However, my position was privileged in relation to that of my respondents. My status as "superior" as a result of my educational level and immigration status was brought up whenever meeting undocumented migrants and refugees in Ethiopia, the Sudan, Italy, and Sweden, while as a foreign student I was seen as "inferior" among migrants who had become Swedish citizens. Even though I was an insider, my ethnic and religious background, gender, and class positions were simultaneously obstacles and advantages in accessing certain groups. Thus, I was aware of and balanced positionalities and power relations with my informants, and sought to build trust and sustain contacts. All interviews were conducted in Eritrean. No personal identifiers were collected, and the names used in this article are not the names of my respondents.

Taking up Schapendonk's (2012) idea of "trajectory ethnography," I managed to follow migrants' stories longitudinally in time and space, conducting migration biographies and meeting some informants before and after their journeys, first in transition locations such as Addis Ababa and Khartoum and in destinations such as Rome and Stockholm. Most of my work occurred in Sweden, where I remained in contact with my respondents over the course of three years. In the sections that follow, I identify the actors and the dynamics of these migration practices, drawing from my respondents' testimonies and recollections of their journeys.

The knowledge and learning of smuggling

Eritrean refugees plan their migration from months to years while gathering necessary resources and information. Finding a smuggler in general, and a trust-worthy one in particular, is not just important but extremely difficult because of the country's militarization and the tough regulations of human mobility described earlier. Yordi, a 26-year-old who escaped from Asmara with her husband and their 5-year-old daughter, narrated the scenario when I interviewed her in Addis Ababa in March 2014:

> We decided to leave the country. But it took us four years of preparation and learning about routes, "pilots," and timings for leaving Asmara. In Eritrea you do not know who is a friend or foe. You have to keep the plan of escape secret, otherwise you end up in prison for unlimited periods of time. The most important thing is finding a reliable pilot. My husband was put into contact with a knowledgeable pilot, who helped us to safely come to Ethiopia, via Internet chats with our family members and friends in Ethiopia and the Sudan.

Until the time and conditions are ripe for escape migrants must keep their plan secret because no one can be trusted. As stated in the above narrative, even the closest relative may be a *sileya* (spy) and expose the prospective migrant and the pilot to the regime for personal advantage or simply out of envy. Planning requires the utmost care and caution to keep both migrants and the smugglers safe. One Eritrean "pilot," named Abraha, shared details on his recruitment patterns:

> [As a smuggler] you should be careful always. Our clients get our phone numbers from our previous clients who successfully escaped by our assistance. When they call us we ask them few questions in our language—who they are, and how they get our phone and so on to crosscheck, you know. … Mostly we have middlemen who make deals with migrants and then they send our clients to the border areas alone and then we pick up migrants there.

It is not only migrants who face risks; smugglers must also develop mechanisms to avoid being scammed into believing they are helping someone escape to find out they are being arrested. For that purpose, they question their clients, or rely on middlemen who can buffer the impact of detection. This is increasingly important if one is planning to escape towns or military camps since there are plenty of spies. In short, in Eritrea it is not just information, but also secrecy that renders clandestine crossings of highly militarized Eritrea-Ethiopian borders possible and migration safe (cf. Alpes 2012; Gerard 2014).

Information from former migrants on their past experiences helps evaluate opportunities and the challenges of using a particular migration route at a particular time. It is important to get the name and address of a dependable broker who may connect migrants to a guide or "pilot," who then accompanies them to the Sudan or Ethiopian borders. In general, valuable information about the journey, safe routes, timings, and contact details of "pilots" can be obtained over the phone, social media (e.g., Facebook), and e-mail chats with former migrants who have either successfully managed their irregular journey or settled in the diaspora. The information can also be obtained from those en route or from those who failed to complete the journey to avoid making the same "mistakes." Yordi for example, "gathered information from everyone including those who had succeeded, failed and were imprisoned to increase our chance of safety. The Internet and social media has [also been of] great help."

As stated earlier, significant amounts of migration knowledge are shared through digital connectivity and technology (e.g., cell phones, social media, etc.). Migration scholars have described how aspiring migrants and refugees in countries of origin or those stuck en route use Internet-based media and communication technologies not merely to stay in touch with families and friends abroad or back in the homeland (Bariagaber 2013; Leurs 2014), but also to learn from others about the specific details that are required for their journeys to succeed. This digital connectivity serves as a mechanism to generate and circulate the necessary knowledge based on collective memory of earlier and ongoing migratory journey experiences. This in turn helps refugees manage risks involved in precarious transitions and mobilize resources while in transit.

Migrants also gather contact details of friends and families en route and those settled in the diaspora for material and social support during the transit, for example, getting shelter, engaging in income-generating activities in transit spaces, and so on. These friends and relatives are also key in meeting the next smuggler who will facilitate remaining phases of mobility until refugees arrive at destinations in Northern Europe or elsewhere.

Kada, for example, was a 28-year-old Eritrean refugee when I met her in 2014. She was hosting three cousins and an older friend from her hometown, Asmara, in her home in Khartoum. She had taken the role of instructing her relatives in the dynamics of Khartoum during their transit and on how to stay safe: "I have been in Khartoum for four years. I know people. I am connecting them for safety with a renowned *delaloch*. I am also training them on how to behave toward police and how to bribe them when necessary." Kada further noted: "It is my responsibility to help them as much as possible. When I arrived in Khartoum, others did the same thing for me. It is my turn now to help others."

It is not only contacts that are shared. Prospective migrants also learn from former migrants which travel documents to get and to carry to move inside Eritrea, and which to use later when applying for asylum. Former migrants also guide aspiring migrants on the practicalities of the journey, from advice over appropriate travel clothes to recommendations for a cotraveler who speaks Amharic if heading to Ethiopia or Arabic if heading to the Sudan. This shows us, unlike popular assumptions, that migrants move with and by their social relations.

"Pilots" as Saviors

Clandestine departures from Eritrea and overland trips toward Ethiopia or the Sudan are extremely dangerous. While reports of kidnapping for ransom and organ harvesting in the Sinai at the hands of organized criminals catch the West's imagination, the shoot-to-kill practices of the Eritrean regime, robbers, the swelling Mereb River, and predatory animals constitute the most pressing risks migrants face in their attempts to escape from Eritrea (see Treiber 2013d; Belloni 2015).

Men known as "pilots" facilitate the transits from within Eritrea to the border with Ethiopia. They are usually Eritrean soldiers or people who work and live in border areas, have experience in crossing borders for trade or other purposes, and possess knowledge of the shortest and safest passages. Many pilots are migrants themselves, in the process of transiting to their destinations:[1] Eritreans in refugee camps in Ethiopia and the Sudan work as pilots and move back and forth to bring migrants. As Abraha, the pilot, stated above, pilots have agents and middlemen who recruit clients in villages and towns in Eritrea and bring them to border areas where they connect with the pilot. Pilots can also be directly contacted by Eritreans in the diaspora who want to assist a family member who is stuck in Eritrea escape to neighboring countries.

I met Abraha in Khartoum in April 2014 through a common friend. Abraha was an Eritrean refugee in his late 30s. Before moving to the Sudan, he had lived and worked in Adi k'yeih, a town along the Ethiopian-Eritrean border. When he was in a refugee camp in northern Ethiopia, between 2012 and 2013, he worked as a pilot, capitalizing on his knowledge of the area and the connections he had along the routes:

> You know this is a dangerous task … to escape from spies and soldiers we travel at night. We instruct travelers how to dress and [give them] masks to disguise their identity including wearing and styling their hair, carrying equipment as the local people along the routes do. We often travel at night. But the hyenas and Rashida kidnappers are active at night. You must know how and when to move to safe routes. A single mistake may lead all of us to a disaster: imprisonment, death or kidnapping by kidney harvesters or ransom in the Egyptian desert.

The previous narrative indicates that, to survive, refugees need not merely have knowledge of particular ways of performing visibility or invisibility in the borderlands but must also have access to a meticulous and efficient smuggling service. Abraha also acknowledged the range of risks involved in his work, from hyenas to kidney harvesters, to kidnappings and the state. It would be amiss to underestimate the role of organized forms of violence in the experiences of migrants; yet it is also important to highlight how these become entangled with the state practices that create the conditions of protracted vulnerability (see Achilli, this volume).

Pilots guide migrants from towns and villages in Eritrea to the border of Ethiopia or the Sudan during the on-foot journey. Once crossed, some migrants stay on the Ethiopian side of the border. Others may go to refugee camps or towns at the Eritrean-Sudanese border on their own, while others may join their families and friends who settled in Sudanese or Ethiopian border towns, and who may help them obtain papers and documents necessary to move toward interior Ethiopia or the Sudan.

Once their task is complete, pilots may connect refugees with another smuggler, through the help of contacts or former migrants, to facilitate the rest of journey. This can be done either immediately upon arrival, or at another time depending on the migrants' economic conditions. In the case of Eritreans, crossing the border into Ethiopia is only one of many steps that will lead them to destinations abroad. Yet many migrants find themselves in a state of limbo, unable to settle and start a new life. This is where the services of other kinds of smugglers or *delaloch* come in handy.

After the pilot, the delala: Negotiating mobility

While cultural and linguistic similarities allow many Eritrean refugees to feel at home in Ethiopia, Ethiopia is still not a preferred destination. Refugees become weary of the limited mobility they have at the refugee camps quite soon.[2] Even if they were able to move into Ethiopian cities informally, finding a sustainable livelihood is challenging. Furthermore, the chances of getting United Nations High Commissioner for Refugees (UNHCR)–assisted resettlement in a third country are extremely limited (see Treiber 2013a; Belloni 2016). Thus, many young, educated Eritrean refugees residing in Ethiopian refugee camps, feeling that they are involuntarily immobile and leading a "wasted life" (cf. Treiber 2013d, 2013c, 2013a), quickly learn about the possibilities of migrating with the assistance of *delaloch*[3] (literary "smugglers" in Amharic) and their connectors.

Migrants find smugglers who can facilitate the rest of the journey into other towns or camps in Ethiopia or the Sudan, and then on to other countries. *Delaloch* facilitate transits to Sudan, from which migrants can travel to Europe across the Sahara Desert or the Mediterranean Sea. Yasin, an Ethiopian *delala* in Addis Ababa, described the process in 2015:

> I assist both Ethiopians and Eritreans in sending them to the Sudan. I have people around the camps. I arrange transport and papers to send them first to [the] Ethiopian-Sudanese border. There they meet their families and friends settled in border towns such as Gedaref and Matama, who would [in turn] assist migrants to meet Sudanese delala to move to Khartoum.

Former migrants work alongside pilots and their *delaloch* to facilitate refugee journeys within specific territories or distances, relying on a combination of skills and specific knowledge about particular locations. Contrary to the narratives of migrants being at the mercy of the smuggler, my respondents' testimonies above reflect a proactive role on the part of migrants and their friends and family members when working with pilots and *delaloch*. It is in fact the collaboration among all parties that allows for the success of the migrants' journey. Mheret was a 23-year-old woman from Eritrea when I met her in Rome in May 2015 while she was transiting through Italy. She described her journey from refugee camps in Ethiopia to Khartoum, the Sudan, as follows:

> My sister and I went to Ethiopia in 2013 assisted by pilots. After three months in a refugee camp in northern Ethiopia we felt it was like prison. We decided to move to Sudan and then to Europe. Our cousin in Khartoum connected us with a *delala* named Ato Getachew in Addis Ababa and agreed to receive us in Khartoum. Ato Getachew put us in contact with an Eritrean broker in the camp, who assisted us to get out of the camp and facilitated our trip to Addis Ababa. From Addis Ababa, Ato Getachew accompanied us and eleven other Eritrean refugees by public bus to Humera [a town in Ethiopian-Sudan border]. Then, he handed us over to two Sudanese *delaloch* on the outskirts of the town. They arranged motorcycles to cross the border and after three days of travel by minibuses, we finally arrived safely in Khartoum.

Mheret's testimony also attests to other aspects of the journey coordinated by facilitators: the financial mechanisms to support a journey. Relying on wire transfer companies or on *hawala* networks,[4] migrants pay their smuggling fees as they go. Facilitators or friends and relatives may also provide alternatives to cover fees, like working them off by gaining employment with specific people or businesses known to facilitators, or by remaining at a specific location to work and save until they are able to afford the next stage of the journey. Mheret explains these alternatives as they were offered to her:

> Those who had to wait for money to be transferred via *hawala* networks could stay in an accommodation arranged by the Sudanese *delaloch*. Those who did not have money to pay for their journey from Ethiopia to Sudan entered into a debt agreement with the *delaloch* and were informally introduced to employers in Khartoum or other places in Sudan [to work]. My sister and I stayed with our cousin who also helped us find domestic work for the coming 11 months.

This testimony reveals the chain of financial transactions and agreements in the economy of smuggling. Yet from the perspective of the smugglers, smuggling refugees from Eritrea is not a mere act of transporting people clandestinely for money. Rather, it involves sound community relations. Smugglers must find ways to build their web of relations and extend them to families left behind, former migrants, locals along the way, informal money transfer agents, and *delaloch* dispersed across diasporic spaces. One smuggler in Rome commented on the transnational and community dimensions of smuggling in May 2015:

> I bring people from Ethiopia and send them from Italy to Scandinavia. But the difficult part of the work is arranging *hawala* money transfer for migrants from Ethiopia to Italy

informally. … we do not want them to transfer money to our accounts. It is risky … [for that reason] we work with migrants, their families in Italy, country of origin and elsewhere. We have agents in those places. It is all about trust and connections by which payments and services are exchanged.

Smuggling relies on transnational social networks (between migrants and former migrants en route and diaspora), economic practices (sending and receiving remittances to finance the migration journey), and communication technologies (appropriating and using the Internet and social media). Mheret further commented:

We do not just move by ourselves. But we move by the help of others and together with others. When I decided to leave Eritrea I contacted my sister in Dubai who financed my journey. When I was in Ethiopia I called my cousin in the Sudan who connected us to the *delala* in Addis Ababa. Internet and mobile phones are indispensable in all the communications and money transfers.

Contrary to perceptions of smugglers as exploitative or violent, pilots and *delaloch* were repeatedly described as supportive and protective by migrants. *Delaloch* are consistently described as saviors, and testimonies attested to the ways they helped migrants to complete their journeys:

You know, pilots and *delaloch* are our visas not to get stuck in refugee camps in Ethiopia and in Sudan. … After working and saving money for two years in Sudan through the support of *delaloch* and our relatives, I finally found a nice *semsari* (smuggler in Arabic) who facilitated my journey to Italy.

Delaloch provide transportation along safe routes, clandestine border crossings, accommodations, and economic support to get employment in the Sudan. *Delaloch* find the appropriate time, condition, and means of transport. They flexibly use a combination of public and private transportation services to pass checkpoints along the Ethiopian-Sudanese borders, and safely place their clients at jobs that will allow them to support themselves while also covering their smuggling fee. Together these factors demonstrate how wrong the dominant academic discourses are about irregular migration and refugee flights from Ethiopia and Eritrea that portray smugglers as exploiters and refugees as silent victims (see Treiber 2013d; Van Reisen, Estefanos, and Rijken 2012; Kubai 2016). Smuggler-refugee relations are diverse and dynamic and involve mutual benefits.

Similar to other African settings (Cooper and Pratten 2015, 2), uncertainty along migration trails generates social agency, collective practices, and creativity in appropriating communication technologies to mobilize and share necessary migration resources such as finance and knowhow, both in the immediate and future locations (cf. Wheatley and Gomberg-Muñoz 2016). Understanding contemporary Eritrean migration should not be reduced to ransom kidnappings and trafficking for organ harvesting in Eritrean-Sudanese borderlands and beyond (see Tesfagiorgis 2013). Rather it must be framed as a local and transnational, community-based, proximity-oriented phenomenon dependent on specific entanglements of social and smuggling networks.

The mainstream scholarship on the practice of smuggling and facilitation of irregular Eritrean refugee migration across Eritrean borderlands and beyond portrays smugglers on one hand as organized criminal actors taking advantage of refugees' vulnerability. Smugglers are seen as exploiters of refugees for sex and labor or as charging unbelievably high costs to transport fleeing refugees or holding them hostage, torturing them, and demanding ransom money in remote deserts; whereas refugees are seen as innocent and silent victims of abuses (see Treiber 2013d; Tesfagiorgis 2013; Van Reisen, Estefanos, and Rijken 2012; Frouws, Phillips, and Horwood 2014; Belloni 2016). This approach not only conflates or mixes up and often reduces smugglers into criminal kidnappers or traffickers but also ignores refugees' social agency and community dimensions of facilitating safe transitions. Smugglers, not surprisingly, prefer to portray themselves as service givers and helpers of refugees rather than exploiters. For instance, a *delala* named Yasin claimed: "I assisted more than 1,000 Eritrean refugees to reach Europe … now they got their residence rights and protection in Europe. I helped them … they helped me… that is it." This reflects the symbiotic relations and mutual benefits that emerge and govern the relationship between migrants and smugglers and how this relationship in turn reproduces clandestine mobility despite restrictions and impediments.

Analysis and Conclusion

Faist (2014) points to three broader network mechanisms that shape contemporary migration dynamics: (1) exchange of information, (2) the norm of reciprocity, and (3) collective action of migrants (p. 38). In this study, all three network mechanisms combined to produce and sustain a community of knowledge among migrants seeking to leave Eritrea for Ethiopia.

Refugees from Eritrea into Ethiopia do not simply escape from their homelands, jump borders, and arrive into Europe. Rather, the migration process, including crossing the highly militarized Eritrean borders, is a long-term task that encompasses careful planning, including the generation and sharing of knowledge and resources among movers (migrants) and nonmovers (friends, families, and community members). Refugees' migration decisions and irregular journeys are individual life projects embedded in, and informed and organized by, former migrations and transnational social formations (cf. Faist 2000, 2014).

The data presented here are examples of how the irregular departure and mobility of refugees continue despite increasing border controls.[5] Models of push-pull factors, structural conditions, and even network analysis are limited in their ability to explain the continued demand for smuggling services. Rather, institutions, actors, social networks, communication technologies, and migration infrastructures (Xiang and Lindquist 2014), operating in transnational social spaces, linking diasporic locations, sustain migratory inflows even with tough migration controls and sophisticated border surveillance at various stages. Refugees produce knowledge and generate resources through community networks; on occasion, they become involved themselves in the provision of smuggling services, further subverting border regimes, surviving violence, and keeping themselves and others on the move.

Viewing irregular migration facilitation as a criminal and organized practice often leads to policy solutions that target the most vulnerable of migrants, who often include facilitators. This perspective ignores fundamental structural conditions behind the practice of contemporary high-risk irregular migration practices. The violence, which Eritrean refugees encounter en route, is not merely about greedy smugglers who perpetrate violence and commit crimes against the state and migrants, as some migration and criminological scholars have argued (Gerard 2014). Rather, it is an extension and part of the structural violence of global inequality and the deprivation of the mobility rights of migrants. In the context of precarious socioeconomic and political conditions, differential access to formal and safe means of mobility rights, or the absence of formal mobility channels, high-risk overland departures and long journeys have become socially and morally accepted practices among migrants, potential migrants, and their families.

Eritreans' collective history and experiences of irregular migration constitute a diasporic system of knowledge (Kibreab 2013; Bernal 2014; Belloni 2015) that challenges immobility regimes and impediments to transit, allowing migrants not just to arrive to their destinations to fulfill their economic goals but also to do so safely. This article's goal is not to simply depict the outcomes that are expected as a result of the irregular journey, but rather to show how despite structural limitations, communities can deploy systems of knowledge across borders that provide protective mechanisms that reduce their members' vulnerability. While accomplishing the migration project allows for the diaspora's further mobility and transnational engagements, migration's importance resides on how it increases and strengthens the collective knowledge that allows for its members' survival. In this context, organizing refugees' journeys becomes a collectively constructed element in the provision of safe transits, as successful smuggling journeys maintain the preexisting culture of social help and brotherhood deeply embedded in clan, kinship, and religious obligations of reciprocity (cf. Faist 2000; Belloni 2015). Even though clandestine mobility often involves violence and trauma, the overland migration of refugees from Eritrea creates and feeds transnational social spaces that connect origin, transit, and destination spaces as legitimate forms of migration knowledge, which become part of the history of the people.

Smugglers and former migrants in diaspora and en route, by constituting the community of knowledge, become refugee protectors as they guide fleeing refugees. Refugees simultaneously take part in a particular performance, such as disguising their identities while clandestinely escaping their home countries, crossing borders, and managing everyday life in transition spaces. They resist forced camp life by moving to towns and cities. Thus, they need knowledge about the ways and precise moment and space they have to perform visibility and invisibility. In the context of state failure, conflict, economic stagnations, and violence in contemporary Eritrea (Kibreab 2013; Belloni 2016), smugglers (pilots, *delaloch*, and their connectors) are viewed by refugees as saviors from violence, a visa to travel, and, hence, their security and protectors from below. In other words, the facilitation of refugees' irregular departures, mobility, and transits forms and endures a collective system of migratory knowledge—rooted in transnational diasporic spaces—that strives to protect refugees from below.

Notes

1. Other researchers have also identified the transition or temporary role of migrants as smugglers in the facilitation of migration journeys. See Achilli (this volume) and Sanchez (2015).

2. According to Ethiopian law, unless exceptional circumstances, refugees are expected to stay in refugee camps in rural areas, owing to the country's limited economic and technical capacities to fulfill the needs of huge refugee flow to Ethiopia (see Belloni 2015).

3. *Delaloch* is the plural of *delala*, "smuggler" in Amharic.

4. *Hawala* is an informal money transfer system by which migrants' family members transfer fees to smugglers.

5. Critical scholarly works have demonstrated that the implementation of tough migration controls at Euro-African borderlands and U.S.-Mexico borders do not stop migration; rather, they produce more illegality and risks since migrants take more dangerous, costly, and long routes (see Andersson 2014; Sanchez 2015; Albahari 2015).

References

Achilli, Luigi. 2018. The "good smuggler": The ethics and morals of human smuggling among Syrians. *The ANNALS of the American Academy of Political and Social Science* (this volume).

Albahari, Maurizio. 2015. *Crimes of peace: Mediterranean migrations at the world's deadliest borders*. Philadelphia, PA: University of Pennsylvania Press.

Alpes, Maybritt. 2012. Bushfalling at all cost: The economy of migratory knowledge in Anglophone Cameroon. *African Diaspora* 5 (1): 90–115.

Andersson, Ruben. 2014. *Illegality Inc. Clandestine migration and the business of bordering Europe*. Berkeley, CA: University of California Press.

Arnone, Anna. 2008. Journeys to exile: The constitution of Eritrean identity through narratives and experiences. *Journal of Ethnic and Migration Studies* 34 (2): 325–40.

Ayalew, Tekalign M. 2016. The struggle of mobility: Organizing high-risk migration from the Horn of Africa. In *Open Democracy, beyond trafficking and slavery*. Available from www.opendemocracy.net (accessed 20 March 2017).

Baird, Theodore, and Ilse van Liempt.2016. Scrutinising the double disadvantage: Knowledge production in the messy field of migrant smuggling. *Journal of Ethnic and Migration Studies* 42 (3): 400–417.

Bariagaber, Assefaw. 2006. *Conflict and the refugee experience: Flight, exile, and repatriation in the Horn of Africa*. Aldershot: Ashgate.

Bariagaber, Assefaw. 2013. Globalization, imitation behavior, and refugee from Eritrea. *Africa Today* 60 (2): 2–18.

Belloni, Milena.2015. Cosmologies of destinations: Roots and routes of Eritrean forced migration towards Europe. PhD diss., University of Trento, Trento.

Belloni, Milena. 2016. Refugees as gamblers: Eritreans seeking to migrate through Italy. *Journal of Immigrant and Refugee Studies* 14 (1): 104–19.

Bernal, Victoria.2014. *Nation as network. Diaspora, cyberspace, and citizenship*. Chicago, IL: University of Chicago Press.

Collyer, Michael. 2007. In-between places. Trans-Saharan transit migrants in Morocco and the fragmented journey to Europe. *Antipode* 39 (4): 668–90.

Cooper, Elizabeth, and David Pratten. 2015. *Ethnographies of uncertainty in Africa*. London: Palgrave.

Faist, Thomas. 2000. *The volume and dynamics of international migration and transnational social spaces.* Oxford: Clarendon Press.

Faist, Thomas. 2014. Brokerage in cross-border mobility: Social mechanisms and the (re)production of social inequalities. *Social Inclusion* 2 (4): 38–52.

Frouws, Bram. 2017. *The Eritrean Exodus: What happened in 2016?* Nairobi: RMMS. Available from www.regionalmms.org (accessed 25 February 2017).

Frouws, Bram, Melissa Phillips, and Christopher Horwood. 2014. *Going West: Contemporary mixed migration trends from the Horn of Africa to Libya and Europe.* Research Report Series 5. Nairobi: Regional Mixed Migration Secretariat (RMMS). Available from www.reginalmms.org (accessed 23 November 2016).

Gammeltoft-Hansen, Thomas, and Ninna N. Sørensen. 2013. *The migration industry and the commercialization of international migration.* New York, NY: Routledge.

Gerard, Alison. 2014. *The securitization of migration and refugee women.* New York, NY: Routledge.

Hannam, Kevin, Mimi Sheller, and John Urry. 2006. Editorial: Mobilities, immobilities and moorings. *Mobilities* 1 (1): 1–22.

Hassanen, Sadia. 2007. *Repatriation, integration or resettlement: The dilemmas of migration among Eritrean refugees in Eastern Sudan.* Trenton, NJ: The Red Sea Press.

Herman, Emma. 2006. Migration as a family business. The role of personal networks in the mobility phase of migration. *International Migration* 44 (4): 192–230.

Kibreab, Gaim. 2009. *Eritrea. A dream deferred.* Oxford: James Currey.

Kibreab, Gaim. 2013. The national service/warsai-yikealo development campaign and forced migration in post-independence Eritrea. *Journal of Eastern African Studies* 7 (4): 630–49.

Kubai, Anne. 2016. Trafficking of Ethiopian women to Europe—Making choices, taking risks, and implications. *African and Black Diaspora: An International Journal* 9 (2): 166–83.

Leurs, Koen. 2014. The politics of transnational affective capital. Digital connectivity among young Somalis stranded in Ethiopia. *Journal of Migration and Culture* 5 (1): 87–104.

Levitt, Peggy, and Nina Glick Schiller. 2004. Conceptualizing simultaneity: A transnational social field perspective on society. *International Migration Review* 38 (3): 1002–39.

Marcus, George. 1995. Ethnography in/of the world system: The emergence of multi-sited ethnography. *Annual Review of Anthropology* 24:95–117.

Sanchez, Gabriella E. 2015. *Human smuggling and border crossings.* New York, NY: Routledge.

Sanchez, Gabriella, and Nicholas Natividad. 2017. Reframing migrant smuggling as a form of knowledge: A view from the U.S.-Mexico border. In *Border politics: Defining spaces of governance and forms of transgressions*, eds. Günay Cengiz, and Witjes Nina, 67–83. Cham: Springer International Publishing AG.

Schapendonk, Joris. 2012. Turbulent trajectories: African migrants their way to European Union. *Societies* 2:27–41.

Schütz, Alfred. 1944/1964. The stranger. An essay in social psychology. *Studies in Social Theory* II:91–105.

Schütz, Alfred, and Thomas Luckmann. 1973. *The structures of the life-world.* Evanston, IL: Northwestern University Press.

Soeffner, Hans-Georg, and Dariuš Zifonun. 2008. Integration – An outline from the perspective of the sociology of knowledge. *Qualitative Sociology Review* IV (2): 3–23.

Tecle, Samia, and Luin Goldring. 2013. From "remittance" to "tax": The shifting meanings and strategies of capture of the Eritrean transnational party-state. *Africa and Black Diaspora: An International Journal* 6 (2): 189–207.

Tesfagiorgis, Mussie. 2013. From troubled homes to human organ harvesters. The odyssey of African refugees in North Africa. In *The Horn of Africa at the brink of the 21st century: Coping with fragmentation, isolation and marginalization in a globalizing environment*, eds. Daniel R. Mekonnen and Mussie Tesfagiorgis. Felsberg: Edition Eins.

Treiber, Magnus. 2013a. Becoming by moving. Khartoum and Addis Ababa as migratory stages between Eritrea and "something." In *Spaces in movement. New perspectives on migration in African settings*, eds. Mustafa Abdalla, Denise Barros Dias, and Marina Berthet, 189–204. Köln: Köppe.

Treiber, Magnus. 2013b. Grasping Kiflu's fear. Informality and existentialism in migration from northeast Africa. *Modern Africa: Politics, History and Society* 1 (2): 111–39.

Treiber, Magnus. 2013c. Leaving Eritrea entering the world. Migrants in the making. In *The Horn of Africa at the break of 21ˢᵗ century. Coping with fragmentation, isolation, marginalization in a globalizing development*, eds. Daniel R. Mekonnen and Mussie Tesfagiorgis, 123–33. Felsberg: Edition Eins.

Treiber, Magnus. 2013d. Lessons for life. Two migratory portraits from Eritrea. In *Long journeys. Lives and voices of African migrants on the road*, eds. Alessandro Triulzi and Robert Mckenzie, 187–212. Leiden: Brill.

Van Reisen Mirjam, Meron Estefanos, and Conny Rijken. 2012. *Human trafficking in the Sinai: Refugees between life and death.* Nijmegen: Wolf Legal Publishers.

Vogt, Wendy. 2016. Stuck in the middle with you. The intimate labors of mobility and smuggling along Mexico's migrant route. *Geopolitics* 21 (2): 366–86.

Wheatley, Abby C., and Ruth Gomberg-Muñoz. 2016. Keep moving. Collective agency along the migrant trail. *Citizenship Studies* 20 (3–4): 396–410.

Xiang, Biao, and Johan Lindquist. 2014. Migration infrastructures. *International Migration Review* 48 (1): 22–148.

Zaitch, Damián. 2002. *Trafficking cocaine: Colombian drug entrepreneurs in the Netherlands.* The Hague: Kluwer Law International.

Zhang, Sheldon. 2008. *Chinese human smuggling organizations: Families, social networks, and cultural imperatives.* Stanford, CA: Stanford University Press.

The "Good" Smuggler: The Ethics and Morals of Human Smuggling among Syrians

By
LUIGI ACHILLI

This article challenges the categorization of smugglers as wicked villains by exploring smuggling's moral economy. I present findings from two years of ethnographic field research on Syrian refugees and smugglers in Turkey, Lebanon, Jordan, Italy, and along the so-called Balkan route (Greece, Macedonia, and Serbia). The relationship between the smugglers and the migrants appeared to be rich in solidarity and reciprocity and grounded in local notions of morality. Far from the dominant official narrative in the West of reckless criminals driven only by profit, smugglers sought and often found moral legitimation by using long-held notions of morality and religious duties when confronting the risky realities of their illicit enterprise.

Keywords: human smuggling; Syrian refugees; irregular migration; Eastern Mediterranean Sea; morality; ethics

Are human smugglers inspired by anything other than greed and disregard for human life? Contemporary mainstream narratives of migration tell us that smugglers are the most immoral people of our time, and that smuggling networks are mafia-like cartels of hardened and greedy criminals dedicated to the systematic deceiving and conning of migrants (see, among others, Ridgwell 2015; Sengupta 2015; *The Guardian* 2015). These facilitators of irregular migration have earned notoriety especially in Western Europe and North America as orchestrators of human massacres, evil geniuses behind criminal trades, amassers of untold riches made at the expense of their victims (see, for example, Perry and Agius 2015), and human predators "waiting to exploit [migrants'] need

Luigi Achilli is a Marie Curie Fellow at the European University Institute and the San Diego State University. He is the author of Palestinian Refugees and Identity: Nationalism, Politics and the Everyday *(I. B. Tauris 2015). He is a social anthropologist with an extensive publication record on forced migration and refugee displacement.*

Correspondence: Luigi.Achilli@eui.eu

DOI: 10.1177/0002716217746641

for assistance and their dreams for a better life" (Europol-INTERPOL 2016, 3). The rhetoric that characterizes human smugglers as greedy and immoral depicts migrants as helpless victims and calls for smashing smuggling rings and tightening borders, something advocates believe would ensure the very safety of migrants (see, for example, Andersson 2014; Van Liempt and Sersli 2013). A profusion of photos of migrants crammed into wretched boats circulates in the media; several accounts report the recklessness of smugglers who do not hesitate to toss human beings in the sea or sabotage their own vessels to force authorities to carry out rescues (e.g., Europol-INTERPOL 2016). On April 2015, for example, an overcrowded fishing boat capsized near the coast of Libya, causing the death of most of the eight hundred people stuck onboard. Survivors claimed that smugglers locked most migrants in the hull and middle deck of the three-layered boat, trapping them when the boat sunk (*The Guardian* 2015).

Human smugglers certainly are responsible for many tragedies that we have witnessed in the Mediterranean and elsewhere. However, while effective in igniting a "moral panic" (Cohen 1980, 9) and demonizing irregular migration, the representations and stories above have consistently failed to account for the dynamics of human smuggling and explain the relationship between smugglers and migrants. Our knowledge of irregular migration facilitation is often plagued with fragmented perspectives on the sociocultural dynamics of the migratory journey and the facilitator-traveler relationship. This is hardly surprising. Scholarship on the facilitation of irregular migration often draws exclusively from the experiences of government or law enforcement entities, or of migrants who were targets of threats, scams, or violence during their journeys (United Nations Office on Drugs and Crime [UNODC] 2010). This research, while valuable in some respects, tends to obscure the perspectives of those playing a role in migrant transit. In this article, I address this lacuna by tracing human smuggling in the Eastern Mediterranean Sea, which reveals patterns of cooperation and mutual support.[1] Challenging the notion that facilitators are merely ruthless profit-driven individuals, I argue that human smugglers feed into shared frameworks of morality with those whom they transport.

Literature Review

I began my field research for this article expecting that my investigation of human smuggling would reveal it to be a fundamentally abusive practice. Persuaded to document the abuses and deception perpetrated by criminals and endured by their victims, I was instead puzzled by what seemed to me an ostensible absence of exploitation. Between March 2015 and July 2016, I conducted field research in the Eastern Mediterranean corridor among Syrian refugees and smugglers. Contrary to my expectations, I learned how human smuggling carries a set of social and moral signifiers among both migrants and smugglers. Most smugglers operated by helping members of their immediate circles to reach the destination that would have been otherwise precluded to them through legal channels. They did it for money, of course; yet deception and exploitation seemed to be less common than popular accounts suggest. As a matter of fact, human smuggling was rooted in patterns of cooperation and support. Where exploitation occurred among migrants and asylum seekers, this was more often the consequence of their protracted condition of deprivation and irregularity than the precise criminal intents of mafia-like organizations. This was, for example, the situation of many refugees from Syria, whose need to support their families back in Syria considerably increased their vulnerability and the likelihood of working in dangerous and exploitative conditions, or getting involved in smuggling networks to enhance their own mobility.

In an effort to better understand one of the most discussed relationships in global migration, I draw on two bodies of literature on the moral scenario that defines the relationship between smugglers and irregular migrants. This article benefits from the empirical value of a growing, yet still small, scholarship that has questioned oversimplistic depictions of the facilitator-traveler relationship and their communities. Doomernik and Kyle (2004) summarized the complex relationship between smugglers and migrants as a spectrum that ranges from the altruistic assistance provided by family members or friends to dynamics of exploitation based on the intent of hardened criminals. Since their work, empirical research has shown that trust and cooperation seem to be more the rule than the exception in the interaction between smugglers and migrants (e.g. Bilger, Hofmann, and Jandl 2006; Koser 1997, 2008; Spener 2004, 2009). Zhang, for example, points out how Chinese migrants coming to the United States often perceive smugglers as philanthropists (2007, 89); while Sanchez shows that the migrant-facilitator relationship in Mexico dwells "on deep, socially cemented ties spanning across countries" (2015, 17). A number of studies on Turkey have remarked the strong bond of trust that ties smugglers and migrants together (Baird 2016; FRA [European Union Agency for Fundamental Rights] 2013; İçduygu and Akcapar 2016).

However, while these studies have begun to dismantle common stereotypes about the smuggler-migrant relationship, the assumption that smugglers are "service-providers" driven exclusively by profit remains evident in much of the relevant literature (e.g., Bilger, Hofmann, and Jandl 2006; Salt and Stein 1997; Staring 2003; Soudijn and Kleemans 2009). This approach represents a clear empirical and theoretical advancement in the field, but it may emphasize the commercial-based and business dimension of the relation between smugglers and migrants at the expense of other questions (Baird 2016). In particular, such an account tends to overlook the contexts in which motivations other than those involving economic utility drive and determine the relationship between migrants and smugglers.

Therefore, as a corrective to this, I turn to another body of literature, one that focuses on moral economy, understood here as "the production, distribution, circulation, and use of moral sentiments, emotions and values, and norms and obligations in social space" (Fassin 2009, 49).[2] This conceptual approach has the advantage of shifting the focus away from a business paradigm toward an analysis of moral landscapes and the sociopolitical context in which smuggling occurs. Such a move may seem counterintuitive at first: extracting money in exchange for help and preying on the misfortune of others could hardly be an instance of moral dispositions. However, for my informants—both smugglers and migrants—the request for money in exchange for services did not necessarily point to any form of immoral behavior.[3] The complex relationship between human smugglers and migrants invites a rejection of abstract models of solidarity and liberal ideals of morality (Meagher 2005, 226; Osella 2015), and it calls for an inquiry into how the moral economies of human smuggling come to be.[4] Such an analysis would be more suitable than a "business approach" to unveil the nuances and complexities that characterize the relationship between facilitators and migrants. It also avoids the pitfall of relegating them into essentialist and culturally deterministic readings while we seek to restore the coherence and meaning of their actions.

Field Methods

This article builds on empirical research largely based on interviews with and participant observations of Syrian refugees and smugglers held in Southern Italy (March–April 2015), Albania (July 2015), Lebanon and Jordan (September–October 2015), Turkey and Greece (April, October, and December 2015, May–July 2016), and the Former Yugoslav Republic of Macedonia (FYROM) and Serbia (November 2015).

The study involved interviews with forty-five men and women formerly smuggled across the Eastern Mediterranean route, and conversations with around fifty migrants—mostly Syrian asylum seekers in Jordan and Lebanon[5]—who were either in the process of being smuggled or considered the possibility to migrate irregularly to Europe. I traveled with some of them during legs of their journey to Europe and sought to shadow their experience. I also conducted twenty-three interviews with border and immigration authorities as well as humanitarians. Perhaps most importantly, I carried out thirty interviews with smugglers who worked, often interchangeably, as organizers, *passeurs*, lookouts, and intermediaries in Lebanon, Greece, and Turkey. In Italy and Albania, I met and spoke with a number of "retired smugglers" who were active during the so-called Albanian Crisis, between 1991 and 2001. I also had several informal conversations with hotel operators, taxi drivers, shopkeepers, and other smuggling market actors along the route who provided their services to both smugglers and migrants. While open and semistructured interviews remained the main and most important mode of my data collection, I also devoted time to participant observation. Since I argue that human smuggling cannot be understood without attending to the interactions between migrants and facilitators, I spent almost three weeks with a smuggling group based in Elgar, a coastal town in western Turkey.[6] The intensive, albeit limited, exposure to the community of smugglers and migrants allowed me to identify their organization and the processes that they rely upon in the facilitation of smuggling, as well as the day-to-day interactions that emerge among the market's participants.

To recruit participants in the Eastern Mediterranean area, I relied on my social contacts in the field and my friendship with Syrian and Palestinian refugees in Jordan, obtained through long-term fieldwork in the Palestinian refugee camps of Jordan (Achilli 2015) and through my involvement in an Italian NGO that worked with migrants and refugees in several countries along the Eastern Mediterranean route and the Balkan corridor. I thus began to meet Syrians and other communities of migrants who had migrated irregularly to Europe, people who claimed to know facilitators. I was able to extend my network of participants to these people's acquaintances, contacts, and relatives across borders.

Because smuggling is not a frowned-upon practice among migrant and refugee communities, I was able to contact more people who migrated irregularly but also some of their facilitators willing to share their experiences. No part of my field data collection involved concealment or deception. I adopted a series of precautions such as disclosing immediately to my informants the exact nature of my research, emphasizing my disinterest in the minute details of their business, and in general limiting my concern to how smuggling was perceived and discussed by those who were involved and their customers. I did not get involved in any smuggling activities. Much of my time in Elgar and my fieldwork across the route was spent figuring out how human smuggling acquires social and moral significance among my informants.

Getting Smuggled: Syrian Refugees' Flight to Europe

At the time of my fieldwork, Syrian refugees had two options to reach Europe: one was legal, through venues such as resettlement programs, family reunification, university fellowships and scholarships, training programs, and private sponsorships. The other option was—for the majority of them—the Balkan route: an exhausting and perilous journey that took them across two continents and several countries (i.e. Turkey, Greece, Macedonia, Serbia, Croatia, and Slovenia).[7] The former was by far the safest route. Yet the transfer of refugees from an asylum country to EU Member States remained for the majority of Syrians a chimera (Achilli 2016).

Turkey soon became a gathering point for Syrian refugees traveling from Syria and its neighboring countries to Europe. However, while Turkey was and still is a necessary step for most Syrian refugees, how a person got to Turkey largely depended on whether he or she possessed valid travel documents. Syrians with a valid passport traveled regularly to Turkey either by plane from Amman, Beirut, or Erbil or by boat from Tripoli in Lebanon. Flying to Istanbul, Izmir, or other urban centers in Turkey, was by far the fastest and safest solution. The flight was relatively cheap, approximately 250 euros. In addition, most Syrian refugees did not need a visa to fly to Turkey. My informants pointed out how even those among them who had lost or never had a passport could easily obtain one from the Syrian embassies in Amman and Beirut. "A year ago, this was almost impossible," a young man from Damascus, whom I met in a coastal city in Western Turkey in November 2015, pointed out: "Now, however, things have become much easier. It is only 200 JOD [Jordanian dinars, roughly 280 USD] if you want to renew the passport; and 400 JOD [560 USD] to have a new one issued. ... As soon as you get the passport, you can take a direct flight from the Queen Alia Airport [in Amman] to Istanbul. It's straightforward, you don't need any *muharrib* [smuggler]!"[8]

On the other hand, most Syrian internally displaced persons (IDPs), Palestinian refugees from Syria, and those without a valid passport embarked on a longer and more dangerous journey that exposed them to greater risks of exploitation. These people had no other option than to cross the border into Turkey illegally. Many of them took the inland route, via the Syrian-Turkish border near the village of Khirbat al-Joz in the northern Syrian governorate of Idleb. Others were smuggled by boat from the Syrian coastal cities of Latakia and Tartus. Both routes were extremely dangerous and expensive as asylum seekers had to travel across areas controlled by armed groups. To do so, they often required the services of drivers and the guides (*dallala*), whose knowledge of the area was pivotal for avoiding checkpoints and smuggling them out of Syria. Stories of exploitation and bribery were not uncommon. Several refugees claimed that they had to pay prices higher than what was agreed upon. Reports also suggested the possibility that armed groups such as Da'ish and the Free Syrian Army (FSA) facilitated internal movement to the Turkish border in the areas under their control in exchange for money (International Centre for Migration Policy Development [ICMPD] 2015).[9] In the last stages of the conflict, the journey seems to be made either independently or with the help of fellow travelers with cars who reportedly charge each passenger up to SYP 150,000–200,000 (Syrian pounds; around 800–1,060 USD) for the trip (ICMPD 2015).

Smugglers operated almost exclusively in Turkey.[10] When Noor and her husband left Lebanon for Turkey, they did not know what they would find, who they would speak to, and what the exact route was. "It was very easy," Noor told me when I met her in Srebrenica, near the Serbia-Croatia border: "You just fly to Istanbul or any other Turkish city and then you go in certain neighborhoods, everybody knows where. As soon as you step in the place, you will be approached by someone who knows that you are Syrian and what you are looking for. And you will find your smuggler or, in the worst-case scenario, someone who knows a smuggler."[11] After having found the smuggler, refugees departed on board wooden and fiberglass boats, rubber dinghies, fishing boats, or big cargo ships. At the time of my field work, the majority of those interviewed indicated that they had reached Greece from the isolated areas near the Turkish port of Izmir and Bodrum. Here, smugglers arranged transportation, for around 1,200 USD per person, to Lesbos or the numerous Greek islands near the border with Turkey. The proximity of the departure point with the Greek islands often meant a one-hour journey in a ten-meter rubber dinghy. Time and price varied based on the type of boat and number of people aboard, the weather conditions, and the relationship with the smugglers.

These connections reveal how unhelpful the description is of smugglers as cruel and reckless criminals driven exclusively by profits can be. Remarkably, accounts about the callousness of smugglers were often dismissed by those very people who risked their lives crossing the Mediterranean. The majority of migrants with whom I spoke did not perceive their smugglers as exploitative. On the other hand, they were vocal in their criticism of the EU failure to live up to the moral and humanitarian ideals it claims to champion. Smugglers offered a way to bypass the inherent shortcomings of a blocked system. The words of Mohammed—a man in his mid-20s from Syria, now an interpreter and social worker in Italy—are indicative of this awareness: "Smugglers are neither good nor evil. You pay for a service and you get what you pay for." Mohammed turned to smugglers when his family was refused a family reunification visa. He paid around 8,000 euros to have his brother smuggled from Syria to Germany. It was a long and tiring journey and Mohammed's brother crossed several states, via land and sea. This was the only available way to Europe, the only bridge to overcome the gap between the EU rhetoric of human rights and free mobility and its restrictive border policies. From his and many others' stories, human smuggling was perceived as part of a system of protection within the context of asymmetric distributions of power where people in certain countries have overarching incentives to move but few legal avenues to do so.

This smuggling process conjures up the "ethical scene" (Cohen 2011), through which migrants and smugglers constitute themselves as a moral community against an immoral "Europe." With few notable exceptions, all interviewed refugees who applied for resettlement had their application either rejected or left pending for an indefinite time. Mohammed's story echoes those of Sharif who concurred that European countries did not leave refugees with any other option than to take the illegal route to Europe. The father of two lived in a popular quarter in Amman. As Sharif's stay in the kingdom was no longer sustainable, he applied for asylum in Sweden. His application was rejected. He then reapplied. He did it three times. All were rejected. When I met him in Amman, he was still determined to leave for Europe. Venting his bitterness against EU embassies, he burst out: "I spent three years waiting for an answer. Nothing happened. I lost money and wasted precious time filing resettlement application forms for European embassies. … Time that I could have used better if I made up my mind earlier." Shrugging his shoulders, he then added: "I will be flying to Turkey next week. From there, I will go to Greece [through illegal channels]. They [European embassies] are encouraging us to go; they need the smugglers to do their job."[12]

Tight Bonds in Flexible and Heterogeneous Networks

A small town on the Aegean coast of Turkey, Elgar is a seaside vacation resort in summer, quite popular among locals and tourists. Around fifty thousand people live in this popular summer resort—mostly Turkish, even though British people have begun to buy summer homes in the town, establishing themselves as a sizeable community of many thousands. However, the number rises in summer when people all over Turkey and Western Europe come to the city for its sandy shores, ancient ruins, and nice weather. Tourism and agriculture have traditionally been the main source of income in this area. However, a new business has boomed recently. When I first visited it, in fall 2015, the city was one of the many centers of human smuggling on the Western shores of Turkey. I went to Elgar because "a friend of a friend" vouched for me with a group of smugglers from Syria. I began my fieldwork with a vivid image in my mind of stepping into a field where secrecy and caution were of the utmost importance. I was taken aback when Abu Hamza—a man in his early 50s who managed one of the smuggling groups that I came to know in Turkey—insisted that he use his real name with me and that I take accurate notes about his job, in part because authorities were already well informed of "what was going on and who was who."[13]

In Elgar, about half a dozen rubber dinghies departed at night when the sea was calm, carrying thirty to fifty people each (a total of three hundred people) to the Greek islands of Agathonisi and Farmakonisi. There were Syrian, Kurdish, Afghan, Iraqi, and Pakistani migrants. The largest client groups were Syrian and Afghan asylum seekers. The majority paid around 1,000–1,300 USD per person. Crossing the stretch that separates Turkey from the closest Greek island takes around 50 minutes. Faster boats took only 15 minutes; for people who could afford, it cost around 2,000–3,000 USD per person.

Working in a market characterized by supposedly high competition did not seem to bother the smugglers who I encountered in Elgar. One of them—Rahell, a man in his mid-20s, from Iraqi Kurdistan—explained how the high demand for his services gave little room for competition or violence among smugglers: "There are many smuggling organizations operating only in Elgar and the areas surrounding. … This does not usually create any problem among us; we actually prefer cooperation over fight. … If I don't have space on my boats, I send people to the other groups to help me to make them reach their destination."

Many benefitted from the revenues generated by this business.[14] The so-called refugee crisis also spawned a black market in fake documents: forged passports, ID cards, work permits, and any other paper for the right price.[15] However, the flow of money did not only stream into the pockets of the "criminals": along with an illicit economy, a licit one flourished. When I visited the city in late fall 2015, Elgar seemed to thrive thanks to the human smuggling industry. Shops, boutiques, restaurants, grocery stores, bus and taxi companies, nightclubs, and pubs were crowded with migrants and smugglers. This coastal town that would have normally sunk into an economic lethargy during the low season found a new impetus in fulfilling the desires and needs of these so-called criminal entrepreneurs and their customers. Hotels offered half or full board accommodations at special rates for families of refugees; bus companies posted special offers and group packages for Syrians and other migrants on the windows of their shops. In the upmarket bazaar, boutique owners participated in the smuggling enterprise, for example, by selling lifejackets showcased on mannequins and helmets with night lights. Grocery stores sold various types of merchandise to migrants and refugees, while restaurants stayed open late to feed the masses awaiting the right moment to depart.

My field work in the Eastern Mediterranean corridor confirms the findings of studies that have shown that smuggling networks active in the area mostly consist of a system of flexible and independent organizations that enter into partnerships with one another for short periods (see Baird 2016; İçduygu and Akcapar 2016; Triandafyllidou and Maroukis 2012). Even though these groups generally lacked centralized and hierarchical structures, a number of roles could be identified within the organizations. Along with the coordinators, who acted as veritable managers by taking the overall responsibility for the operations, there were the boat owners, either an individual or a group, depending on the size of the boat. There were the cashiers, who collected the money. Intermediaries who worked as veritable cultural mediators, serving the organization in a variety of manners from facilitating communication between smugglers and their local associates to taking care of refugees' needs, such as food and accommodation. Drivers took refugees from the hotels where they lodged until embarkation (in Arabic *al-nuqta*, "the spot"). Lookouts would signal the presence of police forces, while bodyguards or "hired muscles" would dissuade potential competitors from taking over the *nuqta* or other bits of the business. Migrants were also involved in smuggling activities. Such was the case of a *chauffeur*, a migrant who would drive the boat for a free ride. These *chauffeurs*—often without any basic nautical knowledge—were instructed by the smugglers on how to pilot a boat a day or sometimes a few hours before the departure. Various shades of involvement—from tacit approval to overt collaboration—defined the collusion of local authorities with the smuggling enterprise.

The groups that I encountered in Turkey and Greece were often based on preexisting kinship and friendship connections and on the idea that helping people reach their destination was not only a legitimate form of labor, albeit criminalized, but a moral duty. This sociomoral proximity and the protracted condition of illegality facilitated a blurring of roles. Asylum seekers and labor migrants might work as recruiters, guides, or intermediaries—positions that were often covered by the same person. They might escort immigrants across the border because of their own first-hand knowledge of the route. They might recruit clients because they share the same ethnic networks. They would provide the various services needed by the migrants (food, accommodation, and so on) because of their long-term relationship with local communities in the transit countries. They would do all this to pay the required fees or have a decent livelihood.[16] This was the story of many people who I met, like Firat, who entered the UK illegally via Greece, Italy, and France. Years after his arrival, British authorities deported Firat back to Greece for residing illegally in the UK. Stranded in Athens with no money, he worked as a *passeur* for the same smugglers—people with whom he shared the same ethnic background—who had helped him to cross the Mediterranean.

Unsurprisingly, many depicted their involvement in a smuggling network as belonging to a family. This family-based understanding of the smuggling network is something that was common among smuggling groups of different origins. The concept of "family" (*'aa'ila*), of course, brings to mind membership in mafia groups.[17] My informants, however, used the word to indicate more the relationship of equality and trust that ties members of a family together than the sturdy hierarchical bond that researchers have observed within mafia-like criminal organizations. Indeed, a high degree of flexibility seems to characterize these groups. For example, a person whose main role in the organization is to recruit prospective clients might also work as a cashier by collecting money if needed. Likewise, people are not bound to the organizations by long-term agreements. The captain of a group operating in the area quit overnight after a two-year involvement in the business. Although the pay was good and his companions were like brothers to him, the risk proved too much for him. Just a week prior to our meeting, Turkish coastguards nearly intercepted him upon his return from Greece. He managed to escape detection, but not without harm. When I first met him in Elgar, he still had deep scars across his arms and chest from hitting a rock after he jumped into the water from the moving boat. He later became a migrant/refugee himself, and embarked on the journey that eventually took him and his brother to Germany.

The smuggling groups that I met were also made up of "freelancers"—individuals who participated occasionally. My informants maintained that these were often locals who provided peripheral services to ensure that the smugglers could operate undisturbed. This was evident with Abu Hamza and his group. While his closest collaborators were mostly Syrian refugees who explained their involvement in the group as a consequence of their ethical commitment to helping their fellow Syrians, a broader nebulous of people—mainly locals—flowed around this inner circle. These people played a number of roles—spotters who would provide specific information about the presence of the authorities, drivers who would take the customers to the *nuqta*, or landowners who would rent a piece of land near the shore to be used as a departure point. Abu Hamza did not consider these people part of his "family," but freelancers who were paid for each service delivered. Abu Hamza compensated his closest collaborators differently: "I give them around 1,500 euro each month, but this is an average. … If they need more money to send to their families back home, I give them more. I am like a father to them."[18]

The Call: Becoming a Smuggler

A plethora of studies and articles have shown how violence and abuse are recurring features of the migrant-smuggler relationship, especially when it comes to collecting money and enforcing contracts (e.g. İçli, Sever, and Sever 2015; UNODC 2010). Even some of the smugglers who I interviewed conceded as much: "Smugglers are not all good," I was told by a few of them. Nonetheless, the majority of smuggling facilitators who I met described themselves as service providers who provided something that people could not get through legal channels. They were aware that they were part of a highly unstable and dangerous market and said that was the reason they asked such high fees from their clients.

They claimed to operate a moral economy by helping people to escape misery and danger (cf. Webb and Burrows 2009). This perception was largely shared by those migrants who had requested their services (see also Van Liempt and Doomernik 2006; Soudijn and Kleemans 2009; Sanchez 2015; Staring 2003; Zhang 2007).

It is obviously impossible to draw a homogenous profile of "the smuggler." Still, a closer look at the inner dynamics of human smuggling draws a complex picture. Violence and solidarity, deception and trust, they all can occur simultaneously in the smuggling business. Studies show, for example, how Chinese migrants smuggled to the United States willingly decided to become smugglers themselves to protect their fellow migrants from the same abuses that they had to endure during their irregular journey (Zhang 2007). Against this backdrop, one may ask: What does honest and ethical smuggling entail? Answers to this question should take into account local notions of morality and the broader sociopolitical context in which the act of smuggling takes place.

Syrians use the Arabic term *muharrib* to indicate the "smuggler." The word does not necessarily have a negative connotation, although it often does. The term can simply refer to someone who sneaks something or someone for either positive or negative intents. Among my informants, for example, smuggling was not just about profiting because the *muharrib* was not necessarily driven only by material gain. It entailed a range of practices encompassing honesty and moral conduct. It involved the smugglers restricting their margin of profit, using good-quality boats, and displaying civilized and refined manners with their customers. They regarded as immoral any misconduct relating to the smugglers' quality of services or treatment of customers and, in general, the intention to profit off migrants. This was the story of Abu Hamza.

Abu Hamza was well known among Syrian refugees for being a *muhtaram* (respectable person). The first time I met him was in Elgar, in the courtyard of a four-star hotel near the city center. He was sitting at a table sipping a cup of tea while juggling three mobile phones. He was arranging the arrival to the city of a new batch of people wishing to cross the narrow stretch of water that separates Elgar from the Greek shores. With him were several boys and young men whom Abu Hamza introduced to me as his crew. As I came to discover soon after, it was a mixed group that comprised both migrants and smugglers. It was difficult to tell them apart. Nothing distinguished "smugglers" or "their clients" as belonging to two distinct social types. They were all Syrians; all stuck along the route to Europe. Even Abu Hamza was seeking asylum to Europe. As many others like him, he left Syria in 2012, taking the route to Italy, via Libya. However, his journey abruptly ended in Egypt, where local authorities detained him for a few months before sending him back to Lebanon. He tried again. The second time he took the Balkan route: Turkey, Greece, Macedonia, Serbia, and Hungary. Again, he did not make it. While waiting on the western shores of Turkey to be smuggled into Europe, Abu Hamza changed his mind: "I could not any longer watch my fellow country mates suffering in Syria or being exploited by smugglers and locals in Turkey. I decided to do something for them."[19]

A smuggled migrant himself, Abu Hamza knew the basics of the job. Hamza owned a jewelry shop back in his village in Syria, so he had some financial liquidity to help set up his business. He found a Turkish associate to help minimize risks—the man's personal contacts and knowledge of the country were crucial to set up the business. This was how Abu Hamza became a smuggler, a good one, as he put it. At the time of my research, around thirty people worked for the organization, helping fellow country-mates to reach their destination in Europe.

Abu Hamza and his group worked for money, of course, yet financial gain did not seem to disqualify the morality of their actions in their own eyes and those of the migrants who required their services. In a recent article, Filippo Osella shows how brokers and middlemen in Kerala are "judged to be immoral when they cheat would-be-migrants by taking money for non-existent visas or jobs, not because they put a price to connections that normally should be provided as part of wider obligations between kin and friends" (2015, 370). Likewise, in Elgar, moral assertions about human smuggling were made on the basis of the quality of the services provided than on the economic dimension of the contracts. As Abu Hamza put it, "I help my fellows [Syrian refugees] cross the sea. They call me *muhtaram* because I charge them much less than any other smuggling group and I give them a far better service: safer boats and better treatment!"[20]

It was not enough to be fair and reasonable in business transactions to be considered trustworthy and respectable. The migrants and smugglers who I encountered in Elgar assessed the moral standards of other smuggling groups by the presence or absence of decency and humanity. The importance of being morally respectable (*muhtaram*) and kind (*tayyib*) was, interestingly, often stressed by smugglers themselves. As Nader, one of Abu Hamza's associates put it:

> There are lot of smugglers in Turkey. Already in Elgar there are six, seven groups. Not all are good. Some of them have no good manners with people [the customers]. They forg[e]t that these people are human beings like them. When you do this job, you should remember that you are dealing with human beings (*'insan*). If you profit off them [it] is no good. If you scare them [it] is no good. Kindness is very important. Sometimes I meet elderly people that when I shake their hands I can feel the[m] tremble [with] fear. I reassure them. I call them "*hajj*."[21] After a while, their mood changes completely; they feel at ease, they are not afraid anymore. ... Each of my new *shabab* [boys] take[s] a course [on] good manners before starting to work with people.[22]

Among my informants, *muhtaram* and *tayyib* were not abstract virtues. However, being a good smuggler implied more than behaving properly and being well mannered. Human smuggling drew social and moral significance from the broader moral and political universe that smugglers and migrants shared. Not only did the majority find no contradiction between smuggling and being pious, they were convinced that facilitating irregular migration was a political and religious duty. Abu Hamza's story is a case in point.

Most of Abu Hamza's customers came from his same village of origin in Syria. His associates—the *shabab*—came from the same place. In the first two years following the outbreak of the Syrian civil war, Hamza's village saw fierce armed clashes between the government forces and the Free Syrian Army. It was subsequently occupied by the Islamic State of Iraq and the Levant (ISIL) in 2013, which still controls a large part of the area. The intense fighting between the various factions over the years deprived the village of basic commodities. The resulting hunger, disease, and high death rate forced many to leave. For Abu Hamza, helping his fellow villagers to escape the extreme misery in which they live was a duty. He felt that his piety influenced his decision to smuggle people:

> We are different from many other smuggling groups. There are smugglers who don't care about their customers. For us it is our duty to help them. These people are not only my customers: they are my *ikhwan* [brothers]. I help the[m] because they are on the wrong side of the world … we all come from the same place. I help them escap[e] the madness of Daesh [the Islamic State of Iraq and the Levant]. … This is *jihad*. Do you know the difference between mine and Daesh's jihad? Daesh is only a bunch of *muta'assibin* [narrow-minded people] who don't understand that *jihad* has little to do with killing people. The real *jihad* is different, it means to strive to become a better person. This is what I do when I help my people, this is the real *jihad*.[23]

Abu Hamza's comment is important in many ways. On one level is his use of "*jihad*."[24] Of particular importance, however, is that Abu Hamza wanted to point out a connection among politics, Islam, and smuggling human beings to make a distinction between different forms of smuggling along a scale of morality. His grievances unveil the deceptive and exploitative nature of some network connections. In what follows, I give some ethnographic texture to this ambivalence as I witnessed it during my fieldwork in Turkey and Greece.

Smugglers and Refugees

The human smuggling that I encountered in Elgar revealed itself to be a business that requires trust. For migrants, smugglers constitute a valuable resource, one that allows them to escape misery and extreme danger. At the same time, smugglers also depend in part on the migrants to refer other prospective "clients" (Triandafyllidou and Maroukis 2012) because their services are tied to specific locations. Those migrants who survive a journey can operate as a pull factor by tempting kin and friends to embark on a similar journey. Some of the successfully smuggled migrants I interviewed relied on smugglers to reunite their families left behind in Syria, Jordan, Lebanon, or Iraq.

Ahmad was one such person. In his late teens when he left Syria for Sweden in 2012, it took Ahmad and his 16-year-old brother around four months to reach their destination. I met Ahmad in Turkey. He flew from Sweden to meet his mother, sisters, and bride whom he entrusted to the same smugglers who helped him and his little brother to reach Europe years earlier. He spent the few days prior to their departure with them, instructing his family on the different legs of the journey. When his family finally departed, Ahmad was able to track his family's journey to Greece using GPS. He left Turkey only when he received confirmation from his bride that they had reached the Greek shores.

Ahmad's decision to entrust his family members to the same smugglers was based not only on cost-benefit calculations but also the idea of relying on the same ethnic and moral community in exile. The time migrants spend with smugglers was functional for strengthening this social bond.[25] For smugglers, many of the migrants are not only customers but friends, fellow nationals, or simply individuals who carry a personal story. The time prior to departure provides migrants and smugglers opportunities to engage that go beyond simple working relationships. Kurdish smugglers operating in Greece, for example, are known to spend a large part of their time with their clients on the mountains of Igoumenitsa, sleeping with them, sharing the same food. I found similar practices among other smuggling groups elsewhere. In Elgar, for instance, smugglers and migrants slept in the same hotels, ate at the same restaurants, and hung around in the same bars. This everyday practice of coexistence among smugglers and migrants formed a bond between both parties. Mahmud, a Syrian man in his early 20s, was an example. The young man spent over a month in Elgar with Abu Hamza and his *shabab*. He first waited for his brother to send him the money to pay for his journey to Greece. He then waited for the sea to be calm enough to allow his departure. When the time finally came, Mahmud no longer wanted to leave: after a month spent living together with the same people who were supposed to smuggle him to Greece, he established a solid friendship with many of them. When I asked him the reason for his reticence to leave, Mahmud replied: "I left my family in Syria; I found a new one here. Now, I don't want to lose again my family." Mahmud eventually left, with a promise to his new friends that he would come back as soon as he obtained refugee status in Germany.[26]

That smuggling may at times be cemented within social ties between smugglers and their customers does not necessarily protect the latter against exploitation and violence. The strong social bonds that researchers have witnessed may be facilitated by the fact that smugglers and migrants share the same ethnic backgrounds or other social ties. In this sense, the establishment of smuggling networks on an ethnic basis serves to reinforce what Ilse Van Liempt aptly calls "chain of trust"—ethnic solidarities between smugglers and migrants that tend to fade the further migrants are from their country of origin (2007, 171). The establishment of a smuggling network would work to protect fellow nationals from the systematic exploitation of smugglers of different ethnic background. However, when border controls intensify and channels of legal entry diminish, migrants' likelihood of being abused and exploited increase precisely within these ties of kinship and ethnicity. One of the main conclusions of a recent study on the effects of the Syrian war and refugee crisis on human trafficking in Syria and the surrounding region indicates "that much of the exploitation taking place is not carried out by organised transnational crime groups, but rather involves family members, acquaintances and neighbours [who] are often left with no viable alternatives for survival other than situations that can be characterised as exploitation" (ICMPD 2015, 6).

A striking example of this comes from Mahdi. When I first met him in Elgar, Mahdi was in his early 20s and had left Syria a year earlier during a period of full-scale conflict. Mahdi came from the same village as Abu Hamza, so he contacted Abu Hamza, who agreed to bring Mahdi's family to Europe if Mahdi would work for him to pay the smuggling fee. When I asked Mahdi whether he was forced into smuggling human beings or got involved in the business voluntarily, he replied: "Look, it's a dangerous job, if the Turkish or Greek police catch you, you can spend up to 10–15 years in prison. So, if I could have chosen, I would have never done that. But—*hamdulillah'* [praise to Allah]—Abu Hamza was there when I needed him. Had it not been for him, my family and I would have died in Syria."[27] While working in Elgar, Mahdi was waiting to have the last member of his family in Syria smuggled to Greece before quitting smuggling and leaving for Europe.

Things, however, did not go as Mahdi had planned. Upon my departure from Elgar, he had agreed to do a last job for Abu Hamza. He had to escort a dozen well-off clients, who could afford a journey on board a fast boat, to the closest Greek island. In theory, this last job should have earned him a few thousands euros, and he could then rejoin his brothers who were waiting for him in Greece to continue their journey to Europe, following the Western Balkan route. On his way to Greece—a few hundred meters from the Greek shores—the boat was intercepted by Greek coastguards. Mahdi, identified as one of the potential smugglers onboard, was arrested.

I saw Mahdi again in Athens on a sunny day in spring 2016. We arranged to meet at a coffee shop in Omonia Square—the once commercial center of Athens that at the time of my research was serving as a meeting point and a makeshift detention camp for thousands of irregular migrants stranded in the capital of Greece. Here Mahdi told me how after being detained in a Greek prison, he was temporarily released to wait for trial. At this meeting, a different picture emerged of Abu Hamza, one that clashed with Mahdi's earlier depiction of his benefactor. "He was good with me when I was in Elgar," Mahdi conceded. Yet, he argued, "Abu Hamza forgets about his associates and friends in the moment of need. I tried to reach him several times, but I never got a hold of him. The only thing that he did was to send my cousin 1,000 euros that served to pay part of the lawyer's fee. Now the lawyer wants more money and I don't have any left."[28] Mahdi felt that he was already a prisoner: if he returned to Syria, he would almost certainly be forcibly conscripted by Assad's security forces. Unable to afford a private lawyer, he was fully aware of the bleak prospect of a court-appointed attorney. Most likely he would serve several years in prison. He could have continued his journey to Europe, but the EU-Turkey agreement went into effect on March 20 of that year, and the decision of Macedonia (FYROM) to seal its border with Greece in February 2016 considerably stemmed the flow of people through the Balkan route. Before bidding farewell, Mahdi asked me to lend him a hundred euros: the money should have allowed him to purchase a bus ticket to Salonica, and then to the border with Turkey, near Edirne. Last I heard from Mahdi, he was in Istanbul looking for a job as a mechanic.

Mahdi's story problematizes simplistic categorizations of smugglers and migrants. Not only does his journey illustrate the limited capacity of refugees to navigate rapidly changing geopolitical scenarios, but, more importantly, Mahdi's ambivalent relationship with Abu Hamza is a potent reminder of the complex ethical and moral dimensions in this illicit enterprise. On one hand, the "morality of smugglers" operates as a sort of counter morality to a discourse that in the name of rescuing poor refugees justifies the criminalization of both migrants and those who facilitate their journeys. On the other hand, the existence of a moral universe equally inhabited by both smugglers and migrants does not prevent ties of reciprocity and mutuality from quickly turning into deception or even exploitation. The fragile status of migrants on the move reveals the ways in which border controls shape transnational mobility. It also recognizes the role of policing and surveillance apparatuses *in generating the conditions for the exploitation of people*. It is hard to say whether Mahdi and many others like him were the exploited, the exploiters, both, or neither.[29] What these stories ultimately tell us is that a protracted condition of illegality exacerbates the vulnerability of Syrians desperate to leave their war-torn country. In this context, more stringent border policies and practices are doomed to fail because they bolster the very phenomenon that they intend to fight.[30]

Conclusion

The discourse and practice of human smuggling among my informants reveal a deeper understanding of how migrants and smugglers perceive, talk about, and take part in human smuggling. Over the course of my fieldwork, I came to recognize the complex system of moral values surrounding smuggling and the strong bonds between the smugglers and migrants.

Media reports constantly point to the brutality of smugglers and the plight of migrants, but they fail to account for the brutality caused by states' efforts to enforce border controls and neglect to acknowledge the ability of smugglers to help people navigate the unequal geographies of mobility. The resilience of smuggling networks amid hostile attempts by nation-states to dismantle smuggling organizations is a reminder not only of migrants' determination to flee their countries but also of the strong bond that forms among smugglers and their customers. This bond, I argued, feeds into a shared framework of morality and piety built and maintained by both parties.

Of course, Abu Hamza and others like him may have used moral tones to appear righteous in their otherwise illicit activities. It can be argued, indeed, that they spoke in these terms to mitigate their involvement in a difficult and unsavory business. This could certainly be true, but it would not be sufficient to explain the social bonds between smugglers and their clients that I witnessed in Turkey and Greece. My fieldwork in Turkey attests to the centrality of ethics in the lives of both migrants and smugglers as they separate from home and prepare for the journey to Europe. Their moral values are intertwined with ideological and political affiliations and come to define the experience of smuggling and being smuggled. While social networks can be supportive, kin and social networks can be deceiving and envious; religion and ethnicity might be used to justify deception and exploitation.

By highlighting the moral economy of human smuggling, I want to draw attention to the relationship between smugglers and their customers. Eradicating these organizations without addressing the causes of clandestine migration may prove difficult because smuggling networks are deeply enmeshed within migratory processes. Most importantly, the militarization of border control may not only be ineffective in stemming migration and smuggling but may ultimately trigger a vicious dynamic. Researchers have demonstrated that the increase in the effectiveness of control policies has accompanied an increase in smugglers' capacity to deliver specialized services to would-be migrants in a systematic and standardized way. In this context, the intensification of border control may lead to the disappearance of "chains of trust" (Van Liempt 2007) and pave the way for a more depersonalized way of conducting smuggling where profits and the commodification of the migrants would entirely replace any other ethical consideration.

Notes

1. In so doing, this article seeks to make a contribution to the small, yet growing, literature on human smuggling in the Eastern Mediterranean. See, among others, Achilli (2017); Antonopoulos and Winterdyk (2006); Baird (2016); İçduygu (2007); İçduygu and Toktas (2002); İçduygu and Yükseker (2012); İçli, Sever, and Sever (2015); Mandić (2017); Papadopoulou (2004); and Triandafyllidou and Maroukis (2012).

2. As of this writing, no studies have systematically examined how ethics and moral values interact with the choice of smuggling human beings. Very few have investigated these dimensions in relation to the migrant experience and decision to leave. For a notable exception, see Julie Chu's (2006) analysis of Fuzhounese migration through human smuggling networks as tied to moral aspirations (see also Ahmad 2011; Hagan 2008; Sarat 2013).

3. For a similar argument, see Osella and Osella (2000).

4. To understand the bond of trust and forms of cooperation that define the interaction between facilitators and migrants, I instead build on Michael Jackson's call to conceive morality and ethics as a field of indeterminacy and struggles, where good and evil are the temporary outcome of mediation processes (2011, 70).

5. In this article, Syrians traveling to the European Union are often referred to as both "refugees" and "asylum seekers." Each term has a distinct meaning that carries different international obligations and consequences. The use of the two terms can be explained by the ambiguous situation of Syrians. Most Syrians who left Syria after the outbreak of the conflict in 2011 and who entered a country of first asylum were registered with the United Nations High Commission on Refugees in the respective countries. However, since their status has not yet been definitively determined in Europe, these people are still asylum seekers while finding a way to Europe.

6. City given a pseudonym to protect anonymity of my research subjects.

7. The situation has changed since early 2016. The EU-Turkey agreement on March 20 and the decision of Macedonia (FYROM) to seal its border with Greece in February seem to have considerably stemmed the flow of people along the Balkan route but increased the dangers faced by Syrians on the move (Achilli 2017; Mandić 2017).

8. Interview, Beirut, October 9, 2015.

9. Also referred to as Islamic State in Iraq and Syria (ISIS), Islamic State in Iraq and the Levant (ISIL), or Islamic State (IS), "Da'ish" is the acronym of "al-Dawla al-Islamiya fi Iraq wa al-Sham" (literally "Islamic State in Iraq and the Levant"). The Free Syrian Army is one of the main armed opposition groups in Syria, founded in July 2011 by officers who defected from the Syrian Armed Forces.

10. For an overview of migrant smuggling flows and trends in Turkey, see İçduygu and Akcapar (2016).

11. Interview with Noor, Srebernica, October 22, 2015.

12. Interview with Sharif, Amman, September 25, 2015.

13. Interview with Abu Hamza, western Turkey, October 28, 2015. Note that other smugglers I encountered during my field work were more cautious and less inclined to divulge the minute details of their business. For obvious ethical reasons, the names of places and people in this article are all fictitious.

14. According to a report published by UNODC (2010), human smuggling along two of the main routes—from Africa to Europe and from South America to North America—generates about $6.75 billion a year.

15. I agree here with those who have argued how the "crisis" narrative is part and parcel of a European discourse on "migration" or "refugees" that fails to reflect the empirics and ultimately depoliticize the context in which migration occurs (see, among others, De Genova and Tazzioli 2016).

16. For comparative literature, see Lucht (2012).

17. See, for example, Gambetta (1993). Human smuggling studies based on criminological models have often overestimated mafia involvement in smuggling networks (Pastore, Sciortino, and Monzini 2006). For a corrective to this understanding, see those studies that have shed light on how smugglers can be part of migrants' social and familial networks (e.g., Bilger, Hofmann, and Jandl [2006]; Herman [2006]; Koser [1997, 2008]; Staring [2004]).

18. Interview with Abu Hamza, western Turkey, October 28, 2015.

19. Interview with Abu Hamza, western Turkey, January 1, 2015.

20. Interview with Abu Hamza, western Turkey, October 28, 2015.

21. The term is an Arabic word for addressing in a respectful manner any elder person.

22. Interview with Nader, western Turkey, December 5, 2015.

23. Interview with Abu Hamza, western Turkey, October 28, 2015.

24. His use of the term *jihad* refers more to the Islamic duty of assisting others, a term without militaristic connotations, rather than the holy war against infidels. Abu Hamza's difference between true and false jihad evokes the distinction in the Islamic doctrine between lesser jihad (*al-jihad al-asghar*) and greater jihad (*al-jihad al-akbar*). On the concept of *jihad*, see Kepel (2002), Roy (2004).

25. Recent scholarship has shed light on the coexistence of friendship and kinship ties with commercial interests within smuggling networks. See, example, Herman (2006), Staring (2004), and Spener (2009).

26. Interview with Mahmood, western Turkey, November 6, 2015.

27. Interview with Mahdi, western Turkey, October 29, 2015.

28. Interview with Mahdi, Athens, May 1, 2016.

29. For comparative literature on how the categories of "victim" and "perpetrator" overlap into the smuggling-trafficking nexus, see Palmer and Missbach's (2017) analysis of underage facilitators of irregular migration in Indonesia, and Shen's (2016) investigation of female child traffickers in China.

30. I have argued elsewhere about the importance of approaching trafficking and smuggling in the area as ultimately interconnected phenomena insofar as different means through which people enhance mobility in situations where channels of legal entry are limited if not absent (Achilli 2017).

References

Achilli, Luigi. 2015. *Palestinian refugees and identity nationalism: Politics and the everyday*. London: I.B. Tauris.

Achilli, Luigi. 2016. *Tariq al-Euroba—Displacement trends of Syrian asylum seekers to the EU*. Migration Policy Centre Research Report 2016/01. San Domenico di Fiesole: European University Institute.

Achilli, Luigi. 2017. Smuggling and trafficking in human beings at the time of the Syrian conflict. In *Human trafficking and exploitation: Lessons from Europe*, eds. Gebrewold, Belachew, Johanna Kostenzer, and Andreas Müller, 129–46. London: Routledge.

Ahmad, Ali Nobil. 2011. *Masculinity, sexuality and illegal migration: Human smuggling from Pakistan to Europe*. Burlington, VT: Ashgate Publishing.

Andersson, Ruben. 2014. *Illegality, Inc.* Berkeley, CA: University of California Press.

Antonopoulos, Georgios, and John Winterdyk. 2006. The smuggling of migrants in Greece: An examination of its social organization. *European Journal of Criminology* 3 (4): 439–61.

Baird, Theodore. 2016. *Human smuggling in the Eastern Mediterranean*. London: Routledge.

Bilger, Veronika, Martyn Hofmann, and Michael Jandl. 2006. Human smuggling as a transnational service industry: Evidence from Austria. *International Migration* 44 (4): 59–93.

Chu, Julie Y. 2006. To be "emplaced": Fuzhounese migration and the politics of destination. *Identities: Global Studies in Culture and Power* 13 (3): 395–425.

Cohen, Laurence. 2011. Ethical publicity: On transplant victims, wounded communities, and the moral demands of dreaming. In *Ethical life in South Asia*, eds. Anand Pandian and Ali Daud, 253–74. Bloomington, IN: Indiana University Press.

Cohen, Stan. 1980. *Folk devils and moral panics*. London: Routledge.

De Genova, Nicholas, and Martina Tazzioli, eds. 2016. Europe/crisis: New keywords of "the crisis" in and of "Europe." *Near Futures Online*.

Doomernik, Jeroen, and David Kyle. 2004. Introduction. *Journal of International Migration and Integration* 5 (3): 265–72.

Europol-INTERPOL. 2016. *Migrant smuggling networks*. Joint Europol-INTERPOL Report. Available from www.europol.europa.eu/sites/default/files/documents/ep-ip_report_executive_summary.pdf.

Fassin, Didier. 2009. Les économies morales revisitées. *Annales. Histoire, Sciences Sociales* 6:1237–66.

FRA. 2013. *Fundamental rights at Europe's southern sea borders*. European Union Agency for Fundamental Rights. Luxembourg: Publications Office of the European Union. Available from http://fra.europa.eu/en/publication/2013/fundamental-rights-europes-southern-sea-borders.

Gambetta, Diego. 1993. *The Sicilian mafia: The business of private protection*. Cambridge, MA: Harvard University Press.

The Guardian. 6 June 2015. Hundreds of migrants rescued from people traffickers in Mediterranean.

Hagan, Jacqueline. 2008. *Migration miracle: Faith, hope, and meaning on the undocumented journey*. Cambridge, MA: Harvard University Press.

Herman, Emma. 2006. Migration as a family business: The role of personal networks in the mobility phase of migration. *International Migration* 44 (4): 191–230.

İçduygu, Ahmet. 2007. The politics of irregular migratory flows in the Mediterranean Basin: Economy, mobility and "illegality." *Mediterranean Politics* 12 (2): 141–61.

İçduygu, Ahmet, and Sebnem Koser Akcapar. 2016. Turkey. In *Migrant smuggling data and research: A global review of the emerging evidence base*, eds. Mary McAuliffe and Frank Laczko, 137–60. Geneva: International Organization for Migration (IOM).

İçduygu, Ahmet, and Sule Toktas. 2002. How do smuggling and trafficking operate via irregular border crossings in the Middle East? Evidence from fieldwork in Turkey. *International Migration* 40 (6): 25–54.

İçduygu, Ahmet, and Deniz Yükseker. 2012. Rethinking transit migration in Turkey: Reality and re-presentation in the creation of a migratory phenomenon. *Population, Space and Place* 18 (4): 441–56.

İçli, Tülin G., Hanifi Sever, and Muhammed Sever. 2015. A survey study on the profile of human smugglers in Turkey. *Advances in Applied Sociology* 5 (1): 1–12.

International Centre for Migration Policy Development (ICMPD). 2015. *Targeting vulnerabilities. The impact of the Syrian war and refugee situation on trafficking in persons*. Vienna: ICMPD. Available from https://www.icmpd.org/fileadmin/ICMPD-Website/Anti-Trafficking/Targeting_Vulnerabilities_EN__SOFT_.pdf.

Jackson, Michael. 2011. *Life within limits: Well-being in a world of want*. Durham, NC: Duke University Press.

Kepel, Gilles. 2002. *Jihad: The trail of political Islam*. Cambridge, MA: Harvard University Press.

Koser, Khalid. 1997. Social networks and the asylum cycle: The case of Iranians in the Netherlands. *International Migration Review* 31 (3): 591–611.

Koser, Khalid. 2008. Why migrant smuggling pays. *International Migration* 46 (2): 3–26.

Lucht, Hans. 2012. *Darkness before daybreak: African migrants living on the margins in Southern Italy today*. Berkeley, CA: University of California Press.

Mandić, Danilo. 2017. Trafficking and Syrian refugee smuggling: Evidence from the Balkan route. *Social Inclusion* 5 (2): 28–38.

Meagher, Kate. 2005. Social capital or analytical liability? Social networks and African informal economies. *Global Networks* 5 (3): 217–38.

Osella, Filippo. 2015. The (im)morality of mediation and patronage in south India and the Gulf. In *Patronage as politics in South Asia*, ed. Anastasia Piliavsky, 367–95. Cambridge, MA: Cambridge University Press.

Osella, Filippo, and Caroline Osella. 2000. *Mobility in Kerala: Modernity and identity in conflict*. London: Pluto Press.

Palmer, Wayne, and Antje Missbach. 2017. Trafficking within migrant smuggling operations: Are underage transporters "victims" or "perpetrators"? *Asian and Pacific Migration Journal* 26 (3): 287–307.

Papadopoulou, Aspasia. 2004. Smuggling into Europe: Transit migrants in Greece. *Journal of Refugee Studies* 17 (2): 167–83.

Pastore, Ferruccio, Giuseppe Sciortino, and Paola Monzini. 2006. Schengen's soft underbelly? Irregular migration and human smuggling across land and sea borders to Italy. *International Migration* 44 (4): 95–119.

Perry, Alex, and Connie Agius. 6 October 2015. Mastermind: The evil genius behind the migrant crisis. *Newsweek*.

Ridgwell, Henry. 6 May 2015. People traffickers make billions in Mediterranean. *Voice of America*.

Roy, Olivier. 2004. *Globalized Islam: The search for a new Ummah*. New York, NY: Columbia University Press.

Salt, John, and Jeremy Stein. 1997. Migration as a business: The case of trafficking. *International Migration* 35 (4): 467–94.

Sanchez, Gabriella. 2015. *Human smuggling and border crossings*. London: Routledge.

Sarat, Leah. 2013. *Fire in the canyon: Religion, migration, and the Mexican dream*. New York, NY: New York University Press.

Sengupta, Kim. 10 June 2015. Mediterranean migrant crisis: The Libyan human trafficker making $50,000 a week. *The Independent*.

Shen, Anqi. 2016. Female perpetrators in internal child trafficking in China: An empirical study. *Journal of Human Trafficking* 2 (1): 63–77.

Soudijn, Melvin R. J., and Edward R. Kleemans. 2009. Chinese organized crime and situational context: Comparing human smuggling and synthetic drugs trafficking. *Crime, Law and Social Change* 52:457–74.

Spener, David. 2004. Mexican migrant-smuggling: A cross-border cottage industry. *Journal of International Migration and Integration* 5 (3): 295–320.

Spener, David. 2009. *Clandestine crossings: Migrants and coyotes on the Texas-Mexico border*. Ithaca, NY: Cornell University Press.

Staring, Richard. 2003. Smuggling aliens towards the Netherlands: The role of human smugglers and transnational networks. In *Global organized crime: Trends and developments*, eds. Dina Siegel, Henk van de Bunt, and Damian Zaitch, 105–16. Dordrecht: Kluwer.

Staring, Richard. 2004. Facilitating the arrival of illegal immigrants in the Netherlands: Irregular chain migration versus smuggling chains. *Journal of International Migration and Integration* 5 (3): 273–94.

Triandafyllidou, Anna, and Thanos Maroukis. 2012. *Migrant smuggling. Irregular migration from Asia and Africa to Europe*. London: Palgrave Macmillan.

United Nations Office on Drugs and Crime (UNODC). 2010. *The globalization of crime: A transnational organized crime threat assessment*. United Nations Office on Drugs and Crime. Available from https://www.unodc.org/documents/data-and-analysis/tocta/TOCTA_Report_2010_low_res.pdf.

Van Liempt, Ilse. 2007. *Navigating borders inside perspectives on the process of human smuggling into the Netherlands*. Amsterdam: Amsterdam University Press.

Van Liempt, Ilse, and Jeroen Doomernik. 2006. Migrant's agency in the smuggling process: The perspectives of smuggled migrants in the Netherlands. *International Migration* 44:165–90.

Van Liempt, Ilse, and Stephanie Sersli. 2013. State responses and migrant experiences with human smuggling: A reality check. *Antipode* 45 (4): 1029–46.

Webb, Sarah, and John Burrows. 2009. *Organised immigration crime: A post-conviction study*. Research Report No. 15. London: Home Office. Available from www.gov.uk/government/uploads/system/uploads/attachment_data/file/116629/horr15-report.pdf.

Zhang, Sheldon. 2007. *Smuggling and trafficking in human beings: All roads lead to America*. Westport, CT: Praeger.

Community Dimensions of Smuggling: The Case of Afghanistan and Somalia

By
NASSIM MAJIDI

This article uses an ecological systems approach to detail community involvement in smuggling in Afghanistan and Somalia—two countries that have similar patterns of irregular outmigration to the West and geopolitical and human security dynamics. I emphasize community connections and family ties as the key points around which irregular migration takes place and smuggling persists. In both of these countries, smugglers are members of local communities. The social organization of smuggling is strongest at community-based points of origin, then weakens as migrants and smugglers get farther from their homes, owing to a growing diversity of actors, cultures, and languages. By analyzing the strength of ties in communities involved in smuggling, the dynamics of referrals and guarantees, and interactions across various distances, this analysis takes the focus away from the causal and economic logic of smuggling to delve instead into its relational dimensions.

Keywords: ecosystem; community; irregular migration; smuggling

Much has been written on smuggling from an organized crime perspective; researchers worldwide have described smuggling as a highly profitable enterprise alongside drug trafficking, organized in vast hidden networks of transnational criminals involved in markets ranging from nuclear weapons to terrorism. Yet smuggling is more than a profit-seeking criminal activity that involves crossing borders illegally. It is a migration-related practice that is deeply rooted in migrants' communities of origin. The more

Nassim Majidi is an affiliate researcher at Sciences Po's Centre for International Studies (France) and a research associate at the African Centre for Migration and Society at Wits University (South Africa). As cofounder and director of Samuel Hall, a think-tank of the Global South, she leads evidence-based research and policy development on migration.

Correspondence: Nassim.majidi@samuelhall.org; Nassim.majidi@sciencespo.fr

DOI: 10.1177/0002716217751895

FIGURE 1
Ecosystem Approach, Adapted from Bronfenbrenner's Ecological Theory

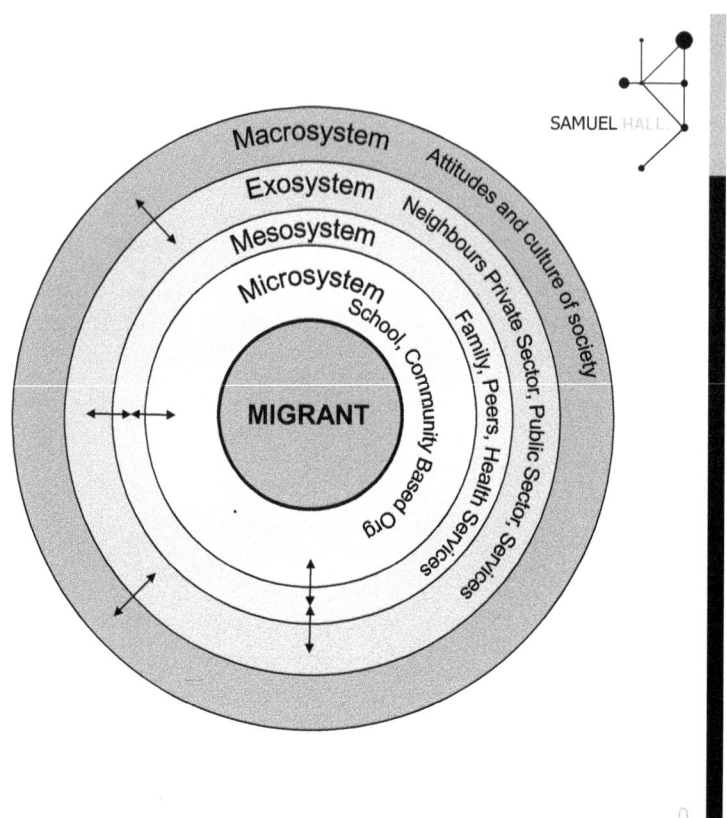

SOURCE: Adapted by Samuel Hall staff from Zubrick (2015), citing Santrock (2007).

engrained migration is as a community practice, the stronger the connections to local smugglers, who are often known directly or personally to the migrant through or as relatives and friends. Those ties represent, in the words of migrants themselves, an opportunity to leave, a source of protection, and a "passport" for a better life. Changing countries outside of legal pathways also relies on trust and community support. The stronger the ties among the individuals behind the migration at the point of origin—from family members to smugglers to money agents—the safer their journey along the way. Yet contemporary migration flows involve traveling over longer distances, thousands of miles away from migrants' places of origin; the ties that bind and protect migrants in their journeys become more and more tenuous the farther they find themselves from home. The way these ties change and play a role in the protection and the vulnerability of migrants in contemporary settings has hardly been the subject of theoretical or empirical inquiries.

This article uses an ecosystem model (see Figure 1) to explain how ties in the migrants' communities of origin impact both their decisions to travel extralegally and their migration experience. Applying ecological systems theory to migration practice means accounting for migration in four environmental layers: the microsystem (comprising family, friends, peers), the mesosystem (involving inter-actions between microsystems), the exosystem (the weight of other private and public vectors), and the macrosystem (attitudes and ideology of society and cul-ture). Together, these four layers influence the decision to migrate extralegally, the choice of migration modality, and ultimately the conditions of the migration. Economic perspectives on migration have long argued that migration is the result of a collective decision-making process "or other culturally defined units of pro-duction and consumption" that seek to minimize risks and maximize benefits for the individual as well as for the collective (Massey et al. 1993, 439). This article provides a model to understand this collective decision-making process and its limitations and reach.

Governments worldwide continue to frame migrant smuggling and the smuggler-migrant relationship in terms of demand and supply, push and pull factors, crimi-nality, and profit-feeding irregular migration. Here, I take a different approach, moving away from the economic logic of smuggling to delve into the relational dimensions present in communities of conflict-ridden countries. The case studies presented here step away from the migrant-smuggler duo to account for the complex sets of actors shaping irregular migration by zooming into their roles in the collective process. The case studies include protection and vulnerability as concentric levels, and present the way migrants deal with these challenges in the context of their journey with smugglers in Afghanistan and Somalia. This article documents the root of the protective connections among families, migrants, and smugglers, and the ways they may vanish over time and space. It relies on the testimonies of Somali and Afghan migrants, their communities, and their smugglers.

Somali and Afghan migrants have been in recent years among the top ten nationalities of asylum seekers arriving in Europe, with Norway and Switzerland being the top destination countries for Somali migrants (with 14 percent of the world's Somali migrant population); while nearly half of Afghan asylum seekers in 2015 applied for asylum in two European Member States, Hungary and Sweden (see Migration Policy Institute 2016; Pew Research Center 2016; Eurostat 2016). Afghanistan and Somalia both share a geo-political past defined by international intervention and conflict, or as Vogt states, "historical trajectories of political and criminal violence" (2013, 764). They also lack legal migration pathways to Europe: most often, the only way out for those seeking to move is to be smuggled. In a context defined by international conflict and military interven-tions, continued confrontation between government and international forces on one hand, and opposition groups on the other, whether Al-Shabaab in Somalia or the Taliban or ISIS in Afghanistan, has translated into growing instability for civil-ians in both countries. One of the main coping mechanisms for the general popu-lation remains migration, with community proximity and personal relationships shaping the ways in which the migration project can turn from aspiration into action. This article provides a conceptual framework to understand this process.

Research Question and Theoretical Background

> When you think of leaving, it becomes like a sickness, an obsession. If someone says
> tonight "I need to go to Europe," that person has to go and will be helped by the com-
> munity to go. Right in your neighborhood, introductions are made. The smuggler I had
> was a friend, I trusted him.

The words of Ahmed, a 35-year-old Somali man who returned from Norway to Mogadishu as part of the "Assisted Return Program" in 2015, echo the voices of migrants who I interviewed in Afghanistan. While much has been written about migrants and smugglers, the role of their communities in the journeys they embark upon has been only peripherally examined. How are migrants' smuggling experiences affected by their social relationships and the environment around them?

The ecological systems theory provides one approach to answering this question. Originally developed by Urie Bronfenbrenner (1981) through the lens of individual development, its relevance to migration processes stands through the provision of a layered analysis of relationships. It involves four levels of interactions to showcase how decisions constitute collective, multilayered processes. The model proposes four levels of interactions ranging from the immediate (migrant-smuggler) to the broader contexts in which migrants and their communities are immersed (institutions, public-private sectors and partnerships, and structural conditions).

The first layer is the *microsystem*. It involves the immediate, personal interactions of the migrants, such as those between migrant and family, migrant and peers. This microsystem is community-specific in the sense that it can be located in the migrants' community of origin and along their transit. Further out is the *mesosystem*, which consists of the set of interactions among migrants' individual microsystems, for instance the family and a community elder, the mosque and neighbors. Then there is the *exosystem*, which is constituted by the public and private structures and partnerships encountered along the migration journey, such as the involvement of financial facilitators or money brokers and those who provide services to the migrants' families and friends when mainstream financial institutions and services would not. The fourth level is the *macrosystem*, which describes the broader political, economic, and social environment where migrants live. A fundamental vector in the macrosystem in the context of this particular article is conflict and the lack of rule of law.

This layered approach maps how relationships shape the decision to migrate and the outcome of the migration. Looking at the role played by the community across the micro-, meso- and macrosystems of migrants' journeys provides an alternative to network-based frameworks, often used in the criminal justice oriented analysis of smuggling. The model proposed here allows for an analysis of transactions and relationships framed around personal, cultural, and ancestral proximity. I argue that these are the defining elements in migrants' decision-making across environments. In other words, networks shape the local culture of migration, making migration more accessible to all (Hagen-Zanker 2017); but it is not smuggler networks alone, it is the interlinkages, interconnectedness, and relationships across these systems that transcend location and time and provide the necessary resources to facilitate migration, including smuggling.[1]

In this conceptual framework, communities are key to understanding the perception of smugglers as a potential source of protection. While the conditions leading to their migration may shape the decisions and timelines of some migrants' journeys, smugglers are found in this fieldwork to be chosen by migrants through a referral and community-based system in their community of origin (what I refer to as the "local" smuggler) or their community of transit. Rather than falling into the smuggler-as-predator trope common in current narratives of irregular migration, I argue that the community ties (or systems) that lead to the selection of a specific smuggler become attenuated as the distance between the place of origin and the destination increases. Consequently, the ability to choose and travel within a specific protective system weakens and risks increase. As Chu highlights in her research on irregular migration from China, mobility is built across a series of signs and symbols built through transactions between people (2010). Yet such signs and symbols are likely to change along the migration route.

As other scholars of smuggling have highlighted, an essential element of smuggling is trust (Sanchez 2014a; Vecchio and Gerard 2014; Bilger, Hoffman, and Jandl 2006; Khosravi 2010). Trust is key to map the nature of the interactions and of the proximity between smugglers and migrants. Before the journey begins, and in transit, relatives and friends, as well as financial facilitators, provide a much-needed connection and resource base to those seeking to move. It is through these mesosystems that migrants come to trust their smugglers. Migrants will be more likely to trust their smugglers operating in those layers of the system because of the ties that link both themselves and their smugglers to a shared community—what Van Liempt refers to as the "chain of trust" (2007). The chain is strongest within communities, strengthened by the proximity and frequency of encounters and transactions that lay out the trajectory and initiate the migration. Once migrants are on the move, they benefit from a transnational community that supports them and from its continued interactions and reach along the way. Ethnic, tribal, and cultural ties bind the community, whether local or transnationally. While some smugglers may engage in unscrupulous practices, it is the ecosystems where they operate that shape their interaction with the migrants and their ability to provide them with protection.

The Case for Afghanistan and Somalia

Afghanistan and Somalia are countries with different political, economic, and social realities, yet they were chosen as examples in this study on smuggling experiences and social relationships for three fundamental reasons. First, Afghanistan and Somalia have been at the center of international geopolitical analyses in the wake of September 11, 2001, and the Global War on Terror. Both countries are often cited as fertile ground for Islamic terrorism, and the potential for Al Qaeda and Al-Shabaab to recruit new members in both regions has been documented. They have also been home to multiple interventions by the international community over several decades—with different occupying forces (from Russia to Ethiopia to the United States), alongside different moments of "withdrawal" and "transition," built into a broader rhetoric of aid, reconstruction, and development. Both countries are also in a constant shift between conflict and postconflict status. Key cities in Somalia and Afghanistan are at the heart of urban warfare, and indiscriminate attacks against civilian and antigovernment opposition are common.

Second, both countries have high levels of internal displacement—more than 1.1 million recorded in Somalia in 2014 and 1.2 million in Afghanistan in 2016 alone (International Displacement Monitoring Centre [IDMC] 2016; Amnesty International 2016)—because of factors ranging from critical food shortages to natural disasters. Last, these structural factors have propelled significant outmigration flows, notably to Europe. Somali and Afghan migrants rank consistently among the top ten nationalities of asylum seekers arriving in Europe (Migration Policy Institute 2016). Somalia and Afghanistan present a similar range of "historical trajectories of political and criminal violence" (Vogt 2013), where mobility constitutes a coping strategy and a mode of survival. They also share a "culture of migration" that begins with cycles of irregular migration at a young age and that connect local communities with large diasporas abroad. Historically afflicted by vast structural challenges, smuggling constitutes virtually the only route for migration from Afghanistan or Somalia to Europe. Through their services, smugglers provide the opportunity for asylum seekers to claim refuge in the West—a role that is recognized and highly sought after. The presence of similar forms of social organization—clans organized alongside ethnic, tribal terms—where members come together to support an individual migration project also make Afghan and Somali migrants a valid comparison. From planning to financing, community members provide the impetus needed to start the project and support those intending to migrate. Local smugglers are part of the community, either hailing from the community itself or having direct ties to it through marriage, or blood or ethnic ties. Smugglers are contacted and selected for their potential to support the common and collective interest, to make the project a reality. In other words, the smuggler is entrusted to play a key role: that of representing the collective goals of the community by virtue of being involved beyond the point of departure in migrants' journeys.

The examples presented here showcase, to a great extent, some of the most extreme cases of human smuggling in response to domestic insecurity and instability, and help us to identify common patterns behind smuggling practices. Although the previously reviewed three factors are fundamental variables defining particular contexts, within these settings, the patterns of smuggling are in many ways similar to those seen in other regions of the world with different levels of development and conflict. As such, our two case studies allow us to also step outside of conflict settings to identify the underlying nature of smuggling as a community-based provision of services and a source of protection.

It is true that there is an inherent transnational element to smuggling, but not in the sense of a vast, well-organized criminal network: smuggling resides rather in the provision of services across borders and space. Smuggling is a succession of travel routes, actors, border crossings, and staged payments, but it is also the collection of everyday, ordinary interactions. In fact, this ordinariness is even evidenced linguistically, through terms like *qachag* in Dari or *tahreebiye* in Somali, both meaning *smuggler* or *trafficker* yet carrying no negative connotations (*tahreb* means "to escape" in Somali). Simultaneously, however, the protective layers of smuggling may crumble in ways that migrants, their communities, or the smugglers are prepared to address.

Methodology

There were three imperatives in the methods used in this study. The *first* was to adopt a methodology that would allow for case-study comparisons and a multisited approach to track the continuum of migrant-smuggler interactions. A multisited approach was required to understand the effect of space on the lived experiences of smuggled migrants and the relationship of migrants to smugglers at different sites. In each of these countries, an inductive approach was used to speak to those who are not heard as often in migration accounts. I took note of the actions and influences of, and roles played by, the brokers, the facilitators, and the smuggling agents. Interviews were conducted in Kabul, Afghanistan, and Mogadishu, as well as in Somaliland, Puntland, and various locations in Norway.

The *second* imperative was to secure access to smugglers through the prism of the migrants themselves: either by being introduced to smugglers by migrants, their friends, and families, or learning secondhand information through the migrants who recounted their relationship to smugglers. The selective factors for participation were therefore to have "tracking strategies" (Marcus 1995) built into the research design, either directly through a physical multisited approach, or indirectly through the secondary accounts of the migrants who had gone through the migration journey.

In Afghanistan, a longitudinal migration assessment was used, through a bimonthly series of conversations led over the course of one year (2015–2016) with thirty-five Afghan men interviewed at different points in their migration journeys: at origin, in transit, at destination, and upon their return. Those who return are mainly those who had exhausted all legal recourse to remain in their destination countries, failed the asylum process, or decided to return before the end of a lengthy asylum process. Data on migrants' journeys and their evolving relations with smugglers were collected through open-ended conversations conducted in person or through phone or Skype.

In Somalia, respondents were selected based on their accounts of using smugglers to pave their way to other countries in the region and to Europe. Between 2014 and 2016, twenty Somalis were interviewed, alongside their family members and friends (members of their immediate microsystem), to map the nature of their relationships with smugglers. Through conversations tracing back the migration journeys of those who had returned voluntarily or due to the lack of any legal option to remain in Europe, the faces of smugglers and their contacts were unveiled.

A *third* parameter entailed interviewing smugglers who were themselves previous migrants, who had failed in their attempts at a life in Europe, or who had returned to their homeland after having been refugees in neighboring countries. In each setting, five smugglers were identified—for a total of ten interviews with smugglers, "brokers," or "travel agents" as many preferred to call themselves—and introduced to the researchers by the migrants. These interviews showed the complexities faced by men who turned their cross-border experiences into a source of income that, while feared by their families, brought rewards.

Interviews were conducted in the national language by local researchers or through a translator when I was conducting interviews with Somali migrants and refugees. In Afghanistan, I relied on my proficiency in Dari, while colleagues spoke Dari or Pashto without translators present; in Somalia, the local language was also relied upon, speaking in Somali with only two exceptions where English was preferred by Somali migrants who opted to converse in English to remove the need for a translator. When interviews were conducted remotely—through Skype or Whatsapp or Viber to speak to Afghan and Somali migrants in transit or at destination in Europe—the question of positionality, and even of multipositionalities (Ryan 2015), was particularly important. In effect, multiple connections were sought to secure interviews remotely: ethnicity and nationality, personal connections or referrals, shared experiences of migration and displacement, class and generation, trust and empathy. Afghan and Somali researchers interviewed migrants who therefore shared multiple similarities and connections to them on these four levels to go beyond positionality to form an ethnic lens and to mitigate for any power imbalance that may have created an insider/outsider or researcher-participant divide (Ganga and Scott 2006).

The Ecosystem of Irregular Migration and Smuggling Facilitation

The start of the migrant-smuggler relationship: A personal connection in the migrant's microsystem

The concept of the "right" smuggler is more often present in conversations than that of the "good" or "bad" smuggler. The smuggler is chosen through a referral process that serves as a guarantee in an otherwise unpredictable journey. Smuggling is a "referral-based activity" (Sanchez 2014b; Zhang 2007), stemming from introductions made within the migrant's community. In the voice of Somali and Afghan migrants, relatives and friends are the best referrals to smugglers. Also key to the selection of the right smuggler are the relationship and proximity of the migrant to those making the referral, as they are well informed of the dangers inherent to the migration journey, including the risk of death, imprisonment, and deportation. Simultaneously, the families and friends of migrants need to know the person who will be taking their relatives through such a risky journey, to have a personal sense of connection that acts as a guarantee and that can also convince them of giving away their most valuable assets—from their relatives to their money, land, or jewelry. The testimony of Khododad, a 17-year-old Afghan asylum seeker in a settlement in Norway, reveals the nature of his journey and the transit:

> My mother found the smuggler. She sold her jewelry and paid him. She told me I could trust him. She paid the local smuggler and told him to take me out of the country. [My journey] started with the local smuggler, someone whom we knew, whom I had seen as a child in our neighborhood. Then he gave me to another smuggler. And [the smugglers] were taking me from one country to another. I did not have any country in mind as my destination but the smuggler brought me [to Norway]. It took me about two months to get to Norway, I don't even know the names of the countries we crossed, nor the exact way we took. [The smuggler would say,] "This country is Macedonia, this country is Hungary, and this country is Serbia."

In Khododad's case, a community link served as a guarantee for both sides. The organization of his journey was led by phone or text message (SMS), with a few smugglers traveling with the migrants. Smugglers remain responsible for migrants and introduce and turn them over to their connections at border points or at locations beyond borders.

Maryan, a 61-year-old Somali returnee from Norway recounted her initial decision to migrate from Mogadishu with her daughter. She openly admitted her reliance on smuggling facilitators. Both Maryan and her daughter traveled with the help of a smuggler whom she referred to as a family friend. Her experience was different from that of Khododad, in the sense that rather than traveling with multiple smugglers, she traveled with someone she knew for the entire duration of her journey:

> Yes, I used smugglers. In my case, a family friend who had successfully helped others go to Norway. Since I was travelling alone with my daughter, I was careful about who I chose. There were a lot of possible choices. But this person was known to me, known to other migrants, I knew he would be responsible.

The experience of entrusting oneself to a smuggler, even when reliable, varies across age and gender. Unaccompanied minors like Khodadad may not have an understanding of their journeys or have a specific destination in mind, while women traveling alone might be wary of their gendered vulnerabilities. Both examples show that the choice of traveling with a specific smuggler is made carefully from the start.

For both Afghan and Somali migrants, the family connection remains the most common source for the smuggling facilitation. On occasion the referral tip may not come from the exact point of origin, but from other locations within the diaspora; in other words referrals can come from friends or family members residing in route or already settled overseas.[2] Communities constitute a transnational resource for finding employment, finding refuge, or finding smugglers while in transit.

The experience of Habib, a 25-year-old Afghan, shows how the responsibility of choosing a smuggler was not made by him alone, but rather collectively taken along the route:

> My family in Iran took care of finding the right smuggler for me. Here, several of our family members living in Mashhad told us that there were a lot of smugglers. So we had to rely on them to find the ones that we could trust, talk to them, before we even left Afghanistan. Then we transferred the money, when [my family] told us their choice was made.

In an interview in Nairobi, Kenya, Abdi, a Somali father of two, also explained the way the decision to travel with a specific smuggler is shared and, as in the case of Habib, at times even made by elder relatives:

> We have come from Dadaab to Nairobi. I will leave my children with their grandparents here so that they can go to school. I am waiting for my in-laws, who are Somali-Kenyans to introduce me to a smuggler they know, one of their friends. We will pay him to take me to Europe. Once I am established there, I will bring along my family.

Not having to think too much ahead or not having to map journeys on their own provides migrants a great sense of reassurance and relief. It also sends a message to the smugglers that there is a family, connections, and guarantees and that, while irregular migration may be a solitary journey in physical terms at times, it is a collective one in its social and economic contexts.

While the positive image of the smuggler holds true across interviews, it is also important to point out that this mainly pertains to local smugglers—those chosen, recommended, and referred to by the family and trusted by the community. Many times these perceptions are connected to notions of ethnic identity and tribal ties, where local or proximate smugglers are defined as better than those belonging to other classes or groups. Parviz, an Afghan from Takhar, described how ethnicity and proximity were central in the decision to hire specific smugglers:

> The local Afghan smugglers are good but the other smugglers are different. We went with Afghan smugglers who were from Takhar province, our province of origin and known to our villagers, and were very good but most other smugglers are liars. They ask for more money and will ask for US$2,000 or US$3,000 when the cost for that [service] is only US$1,000.

These testimonies show the prevalence of the role of the community—being it in the province of origin, or while in transit—in the decision to travel with a specific smuggler. The choice of a smuggler starts within the community. Smugglers work with migrants who they know (and whose families they can locate), as much as migrants work with smugglers they know through family and friends. Rather than a transnational criminal network, "it is a referral network," in the voice of many migrants interviewed.

The mesosystem: Interactions among smuggling facilitators

> A smuggler is a smuggler, wherever he is, the main concern is money. If you don't give them money they won't help you so their behavior and action depend on whether you give them money. They will treat you well, but without money you will be mistreated. Generally smugglers are not kind. Their kindness is linked to money. Without money they are cruel. We choose them by asking others especially other people they have assisted before and took them abroad and also through asking relatives and I identified the ones that were good. (Hassan Ali, 33, Mogadishu)

Although they trusted their smugglers, migrants and their friends and families also knew that money was a smuggler's main motivation to provide help. Migrants and smugglers alike wanted to ensure that they can afford the journey financially—a calculation that they need to make from the onset. Will migrants have enough money to finance the migration project? Will their families be able to pay and release the sums on time? Will smugglers need additional money along the way?

According to Legorano and Parkinson (2015), 90 percent of human smuggling is done through money transfers, and the money transferred equates to close to $2.5 billion annually. Financial calculations are a significant part of the conversations that take place in the migration experience, and a constant cause for tension. Facilitators of money transfers—*dahabshiil* in Somali or *hawaladar* in Afghan—are there to reduce some of the financial challenges that smugglers, smuggled migrants, and their families face.

Financial facilitators fulfill a fundamental function between migrants and smugglers along the migration trail: they protect the integrity of the financial interests involved in the transaction. The security provided through these financial interactions and their guarantees are key for migrants being smuggled and those behind their transits. Money does not need to exchange hands: transactions occur with no physical movement of cash. Only a code is needed, which is given to clients in both countries of the operation. Furthermore, the absence of physical money means neither migrants nor smugglers have to carry the large sums involved in smuggling, which prevents them from becoming targets of crime. The possibility of paying in installments means that payments are linked to results: increasingly, each segment of the journey is paid for separately.[3] Because money is not physically moved between migrant and smuggler, the transfers can be completed instantly, and even faster if agents from both sides are present at the broker's office simultaneously. Salad, a Somali returnee, described his experience working with *dahabshiil*:

> We trust them because there is no direct transaction. You deposit the money with *dahabshiil* in an account. Once you reach your destination, as per the agreement, [the smugglers] will receive the money. So the smugglers have someone who represents them with *dahabshiil*, and I have someone representing me at *dahabshiil* too. We are both protected. If [the smugglers] treat me well, they will receive their money.

As Salad's case shows, working with financial facilitators also improves the chances that the smuggling service will be provided efficiently and smugglers will be paid only upon completion of the journey. Nashrullah, a 25-year-old Afghan migrant who found his smuggler through friends in Tehran, also explained:

> My friends found the smuggler over the phone, and I paid them [the smugglers] over *hawala*. I paid 2,200,000 toman for the smuggler to arrange for [my] passage through Turkey. [Once I was in Turkey I] then paid 6,800,000 toman to Greece.[4] [I] had given the money to [my] relatives and to a trusted *hawaladar*. Whenever [I] reached [a segment towards my] destination, [I] would make one phone call for the *hawala* dealer to give the money to the smuggler.

Money is deposited at the point of departure or transit, where the initial smuggler is chosen. The guarantee payment is linked to a guarantee of safe passage. The contract is built on incremental payments, alongside a step-by-step communication between four key actors: the migrant, the smuggler, the financial facilitator, and a representative from the migrant's community. The ties may be weak between the migrant and the smuggler, but they are close between the smuggler and the migrants' relatives, and the relatives and the financial dealers. Elements of trust bind them all, as a guarantee of delivering on the promises made.

"There are tens of smugglers across the points of travel, in Afghanistan, Iran, and Turkey. But agreeing on the financials is key," explains Naser, a 21-year-old Afghan returnee. This is because the sums charged by smugglers tend to be significant—at the time of data collection, an Afghan's transit to Australia by land and boat was in the US$5,000 range, while traveling by plane cost US$18,000.

The ties that bind the financial facilitator and the smuggler (from the micro to the mesosystem) are not immediate; yet the nature of the financial transaction as provided by a third party protects them both. The fact that the money is held in deposit by a *hawala* dealer pending delivery of the services is a source of reassurance for many Afghans who I interviewed.

While the services provided by financial facilitators on behalf of migrants are often described or depicted as illicit or criminally organized, *hawaladar* are officially sanctioned businesses. The *hawala* system is important in contexts such as Afghanistan and Somalia where the low penetration of the banking system, the low levels of literacy, and the lack of official identification or documentation are all obstacles to transfers through formal banking institutions. The testimonies shared by Somali migrants resemble those of the Afghans interviewed.

Yet it would be naïve to claim that financial transactions are free of tension. Some smugglers may opt to change the terms of the agreement, imposing new fees or threatening migrants who do not abide by changing demands. Maryan's interaction with a smuggler was more cumbersome than expected. Already the trip itself was risky, but she found herself "gambling with my last savings and my life at the same time." Traveling with fake documents, crossing the border of Kenya to reach Nairobi, passing checkpoints filled with fear, and maneuvering to pass into Jomo Kenyatta International Airport were all expected, but she did not expect the changing behavior of the smuggler. "At the airport, he asked for more money. Every time he tried to push for more than what was originally agreed upon. He threatened to leave me there if we did not pay. He told me I would face the consequences. Finally at my final destination in Norway, he disappeared, and got arrested by the Norwegian Police."

The impact of the exosystem: Relationships and factors beyond the migrants' control

The story of smuggling is not uniform from start to finish. The faces of smugglers change, as do the experiences of the migrants. There are smugglers who prey on migrants, while some migrants say smugglers provide a life-saving service. The reality is somewhere in the middle. Smugglers provide mobility where the state's migration frameworks do not. Findings of field-based research "challenge the often simplistic depiction of facilitators as ruthless smugglers who are routinely endangering the lives of refugees and migrants. … Whilst there are many stories of violence and death on the journey, it is also clear that many smugglers provide the only opportunity to secure access to Europe in the absence of safe and legal routes for protection and work" (Crawley et al. 2016, 9).

The layers of protection provided by smuggling are set in motion even when communities—like those of the Somalis and Afghans—are not bound to one single place or space. Yet the presence of relatives and financial facilitators alone does not always protect migrants through the entire span of the migration journey. As new routes must be devised to avoid increasing immigration enforcement, community dimensions fade out, and the dangers and risks of migration emerge.

Control, surveillance, and extraterritorialization of borders have led people to travel on riskier, more remote routes where the likelihood of obtaining help or contacting friends and relatives in case of danger is remote. Environmental conditions and exposure play a larger role than violence in the injury and death of migrants in transit (Slack and Whiteford 2011). Many migrants have no choice but to rely on smugglers who they do not know or trust. Fereydoon, a 22-year-old Afghan returnee, explained:

> If you don't know the smuggler, the result will be uncertain. The main problem for me, as a deportee, was that I did not know the smuggler. If as a client who knows the smuggler he is vested in you; he can take [you] to the country of destination without any problem and very [fast]. Otherwise they won't invest on your care and you will be caught and deported.

In this transnational game of choosing the "right" smuggler, and the logistics of crossing borders, surprise and happenstance often take over an otherwise organized process of selection, transactions, and logistics.

Migrants realize that journeys are unpredictable; there is no miracle solution, and they must learn to be flexible. Migrants often adapt to new contexts along the way (Brigden 2016). A Somali returnee, for example, explained that he did not rely entirely on the smuggler. On his way to Norway from Somalia, he traveled to Greece, where he was given a real passport of an Italian who resembled him. He was caught but managed to get away and stayed with friends in Greece. He got another fake passport from another smuggler and traveled to Vienna by bus, and from Vienna to Sweden by plane, and finally from Sweden to Norway by bus. It was not his initial plan, but he gave up his hope of what a smuggler could do for him, and focused instead on how he could regain control of his migration journey.

Narratives of negative experiences with smugglers were common among those whose migration journey had failed. Even those who had a successful journey but were either returned by force or because they lacked any other remaining choice, raised concerns about smugglers. Hamed, a 24-year-old, expressed his view:

> If you are vulnerable, the smuggler will not care. Even if the smuggler is your brother he won't have mercy [on] you. [A] smuggler is a wild person: they just look for their money, they are not kind and sympathetic, there were some people who were sick and [smugglers] don't care about sick and injured people.

Negative views of smugglers abounded in the discussions with returnees to Afghanistan. Rahim, for example, explained that he was aware that smugglers "use the migrants and sometimes sell them. They take the migrants into custody and demand for more money from families." Rahim's statement alludes to elements of bonded labor and trafficking in the smuggling practice. Experiences of this kind were rare in interviews that I conducted, but they show the thin line that may exist between smuggling and trafficking, and where smuggling may fall into patterns that resemble those of organized crime. Interviewees also referenced human smuggling that coincided with the smuggling of goods, drugs, and other illicit materials along remote border areas, but this, they said, was more because the goods were illicit rather than an indicator of market convergence.

Certain groups of migrants, such as women, children, and the poorest of migrants, are particularly vulnerable. Those who cannot afford fake documents or plane tickets will need to walk most of the way, and not all will have the endurance to survive the journey by foot. Returnees recounted stories of women who could not continue walking, and who would not get the sympathy of smugglers. They blamed the smugglers for lying to female migrants. Bostan, a returnee to Afghanistan whose migration dreams were dashed by the realization that his migration plan had gone sour, stated: "[The smuggler] said that we would walk for three hours but then we walked for 16. Women can't walk this long. [Smugglers] are liars and they just want to get their money. If women and girls can't continue, they will then take them to their home and would do anything with them that they want. Most of them are drug addicts. All smugglers are people who live near the border, and they do anything that they can." Other migrants confirmed similar accounts, explaining that smugglers took advantage of young women, "bringing shame to them."

Not everybody had negative experiences with smugglers, however. Other migrants spoke highly of the treatment they received, but would admit that "not everyone can make it." The smuggler was not the biggest danger, however; the environment was. This was particularly the case for Afghan and Somali migrations who traveled by boat, with migrants spending between four to six hours in the water. A female migrant stated: "There were so many people in the boat, water was coming inside. We had already walked in Turkey's mountain areas for about nine hours. Most of the children and old people who were weak were not able to continue anymore."

Whether it is relying on stranger smugglers, or counting on luck and improvisation, encountering border police, or facing environmental challenges, migrants gradually lose the layers that protect them the farther they move from their microsystem. Their journeys involve the continued entering and existing of a vast realm of foreign communities, with their own rules and their own ethnic, tribal, and cultural ties. Furthermore, the data show that in some instances, smugglers often encounter environments that are more constraining for them than for the migrants, and that the conditions of their markets have also changed. Given the tightened border controls on the way to and within Europe, many of the smugglers are also prior migrants and returnees themselves who are unable to benefit from their other skills, or are stranded while in transit; they turn their migration experiences into assets. Faced with an abundance of competition, some smugglers have had to change their tactics, only charging fees if migrants make it to their destination, often without the guarantee of the financial facilitator. In other words, the money is held by the family of the migrants or by the migrants themselves and released only if the final destination is reached. This does not necessarily translate into profits or significant profits for all. In Calais, for example, there is a complex hierarchy of smugglers. Migrants distinguish between different types: the "Mercedes Benz smugglers," in the words of an Afghan in Calais (facilitators make the most money from the irregular passage to the UK) and "those who live among us" and who are the day-to-day focal points who advise on the best passage to the new arrivals. The latter are often very hard to differentiate from migrants themselves, as they share the same profiles, backgrounds, and histories as the migrants themselves. The complexity and hierarchy of the facilitation process are therefore also consequences of the exosystem: the heavily guarded, restricted, and, at times, closed borders and the policies that enforce these restrictions.

Conclusion

This research shows how migrants' smuggling experiences are affected by their ecosystem. Relationships in the microsystem (point of origin) and the mesosystem (point of origin and transit) can provide the needed guarantees to trigger irregular migration through known smuggling facilitators.

Similar to other studies that have shown the migration journey to be an ad hoc process (Crawley et al. 2016), my study has shown that while the smuggler at the start of the migration journey is chosen carefully, the migration journey may not be planned through to the end when this smuggler is chosen. The smuggler is chosen, the money is set aside, and arrangements are made with financial facilitators, such as the *hawala* dealers in Afghanistan or the *dahabshiil* agents in

Somalia. The microsystems and mesosystems protect the migrant's irregular migration journey and secure the services of a smuggler. Yet beyond the community of origin and the initial environment of departure, the journey is unknown. During the journey, the smuggler's role evolves. In foreign lands and away from their own community, migrants find themselves facing unexpected realities. As a well-known "helper" or as the "predator," the smuggler can wear different hats: the "right" smuggler may not be the same smuggler throughout the journey. While the migration journey was planned based on trust and guarantees at the point of origin, through layers of relationships—trust in the local smuggler, trust in an informal money transfer system—the trust fades away the farther one is from home.

Strengthening the migrant's ecosystem can increase safeguards, while also eliminating smuggling facilitators who can put migrants in harm's way. The trust, guarantees, and safety of migrants are secured through the community—the stronger the ties across borders, the more positive the journey and its outcome.

All of this suggests that layered interventions are necessary from a policy perspective—not to "combat" trafficking and smuggling, but to open discussions around legal pathways for migration that can engage different members of the microsystem, mesosystem, exosystem, and macrosystem to ensure a more humane approach to migration management across borders. Unpacking the "community" behind irregular migration will allow practitioners and policymakers to fully comprehend the social environment that enables smuggling facilitation, and the societal impact of communities on human migration.

Notes

1. Vogt (2013) uses a similar model, whereby care and protection provided by and for migrants during their clandestine journeys create—as intimate forms of labor—spaces conducive to protection.

2. Over four million Afghans alone still live in neighboring Iran and Pakistan as refugees or undocumented migrants, while the Somali diaspora expands across East Africa, with a large population in Kenya, all the way to Europe.

3. Migrants traveling along other routes and mechanisms may be more vulnerable than others to violence, as in the case of kidnapping among Eritrean migrants in Libya or Central American migrants in Mexico.

4. Approximately US$2,800 from Tehran to Greece.

References

Amnesty International. 2016. *Afghanistan: Number of people internally displaced by conflict doubled to 1.2 million in just three years*. Available from https://www.amnesty.org/en/latest/news/2016/05/afghanistan-internally-displaced/.

Bilger, Veronika, Martin Hoffman, and Michael Jandl. 2006. Human smuggling as a transnational service industry. *International Migration, Special Edition on Human Smuggling* 44 (4): 59–93.

Brigden, Noelle. 2016. Improved transnationalism: Clandestine migration at the border of anthropology and international relations. *International Studies Quarterly* 60 (2): 343–54.

Bronfenbrenner, Urie. 1981. *The ecology of human development: Experiments by nature and design*. Cambridge, MA: Harvard University Press.

Chu, Cindy Yik-Yi. 2010. Human trafficking and smuggling in China. *Journal of Contemporary China* 20 (68): 39–52.

Crawley, Heaven, Franck Duvell, Katharine Jones, and Dimitris Skleparis. 2016. *Understanding the dynamics of migration to Greece and the EU: Drivers, decisions and destinations*. MEDMIG Research Brief No. 2. Available from http://www.medmig.info/research-brief-02-Understanding-the-dynamics-of-migration-to-Greece-and-the-EU.

Eurostat. 2016. *Asylum in the EU Member States*. Eurostat. Available from http://ec.europa.eu/eurostat/documents/2995521/7203832/3-04032016-AP-EN.pdf/.

Ganga, Deianira, and Sam Scott. 2006. Cultural "insiders" and the issue of positionality in qualitative migration research: Moving "across" and moving "along" researcher-participant divides. *Forum: Qualitative Social Research* 7 (3): Article 7. Available from http://www.qualitative-research.net/index.php/fqs/article/view/134/289.

Hagen-Zanker, Jessica. 2017. *Why do people migrate? A review of the theoretical literature*. MPRA Paper No. 28197. Available from https://mpra.ub.uni-muenchen.de/28197/1/2008WP002.

Internal Displacement Monitoring Centre (IDMC). 2016. *Afghanistan—Country information 2015*. IDMC. Available from http://www.internal-displacement.org/database/country/?iso3=AFG.

Khosravi, Shahram. 2010. *"Illegal" traveller: An auto-ethnography of borders*. New York, NY: Palgrave Macmillan.

Legorano, Giovanni, and Joe Parkinson. 30 December 2015. Following the migrant money trail. *The Wall Street Journal*.

Marcus, George E. 1995. Ethnography in/of the world system: The emergence of multi-sited ethnography. *Annual Review of Anthropology* 24:95–117.

Massey, Douglas S., Joaquin Arango, Graeme Hugo, Ali Kouaouci, Adela Pellegrino, and J. Edward Taylor. 1993. Theories of international migration: A review and appraisal. *Population and Development Review* 19 (3): 431–66.

Migration Policy Institute. 2016. *Migration Policy Institute data, 2008–2016*. Washington, DC: Migration Policy Institute. Available from http://www.migrationpolicy.org/programs/moving-europe-beyond-crisis?gclid=CMuSl_ut49QCFXEo0wodTA0HLg.

Pew Research Center. 2016. *5 facts about the Somali global diaspora*. Washington, DC: Pew Research Center. Available from http://www.pewresearch.org/fact-tank/2016/06/01/5-facts-about-the-global-somali-diaspora/.

Ryan, Louise. 2015. "Inside" and "outside" of what or where? Researching migration through multi-positionalities. *Forum: Qualitative Social Research* 16 (2): Article 17. Available from http://www.qualitative-research.net/index.php/fqs/article/view/2333/3784.

Sanchez, Gabriella. 2014a. *Human smuggling and border crossings*. New York, NY: Routledge.

Sanchez, Gabriella. 2014b. Human smuggling facilitators in the U.S. Southwest. In *The Routledge handbook on crime and international migration*, eds. Sharon Pickering and Julia Ham, 275–86. New York, NY: Routledge.

Santrock, John W. 2007. *Child development*. 11th ed. New York, NY: McGraw-Hill.

Slack, Jeremy, and Scott Whiteford. 2011 Violence and migration on the Arizona-Sonora border. *Human Organization* 70 (1): 11–21.

Van Liempt, Ilse. 2007 *Navigating borders: Inside perspectives on the process of human smuggling into the Netherlands*. Amsterdam: Amsterdam University Press.

Vecchio, Francesco, and Alison Gerard. 2014. Surviving the politics of illegality. In *The Routledge handbook on crime and international migration*, eds. Sharon Pickering and Julia Ham, 179–92. New York, NY: Routledge.

Vogt, Wendy. 2013. Crossing Mexico: Structural violence and the commodification of undocumented Central American migrants. *American Ethnologist* 40 (4): 764–80.

Zhang, Sheldon. 2007. *Smuggling and trafficking in human beings: All roads lead to America*. New York, NY: Praeger.

Zubrick, Stephen. 2015. *The lingitudinal study of Australian children: Review and revision of key research questions*. With Helen Rogers, Jan Nicholson, Ann Sanson, and Lyndall Srazdins. Melbourne AU: Australian Institute of Family Studies.

"I Want to Be Trafficked so I Can Migrate!": Cross-Border Movement of North Koreans into China through Brokerage and Smuggling Networks

By
KYUNGHEE KOOK

This article draws on ethnographic fieldwork and in-depth interviews with forty North Korean escapees involved in smuggling and brokerage networks and explores North Korean escapees' cross-border mobility to China. It addresses the complexities of *smuggling*, showing how the category spans a continuum of actions that might be described as *saving* or *rescuing* at one pole, and the kind of exploitation generally termed *trafficking* at the other. By focusing on the multiple and varied interests and motivations of different actors who assist with North Korean women's migration, I argue that differences among trafficking, smuggling, and migration are constructed rather than essential, and reflect a continued tendency among policy-makers to imagine human mobility through the lens of a fictional opposition between actions that are forced and those that are voluntary. The North Korean women's migratory processes demonstrate the complexities of brokerage and smuggling networks, revealing how they can, but do not necessarily, entail the kind of exploitation generally termed *trafficking*.

Keywords: North Korean migration; human smuggling; human trafficking; brokerage

North Korean authorities made no discernible efforts to prevent human trafficking during the reporting period. While internal conditions in the DPRK have prompted many North Koreans to flee the country in the past, which has made them vulnerable to human trafficking, border security increased during the reporting period, which led to a decrease in the rate of refugees resettled in the Republic of Korea. Nevertheless, *there was no evidence that the DPRK government attempted to prevent human trafficking by screening migrants along the border.* DPRK authorities made no discernible efforts to reduce the demand for commercial sex acts. (U.S. Department of State 2013, 222, emphasis added)

Kyunghee Kook is a PhD candidate at the School of Sociology, Politics and International Studies, University of Bristol. Her research interests are irregular migration and smuggling networks, trafficking, and North Korean mobility. She is currently working on a dissertation on North Korean migration to South Korea.

Correspondence: kyungheekook@gmail.com

DOI: 10.1177/0002716217748591

This extract from the U.S. Department of State Trafficking in Persons (TIP; 2013) report shows the contradiction of dominant discourse on North Korean trafficking. While the U.S. administration has described the North Korean government as a system of political repression, operating through prison camps, violating basic human rights of its citizens in every conceivable way, it also presents the government as a "normal" nation responsible for preventing human trafficking.

Two-thirds of North Koreans who cross the border into China are women, escaping from food shortages, economic disaster, and political persecution (South Korean Ministry of Unification 2016). The journey is extremely perilous, and escapees are not safe once they cross the border. In China, they are vulnerable to arrests and repatriations because of their illegal status. This vulnerability in China often leads them into conditions and relations that are associated with various forms of exploitation and violence, including human trafficking. There is a good deal of evidence on the exploitation and abuse endured by North Koreans in China, prompting many human right groups, individual researchers, media, and international bodies such as the UN to describe them as victims of "modern slavery" and "human trafficking" (Amnesty International 2006; Muico 2005; Human Rights Watch 2002; International Crisis Group 2006; Liberty in North Korea 2013).

These narratives of human rights violations on North Korean escapees focus heavily on their illegality in China and the horrific consequences of repatriation, such as imprisonment and hard labor in North Korea. In 2006, in the regions of China bordering North Korea, for instance, John Miller, then-director of the U.S. State Department's Office to Monitor and Combat Trafficking in Persons, asserted that almost 80 to 90 percent of North Korean escapees were victims of human trafficking, and that women were more likely to be trafficked than men (Office of the Under Secretary for Global Affairs [OUSGA] 2006). North Korean women fleeing into other countries are generally considered "victims of trafficking" and as taking part in "forced" migration (Hawk 2003; M. Kim 2010; Lankov 2004).

Discourse on human trafficking often misrepresents North Korean women's migration process. Much of the literature views North Korean female border crossing as a form of trafficking (Amnesty International 2006; Hughes 2005; Refugees International 2005). Davis (2006, 123) observes that many North Korean women who seek better lives in China become victims of cross-border trafficking through a number of means, including being sold by their families and acquaintances, or by professional traffickers involved in transnational criminal groups. Women are often promised better jobs or good lives as wives in China, but their situations rapidly deteriorate when they fail to find jobs or suffer from abuse by their new husbands, and some women are even kidnapped and forced to work in the highly exploitive sex industry. E. Kim et al. (2009, 166) conclude that cross-border trafficking of North Korean women is "modern day slavery" and should be recognized as a major human rights violation:

> Most North Korean women sold to karaoke or brothels were often deceived or kidnapped by traffickers in the first place. An interviewee revealed the following story,

"Two traffickers who bought me from the North Korean trafficker and took me to a remote country side by taxi. When I arrived there about 30 to 40 dirty and old Chinese men were gathered and they began to rape me one by one all night. The very following afternoon, the trafficker took me to a city and sold me to a pimp for prostitution.

These people treated us badly. I was beaten with fists, threatened with knife, and was never paid. These people kept threatening me by saying that if I am not submissive they would kill me or report me to the Chinese police which will eventually send me back to North Korea which is the most horrible case that I could imagine." (E. Kim et al. 2009, 165)

Smugglers and brokers are often demonized or indistinguishable from traffickers in academic and international nongovernmental writings. In mainstream policy discourse, brokers and smugglers are stereotyped as unscrupulous individuals willing to deceive and exploit for their own personal gain. However, growing empirical evidence suggests a much wider range of experiences in North Korean women's mobility that contradicts the one-dimensional concept of trafficking. The following case is illustrative:

In January 2003, I crossed the Tumen River with my mother with the help of professional brokers based in Yanji. ... I heard that North Korean women like me usually work in the karaoke bars. I had to earn money to pay the debt and also, if possible, buy the household registration. ... Now I work at a boarding house where there are three ethnic Korean women and two North Korean women, including me, living together. We are sent to a number of karaoke bars where most of the customers are ethnic Korean and South Korean men. On average, I earn 300 Yuan per day. Out of about 10,000 Yuan I earn every month, I can save 4,000–5,000 Yuan. I send some of this money to my Chinese family in Jiaohe and sometimes I visit them. This kind of life is not easy, but I am doing this for a better future for myself and my family. (Miss Kim, Committee for Human Rights in North Korea 2009, 44)

As illustrated in Kim's case, brokers along the China–North Korea border can deviate from the dominant stereotype of human traffickers preying on vulnerable women desperate to escape poverty or political oppression. The stereotype of smugglers and brokers has been increasingly challenged in recent years by ethnographers who study smuggling networks and the multiple roles, motivations, and identities of brokers. Lindquist, Xiang, and Yeoh (2012) found that human smugglers enable mobility by procuring documents and transportation, challenging the distinction between "profit-oriented" industry and "altruistic" social networks. This false dichotomy appears in Collins's study (2012) on students' migration—students in Collins's study became brokers themselves; they and their smugglers relied on their social and personal networks for the migration process.

This article presents research on the movement of women out of North Korea, investigating the smuggling networks that include family members, informal smugglers, recruiters, and brokerage networks. The result of my investigation is a critical interrogation of the divergent interests of the individuals taking part in the smuggling enterprise. While the interest of some individuals in smuggling may derive purely and simply from greed, others have more altruistic interests in assisting North Koreans seeking to live in China. My research attempts to tease out the complexities of North Korean women's migratory processes through brokerage and smuggling networks, revealing how they can, but do not necessarily, entail the kind of exploitation generally termed *trafficking*. Rather than merely comparing the dichotomous concepts—*smuggling* and *trafficking*—this study highlights the diversity of experiences in smuggling and of smugglers.

Research Methods

The research was carried out over eight months in two waves between June 2014 and October 2015 in Seoul, South Korea. During these eight months, I conducted participant observations as well as in-depth interviews through a part-time voluntary post in a Korean nongovernmental organization (NGO) founded by North Korean defectors. At first, I created research projects and public awareness campaigns about North Korean refugees' human rights. Initially, I was not allowed to work with the rescue team. They wanted to be sure that I was not a spy sent by the North Korean government or a member of China's secret police or South Korea's National Intelligence Service (NIS). Believing that my legal documents would dispel these suspicions, I presented the head of the rescue team with my identification card, certificates from schools, and a copy of my resident registration. Nonetheless, he was concerned that these documents could be forged.

After three months, I was given a position on the rescue team. I not only worked as an assistant in Seoul for the rescue teams that operated along clandestine routes for smuggling defectors into China or South Korea, but I also supported North Korean defectors' settlement in South Korea. This position provided me not only the access to many North Korean escapees (by helping them set up bank accounts or submit paperwork to government offices, for example), but also the ability to document the roles of smugglers, brokers, and other NGOs who have assisted North Koreans' journey to South Korea—contact between activists in Seoul and others traveling to China gave me access to these clandestine groups.

Some of the North Koreans involved in the NGO regarded me only as an activist, rather than a researcher, which allowed me to conduct participant observations in one of the underground churches that supported North Koreans living in South Korea. I spent time with these escapees while attending Sunday services, meetings, and other events. The new arrivals often asked me to help them in their day-to-day lives. I followed them to their homes, as well as into banks, public offices, and shopping centers. These informal interactions allowed me to develop a close and abiding relationship with them. Throughout my fieldwork, I did not attempt to conceal my identity and introduced myself as a researcher who had studied and lived in the United Kingdom (UK). My experiences and knowledge of the UK helped me to earn popularity among North Korean defectors who wished to migrate to the UK. They quickly regarded me as a broker who could help them in their migration (e.g., to apply for refugee status in the UK) regardless of my lack of knowledge about the process. Some women asked me to arrange matches with English men so that they could acquire UK residency through marriage.

The second phase of my fieldwork involved in-depth interviews with twenty-seven North Korean women and thirteen North Korean men. The NGO and church networks were used to conduct the interviews, and research participants were collected through the snowball sampling method. All of the participants studied were over the age of 18 years and had escaped from North Korea between 1998 and 2015. The high proportion of women among interviewees reflected the fact that around 70 percent of North Koreans in South Korea from 2005 to 2015 were women. All the female interviewees had married Chinese men in China or had been sold as brides. Their illegal status in China and their subsequent divorces from their Chinese husbands led them to South Korea with the aid of smuggling networks and brokers through a third country, for example, Cambodia, Laos, Thailand, or Mongolia. Two-thirds of my interviewees, men or women, had at some point provided smuggling or brokerage services to other North Koreans in North Korea and China. Some of them had continued working as smugglers or brokers after arriving in South Korea.

All interviewees were informed of my identity, and the purpose and process of the research. All expressed consent to participate. All interviews were conducted in Korean. Every interview was conducted one-on-one to ensure privacy and confidentiality. No identifiable information was collected. Additionally, to ensure that confidentiality was not breached accidentally, pseudonyms were applied to participants and locations. Some of the initial interviews were conducted in the NGO office where interviewees would feel more comfortable. After sufficient trust was established, formal interviews were conducted in the participants' homes or workplaces, which allowed me to gain further understanding of their lives. In addition to participant observation and in-depth interviews, document analysis was also used to gain additional knowledge relevant to the background and context of North Koreans' irregular migration. By triangulating these three different data sources, I hoped to achieve a more insightful and more valid account of North Korean migratory experiences than that offered by the mainstream news media or government reports.

This study has limitations. Safety was one of the primary reasons for choosing South Korea as the fieldwork area. In China, North Koreans are considered illegal migrants, and anyone who is suspected of aiding them is subject to the penalty of law, including fines and imprisonment. To avoid placing both myself and the participants in any danger, I conducted fieldwork in South Korea where they and I had legal status as citizens. Therefore, findings and analysis in this study reflect only the experiences of those who managed to settle in South Korea.

Escaping from North Korea and Smuggling to China

In the early 1990s, the North Korean economy began to collapse. The dissolution of the Soviet Union in 1991 marked the end of its subsidies to North Korea, and

China established economic and diplomatic ties with South Korea in 1992, result-ing in worsening trade relations with North Korea. The lack of subsidies, support, and trade with Russia and China had a drastic impact on the agricultural sector in North Korea. Moreover, crops failed because of continual natural disasters between 1993 and 1995 such as drought, hailstorms, and flooding (Muico 2005). These severe agricultural disasters between 1993 and 1994 compounded the food shortage. As a result, it is estimated that more than 2 million North Koreans, or 10 percent of the total population, died from starvation between 1994 and 1998, a period known as the Arduous March (Haggard and Noland 2007; Lankov 2004, 832). Daily food rations were reduced from three to two meals a day during that period, and even after. In particular, the regime stopped providing food rations and daily necessities to North Koreans living in the northernmost province of North Korea, Hamkyung, bordered by China. Since 1994, Great Leader Kim Jung-Il announced that the people of Hamkyung had to be self-sufficient because the national railway transportation had stopped. Hamkyung is surrounded by mountains, with little land suitable for agriculture. North Koreans living in that province are dependent on receiving food and goods from other regions by rail. Since 1994, a large number of North Koreans near the border began to cross the border into China through the Tumen and Yalu rivers (Kirkpatrick 2012).

Tens of thousands of North Koreans have sought refuge, employment, and relative freedom in China. The North Korean regime authorizes its people to travel abroad only in very exceptional cases and criminalizes leaving home with-out permission, and China only grants entry visas under very limited circum-stances. Almost all North Koreans seeking food and shelter have illegally crossed the border into China. The journey is extremely perilous, and escapees are regarded as illegal economic migrants in China and repatriated if discovered by the authorities.

Today, North Korea and South Korea remain cut off from one another with no direct interaction since the Korean Peninsula was officially divided into two zones between 1950 and 1953—the communist-backed North and the U.S.-supported South. Since the mid-1990s, the Chinese government has rejected North Korean immigrants as refugees and has regarded them as unwanted illegal aliens (Kivisto and Faist 2000, 223). Until the time of this writing, the Chinese government has continued to repatriate North Koreans (UN Commission of Inquiry 2014) for the following two reasons. First, granting them refugee status may encourage further defections, which would not only destabilize the North Korean regime but also worsen China's good relations with North Korea. Second, repatriating North Koreans costs much less than recognizing them as asylum seekers or refugees (Lankov 2004, 872–3).

Because of their illegal status, North Koreans in China are hidden from the public and invisible to any official population assessments. Accurate data on the North Korean population in China are virtually impossible to gather, and esti-mates of the number of North Koreans vary widely depending on the sources. In the early 2000s, the South Korean government estimated the number at 30,000 and the Chinese government at 10,000. Meanwhile, the U.S. State Department estimated 75,000 to 125,000, while the United Nations High Commissioner for Refugees (UNHCR) responded with 50,000 to 100,000 (Song 2013, 401).

When North Koreans are repatriated, the North Korean government views them as political criminals, and they are charged with treason and punished severely. They are sent to North Korea's concentration camps, called *Rhodongdanryendae*, or prisons called *Kyohwaso*, also known as labor camps. In some cases, they are sentenced to death. Prisoners in the camps are subjected to forced labor (Davis 2006, 134–35), and numerous witnesses have reported human rights violations such as beating, torture, starvation, and human experimentation (Margesson, Chanlett-Avery, and Bruno 2007). Sentences for North Koreans deemed treasonous tend to differ according to the individual's intentions and motivations for illegal border-crossing. Motivations are understood to be either political or economic, and lighter sentences are given to those deemed to have crossed into China only temporarily and out of desperation for food and shelter. They are typically sentenced to only one to three years in the labor camps, while those who cross for political reasons are given more severe punishments. If they are attempting to stay in China or reach a third country, South Korea in particular, they are sent to a *Kyohwaso* for five years or more. If they are caught near the Chinese border in a third country or are involved with Christian missionaries, they are sent to political camps for lifelong imprisonment. Despite this risk, many North Koreans aim to move on to countries such as South Korea, where they would be legally recognized as citizens if they can successfully cross the border. They almost always depend on a smuggling network to do so. Since the Korean Demilitarized Zone (DMZ) formed as a de facto border barrier, around 30,000 North Koreans have reached South Korea by traveling through Mongolia, Laos, and Thailand. Approximately 70 percent of North Korean migrants in 2016 were female (South Korean Ministry of Unification 2016).

Push and Pull Factors for Gendered Migration

The proportion of women to men among North Koreans illegally present in China is around 7:3, and this ratio reflects their particular social and cultural circumstances in both North Korea and China. In North Korea, men are required to do military service for 10 years, and are involved in political parties and national industries that keep them under high levels of surveillance. North Korean women, by contrast, are less visible than men since they are primarily located in the private sphere. Their relatively less prominent position allows them to become more mobile than men. Since the economic crisis, the traditional gender roles have been dismantled. As men no longer receive food rations from the government, women have been pushed to be the breadwinners, and this has encouraged them to become engaged in smuggling and the sale of necessities on the black market (S. Kim 2014, 557).

In China, women's subordinate social position also allows North Korean women to stay there more easily than their male counterparts. North Korean men mainly find temporary, outdoor-based, manual labor such as construction and farming in China, and working outside makes them highly visible and thus vulnerable to arrest or deportation. For this reason, North Korean men tend to stay in China for only short periods, returning to North Korea once they have gained sufficient monetary resources. North Korean women, by contrast, can find employment in more concealed places. They often work in private houses as domestic workers, in textile factories, or in the sex industry. North Korean women even use marriage to Chinese men as a strategy for hiding. The hidden nature of these opportunities in China is a double-edged sword. It places North Korean women in the contradictory situation of being simultaneously less susceptible to immigration crackdowns and more vulnerable to exploitation. Absolute poverty and gender inequality combine to "push" North Korean women to cross the border. The demand for "wives" in northern China, on the other hand, "pulls/attracts" them.

China's one-child policy and son preference, particularly in the countryside, have contributed significantly to sex-selective abortions that have caused severe sex ratio imbalances (Barot 2012). This imbalance has resulted in a disproportionate number of single men at marriageable ages. In 2010, around 19 million single men in China looked for brides, and the number will likely increase to 30.9 million in 2040; and the proportion of men remaining single was 11.4 percent in 2010 and will likely increase to about 23.3 percent by 2040 (Tucker and Hook 2013, 209, 219). In China, there has also been massive internal migration from rural to urban areas. Since the Confucian tradition requires sons to take responsibility for their parents' care and therefore stay in the countryside, while daughters have the freedom to migrate to cities for the job opportunities afforded by industrialization, this migration has largely been of women (Wang and Hsiao 2009).

Poor and isolated Chinese men, mostly farmers, in the remote rural areas of northern provinces need wives to reproduce and sustain families, but also to work the farms (S. Kim 2014, 561). North Korean women's illegality in China has led them to be commonly considered as "proper" wives, because they are respectful and obedient to their husbands in order to remain hidden from authorities. Chinese men looking for "proper" wives are positioned at the margin in the marriage market. These men are usually from lower socioeconomic backgrounds and are, therefore, not popular among Chinese brides. The North Korean women I interviewed often recounted that their Chinese husbands were old, poor, and disabled. Considering the marginalized positions of both Korean women with illegality in China and Chinese men neglected by local brides, these marriages have been considered "fair" (*jeockdanghan*) and the two "suitable" (*jeockdanghan*) for each other. A clear example comes from the marriage between poor and relatively isolated South Korean grooms and brides from South Asia who wish to migrate through marriage based on the economic difference between the two countries. These brides are commonly considered to be "proper" wives (Freedman 2005; Lee 2009).

At the same time, these North Korean brides are also considered "dangerous" because they tend to run away and thus put their husbands at risk of being charged with helping illegal migrants. North Korean women are notorious for being run-away brides (J. Kim 2010). "Dangerous" is translated as *wiheomhan* in

Korean. *Wiheomhan* means to put others in danger or oneself at risk. North Korean women in China are obedient to their husbands so as not to be reported by them to Chinese authorities, which makes them "good" (*jeockdanghan*) wives. But their illegality may put their husbands in danger, and if they are caught by the authorities, their husbands are punished by law, including paying a fine or being put in detention for a few months. My field data revealed that Chinese husbands were active in watching their wives and followed them around to preempt any attempts to run away. In some cases, when the wives ran away, their husbands sought help from the smugglers who had brought them to China or brokers who had arranged the marriage. By tapping into the wives' social networks, these Chinese husbands were able to "recover" their wives. The growing need for women willing to enter into marriages with these single men far outweighs the concerns and risks prompted by those who run away from their husbands, thus creating strong smuggling and marriage brokerage networks.

Caught in the Trafficking/Smuggling Dyads

North Korean women's migration to China through smuggling networks has been characterized as two distinct phenomena in the research literature. On one hand, North Korean migrant women are frequently depicted as "victims of trafficking" who are forced into prostitution, evidence for which has been amply supplied by academic research. E. Kim et al. (2009, 160), for example, described how North Korean women were "trafficked" in one of two ways. The first was through transnational criminal organizations, which were dominated by the ethnic Han Chinese who were involved in the sex industry. In some cases, these gangsters kidnapped and forced North Korean women to work in the sex industry on highly exploitive terms. The other way was through informal networks based on personal links with Korean-Chinese people living in China, such as cousins and kin. These networks were known to be involved with marriage migration, through which North Korean women crossed the border to marry Korean-Chinese or Han-Chinese. According to E. Kim et al. (2009), because the sex industry was not well-developed in the northern parts of China but the demand for wives was strong, the marriage-migration market was far more active in recruiting North Korean women. The fact that kin are involved in arranging migration does not necessarily protect the women. North Korean women are often promised better jobs or good lives as wives in China; but their situations rapidly deteriorate when they fail to find jobs or suffer from abuse by their new husbands.

Another view, advocated by many NGOs and some recent academic research (Chang, Haggard, and Noland 2008; Committee for Human Rights in North Korea 2009; S. Kim 2014), describes North Korean women as "smuggled migrants," who voluntarily migrate to seek greater economic opportunities in China. Some NGOs have reported that North Korean defectors generally cross the border to China either through their own networks of friends and relatives in China, or by hiring smugglers (International Crisis Group 2006). This, they argue, means that North Korean transportees actively agree to violate border controls in China, and they can be legitimately defined as smuggled migrants. This view is supported by a survey conducted by Chang and her colleagues (Chang, Haggard, and Noland 2008), which shows that three-quarters of thirteen hundred North Korean border crossers in 2008 (80 percent of whom are women) currently in China received assistance to escape North Korea. Some of these migrants reported that they paid for assistance, suggesting that bribery of officials and/or networks of smugglers play a role in such escapes.

How should these contradictory representations be interpreted? The most obvious answer to this question is that these descriptions relate to different types of migrants. There seems to be a general agreement among politicians, journalists, NGO workers, and even some academics that several dichotomies can be made between different groups of migrants: those who are forced to work versus those who choose to work, those who are trafficked versus those who are smuggled, those who are exploited versus those who make money, those who should be protected versus those who should be deported. The problem is, however, that these sources cannot always identify or agree on, as Derks (2010, 916–17) puts it, which migrants should fit with which group. This complexity in classification indicates that the differences between groups of migrants are not fixed, but rather constructed categories (O'Connell Davidson 2010). As de Haas (2009, 11) argues, "the sharp distinction between forced and voluntary migration is primarily a policy and legal distinction driven by the interest of states in classifying migrants." This is no less true for the "forced" and "voluntary" North Korean migrants in China. The different statuses of North Koreans in different countries provides a good illustration of the changeable legal positions of migrants. In China, a popular transit country where approximately 80 percent of North Korean escapees live, the government has labeled them as illegal economic migrants for diplomatic reasons. In Europe and North America, North Korean escapees are defined as refugees or asylum-seekers (Chan and Schloenhardt 2007). Therefore, whether one is deemed to be a smuggled migrant, who has voluntarily chosen to cross the border illegally, or a refugee, who has been forced to move, rests in part on the foreign policies and immigration regimes of the receiving countries. However, the question remains, How do we deal with the blurred distinctions? Some scholars have suggested that researchers will be better able to analyze migration in a range of contexts if they consider a continuum from low to high constraints under which migration occurs (de Hass 2009; Turton 2003). In my view, these dichotomies fail to capture the complexity and the fluidity of their situations. The complexity inherent in the North Korean women's migratory process suggests that the forced-voluntary dyad overlaps with the distinction between trafficking and smuggling.

North Korean Women's Migration Process: Neither Trafficked nor Smuggled

The migration of North Korean women into China has been viewed as a form of trafficking with emphasis on traffickers' cruelty in the media, research, and humanitarian groups' reports. However, my field data show that their migratory experiences do not fit either the concept of trafficking or of smuggling and reveal neither evil traffickers nor powerless victims of trafficking despite exploitative situations during their migration. Their movement to China consists of two stages, involving two groups of smugglers or brokers: first, informal smugglers who facilitate undocumented border-crossing; second, marriage brokers who link North Korean women with local Chinese men. Human smugglers and marriage brokers work independently or collectively depending on the situation. In the following sections, through the analysis of my field data, I illustrate how neither trafficking nor smuggling is helpful in categorizing these women's experience or explaining violations of their human rights.

Crossing the border

North Korean women's movement into China has been described as human trafficking involving being kidnapped or lured by traffickers who are members of criminal organizations (for example, see Muico 2005; E. Kim et al. 2009; J. Kim 2010). On the other hand, my empirical work shows that North Korean women cross the border illegally in the following three ways: (1) they move illegally across the border independently, (2) they find themselves a smuggler to assist them, or (3) they are introduced to a smuggler by a broker at the first stage of the migratory process. A third of the North Koreans who I interviewed, all now living in South Korea, crossed the border into China illegally without a smuggler and explained that when they did so years earlier, it was reasonably easy to do so. Ra-Soon and Jin-Hee who crossed the Tumen River independently in the early 2000s remembered:

> If you are knowledgeable about the lay of the land around the Tumen River, it is not that difficult to get across.

> If you bribe the border guards with some food or few packs of cigarettes, they tell people how to cross the river. Often, the guards even accompany the border-crossers to the Chinese side of the river.

These statements reflected a different reality from that created by the dominant discourse or other research findings. I suspect sources of information and statements gathered from subjects in different situations may contribute to the differences in findings. For example, the interviews conducted by E. Kim et al. (2009) were with North Korean women who lived in refugee shelters in China and who were defined by the researchers as victims of trafficking for sexual exploitation based on the UN protocol. Many of the interviewees lived in the same shelter operated by a South Korean Christian NGO and were initially contacted by NGO activists for interview. In my study, the participants were not recruited from any shelters but through snowball sampling among North Koreans already living in South Korea.

Since the mid-2000s, the border patrol has been tightened, and ordinary North Koreans have been unable to bribe border guards and to circumvent border controls as easily as before. An increasing number of North Koreans therefore cross the border by river by hiring smugglers. The smugglers take them to the Chinese side in exchange for some money or the promise of repayment on a later date. Some of the migrants keep their promise and pay their smugglers while others do not (based on the accounts of interviewees in my study). Some North Koreans who manage to cross the border independently then go on to offer smuggling services to other North Koreans. As their successes in assisting people with border crossings grow, they become "smugglers" of North Korean escapees. Some North Korean smugglers work only through their personal net-works with family, cousins, friends, neighbors, and acquaintances, while other smugglers have extended networks that include military, border guards in North Korea, and even partners in China. Those who have connections with the military and border guards are most successful in their smuggling ventures, and it is therefore not surprising to find that many informal smugglers are men who have been previously discharged from the military.

In addition, some informal smugglers are encouraged to play the role of recruiter by brokers in China. For example, the smugglers in North Korea and their Chinese-Korean brokers in China, who assisted my study subjects in their migration, were close or distant relatives. Demand for women for marriage in China increases North Korean smugglers' recruitment of women. Young-Jin, who had worked as a smuggler in North Korea for four years between 2008 and 2012, encountered Chinese brokers through kinship networks and became a marriage recruiter:

> I used to just take North Koreans to borderland in China through the Tumen River and then to drop by my aunt's house to get some food on my way back to North Korea. One day, I came across my aunt's distant uncle in her house. He asked me about my job and told me that if I took North Korean women to him, he would pay me. A month later, I took two North Korean women to his house and received 3,000 Chinese yuan. This amount of money was more than ten times as much as what I was paid for one person's smuggling service. I wanted to make more money and so I asked around most North Korean women whom I knew if they wanted to go to China.

While many of the female North Korean interviewees in my study voluntarily contacted their smugglers for assistance to cross into China, a few who lived close to the border left for China at the suggestion of a marriage recruiter. Four of my interviewees, for example, lost their family during the 1990s. They engaged with the Chinese black market in the nearby border zone, commonly known as *jang-madang*, both selling products such as dried or salted foods and looking for jobs in China. The recruiters suggested to them that they could go to China and promised to arrange marriages with Chinese men or to find them jobs in restau-rants, factories, or the care industry. The recruiters then accompanied them across the border, where they met other brokers in China. Youn-seo, one among those who escaped from North Korea in 2008 on such a route, recounted:

> I used to sell tofu in Jangmadang. But I barely managed to break even. Right after eating breakfast, my family would start to worry about lunch. Even the beans for tofu were

running out. There was no hope. I could not let my family die. At that time, I was often advised to go to China by a man—I did not know him very well except that he sometimes bought tofu from me in Jangmadang. He told me that he could take me to China for free and introduce me to some jobs. So, there was no reason not to follow him.

Most of my interviewees, however, initiated contact with smugglers directly. They found the smugglers through their social networks. During the first stage of their migration, all my interviewees crossed the border into China voluntarily, albeit illegally. The informal smugglers assisted or arranged their irregular border-crossing. Even though in some cases, crossing the border was recommended by recruiters, it was nonetheless these women's choice to go. And yet, when North Korean women's mobility is conceptualized as trafficking, this recruiting stage is often described as forced. In other words, voluntary participation in smuggling disappears in this victim-focused discourse.

Neither traffickers nor criminal organizations but "seon" brokerage networks

After crossing the border either with or without the assistance of smugglers, most North Korean women who wish to hide in China through marriage meet and stay with other brokers until they can live with their Chinese grooms in other cities or the countryside. At this stage, antitrafficking discourse represents North Korean women as trafficked into forced marriage by traffickers. Once they had been moved to China by the traffickers from North Korea, they were sold or resold to the Chinese traffickers who work independently or are the members of organized crime groups of Han Chinese (E. Kim et al. 2009, 161–62). A typical example comes from a 21-year-old North Korean woman who was sold by Chinese traffickers once she crossed the border (Muico 2005, 5): "A human trafficker sold me to an anonymous man living deep in the mountains of China. He had a dark complexion and was around 40 and below 160 cm tall. He spoke incomprehensible Chinese and confined me."

According to the subjects in my study, however, the traffickers' main business is in arranging marriages between North Korean women and Chinese men rather than finding employment for the women. They are commonly called traffickers or *seon* in Korean by North Koreans. The term *seon* translates literally and interchangeably into three English terms: networks, brokerage, and matchmaking for marriage. In this article, *seon* is used both as a singular and plural noun (an uncountable noun), as it is in Korean. Because the words *smuggler* and *broker* do not exist in Korean and the use of English in North Korea is prohibited, North Koreans did not know these two terms until crossing the border into China. For those reasons, *seon* is used to refer to brokers, particularly when North Korean women call on "good" marriage brokers. They call "bad" brokers *inshinmaemaebum*, which translates into *traffickers* in English.

Marriage brokers are loosely connected ethnic Koreans in China and mostly work independently. These brokers are also the intermediaries between North Korean women in search of shelter in China and bride-seeking Chinese grooms.

Their key function is to bridge the gap between supply and demand in the two countries. And yet, they work together with smugglers who help migrants cross into China. The fact that they are both Korean and Chinese enables them to play a key role in smuggling and as marriage brokerage. They are bilingual and maintain family and social networks in both countries. In the borderland, marriage deals between North Koreans and Chinese brokered or facilitated by well-established Korean-Chinese kinship networks have become common. These different ethnic groups, North Koreans, Korean-Chinese, Han-Chinese, work together to facilitate the migration of North Korean women.

Not forced into marriage, but choosing to be "sold" to move

In contrast to the dominant antitrafficking narrative that women are forced and coerced by traffickers into irregular migration and forced marriage, many North Korean female interviewees in my study were determined to cross illegally into China and agreed to marriage through brokerage networks, *seon*. In their accounts, *seon* did not emerge as "bad traffickers" but "good brokers." The interviewees recounted that they had a choice to agree to or reject a marriage with Chinese men. In a few cases, North Korean female escapees rejected a proposed marriage and asked the brokers to find them jobs instead. One example is 37-year-old Geum-soon, who failed to cross the border independently three times and ended up using *seon* to cross into China. She rejected a proposal to marry a Chinese man. Geum-soon commented: "I stubbornly rejected to marry and even threatened him if there is no way that I will be a bride, if so, you will pay for it." She refused to eat for three days and her broker finally found her a job at a restaurant. Some of the women I interviewed did not reject marriage outright, but insisted that the marriage brokers offer them a choice of Chinese grooms. Many narratives revealed that North Korean women made the decision to marry and were not "sold" into a "forced" marriage.

Many of my study subjects' accounts recognized *seon* as good matchmakers, not traffickers. They also explained that their marriages were arranged but not forced. As Kyung-suk, a former school teacher who escaped from North Korea after her father died from starvation, remembered: *seon* was a marriage matchmaker, rather than trafficker, who helped to get her out of poverty:

> If I had not connected with *seon*, I would have died of starvation or suffered from absolute poverty in North Korea. Even though *seon* led me to marry my ex-husband who had tortured me for many years, they did not know his character and personality. So it is not their fault. I do not think they really sold me but introduced him to me. In my mind, they just wanted to help me as it was better to marry a Chinese man due to my illegal status in China. So I did not reject their proposal.

Half of all my female respondents who repatriated to North Korea escaped again. When they had a plan to cross the border into China, they looked for *seon* who worked together with marriage brokers in China. Time and again, they reiterated that *seon* were "good brokers" who provided them with an opportunity to go to China. They strategically chose to use *seon* because of costs and safety. Most of them could not afford the fee to hire smugglers. Using *seon* was central in interviewees' narratives: "Using *seon* is a free-pass to go to China." As Ji-Young, a 42-year-old, who wanted to be sold by *seon* to "go to China safely" recounted:

> I learned from my first escape from North Korea. Then, I crossed the border into China independently and, right after that, I got caught by Chinese border guards because I was not protected by anyone. When I planned to move to China for the second time, I realized that I needed to look for *seon* who could guide and protect me. I contacted the *seon* and asked him to sell me as a bride in China. I wanted to be trafficked so I can migrate. It is a win-win relationship. He made money by selling me and I could live in China through marriage, which was a safer way to move.

Similarly, 55-year-old Seon-hee, a formal smuggler who smuggled home appliances from North Korea to China, tried to be "trafficked" to China through *seon* but failed:

> I was a smuggler and had known some traffickers involved in *seon* well. I expected that as long as I was trafficked by them, I could go to China for free. I had known one of [the] female traffickers who was most successful among the traffickers. I asked her to sell me to the trafficking market for marriage in China. But she told me that it would be impossible because I was too old to be sold.

Seon-hee kept looking for *seon* for a year and finally negotiated a deal to be sold as a bride with traffickers. She continued: "No time to be picky. I convinced traffickers to look for my potential husband; anyone is ok to me." She ended up marrying a 65-year-old Chinese man. Many narratives revealed that *seon* was the only means to be mobile for these women. It has been shown in much of the literature on women's illegal migration that a high proportion of Eastern European women who migrated to Western European countries used "trafficking systems" as a means to migrate and consented to work in the sex industry (Gülçür and Ilkkaracan 2002; Orfano 2003). Andrijasevic (2007) also observed in her study that Ukraine women entered the trafficking system to move to Italy and they negotiated on their own behalf with traffickers.

My data contradict the dominant abolitionist discourse about North Korean women, who, it is said, are forced by traffickers to move for marriage. For example, according to an interview quoted in Anti-Slavery International (Muico 2005, 9), "If you are a North Korean woman crossing the border, it is almost impossible to survive without being abused or sold." Similarly, one of abolitionist feminists, Robin Morgan (cited in Priscilla 1997, 92), once said that "women should stop migrating ... to avoid being caught up in trafficking and prostitution." These two narratives reflect a new abolitionist discourse that women are only objects to be sold and, therefore, there is no distinction between "forced" and "free choice" (Anderson and Andrijasevic 2008). According to this discourse, North Korean escapees in China have not freely chosen to be there; they are tricked and coerced into prostitution or forced marriage as a way to survive. They are also subjected to various forms of slavery, such as forced labor and slavery-like conditions (Amnesty International 2006; Davis 2006; Hughes 2005; E. Kim et al. 2009; J. Kim 2010).

These claims run against the ethnographic data collected in my study. While it is possible for North Korean women to find themselves in exploitative situations, and being sold could mean they are exploited, it simultaneously means that North Korean women are offered opportunities to move to China without the expense of hiring brokers. This contradicts the dominant discourse in contemporary literature of "trafficking as modern slavery." How can such reciprocity in the relationship between "trafficker" (slave trader) and "victim" (slave) reconcile with the notion of trafficking as modern-day slavery (O'Connell Davidson 2013, 7)? Although marriage brokerage networks profit from these women's mobility, there is a reciprocally beneficial relationship between North Korean women. The North Korean women migrants in my study trusted brokers in their marriage-migration process.

My research findings also demonstrate that the women voluntarily committed themselves to this migration situation. My findings seem to show that North Korean women determine their migration and strategically use marriage as a means of becoming mobile and surviving in China. This challenges the abolitionist discourse, which leaves no space for North Korean women's agency and instead reduces them to helpless and powerless victims. Turton (2003, 8) notes that all migrants including victims of trafficking or refugees exercise agency in migration because to migrate is to make a decision.

My discussion is not meant to imply that there is no exploitation in this marriage-migration scheme. Quite the contrary: North Korean women "being sold" into marriage can become vulnerable to exploitation and abuses. Chinese husbands and their families often stressed that they "bought" North Korean brides, and therefore these North Korean wives must play the role of a "proper" wife worthy of the price. Some women in my study who had been married to both a North Korean and a Chinese man noticed the differences between the two. Eun-Kyung, who migrated to China through marriage, said, "the most different thing in my married life between North Korean and Chinese husband is that I could not refuse what my Chinese husband asked me to do."

Moreover, their illegal status, and a lack of Chinese language skills and cultural knowledge about China in general, left the North Korean women in my study vulnerable to exploitation. These "bad" brokers appear as "traffickers," or *inshin-maemaebum* in Korean, in the interviewees' narratives. In a few cases, for women in my study, once they crossed the border into China, they were deceived by recruiters or, in some cases, by family in China who had helped them migrate. Some of my subjects had hoped to find a job in China, but were instead forced into marriage. One such woman was Mi-Seon, a 37-year-old:

Once in China, I was deceived by a broker who later turned out to be a trafficker. He told me he would find a job in a Korean restaurant for me. When I stayed in his house, he said that he would take me to the restaurant but instead he took me to a house in an unknown place. I had no idea what location I was in. I thought it was a restaurant. I stayed with a few other North Korean women there for one month until I was sold to a Han Chinese man in one of [the] rural villages in Heilongjiang Province for the price of 800 yuan.

Since the broker deceived Mi-Seon, he was regarded as a trafficker, *inshin-maemaebum*, by her. She identified herself as a victim of trafficking in later accounts. While *deception* is used to help define human trafficking under the UN Protocol, the ambiguity lies within the very concept of deception itself (Anderson and O'Connell Davidson 2003; Andrijasevic 2007). Maluccelli (2001) has observed in her research that the concept of *victim* is not adequate in representing migrant women who were not forced to move but lured by traffickers. In my study, nevertheless, the women concurred that deception and confinement constitute the conditions of trafficking. Therefore, their *seon* were regarded as traffickers.

Conclusion

Contrary to the common discourse on bride-trafficking of North Korean women, data from this study showed that not all of these women were trafficked into forced marriage and, in fact, their movement across the border was rarely coerced. North Korean escapees often fall between the dichotomy used in international law and by states to group migrants into the "deserving" and the "undeserving"—forced or voluntary, trafficked or smuggled. Using North Korean migrant voices, this study found that the smuggling/trafficking distinction does not match well with the lived experiences of these women.

To frame escapees' situation as *trafficking* does not help to protect them from the consequences of this label. On one hand, adopting the trafficking label limits the scope of concern to those who have experienced a very narrow and particular constellation of abuse and exploitation. North Korean women interviewed in this study chose to be "sold" into marriage. From an abolitionist perspective, these women might not be defined as victims of trafficking but smuggled migrants under the UN antitrafficking, or the Palermo Convention, protocol. Smuggling involves voluntary participants, whereas trafficking occurs "by means of the threat or use of force or other forms of coercion or of fraud and/or deception for the purpose of exploitation" (Gallagher 2002, 26). Since the North Korean women in my study voluntarily crossed into China, they are technically smuggled migrants. Five among a total of twenty-seven North Korean women interviewees were deceived, confined, and sold by traffickers. In these cases, trafficking and smuggling become difficult to separate because someone can be a smuggled migrant one day and a victim of trafficking the next (Bhabha 2005, 3). Moreover, the concept of exploitation is not well defined. The UN protocol cannot fully capture the complex situations that migrants face in their migration process (Bhabha and Zard 2006) because the protocol prioritizes strengthening border controls to ensure national security and to combat transnational organized criminal activities, not to protect migrants' human rights (Lobasz 2009).

Even those who manage to obtain the status of "victim of trafficking"—not an easy status to attain because of the burden of proof—are not necessarily protected from repatriation. North Koreans afforded the status of victims of trafficking by the Chinese authorities have been repatriated (J. Kim 2010). Once back in North Korea, they face punishment in labor camps. The Chinese government has been criticized by international communities for its failure to protect North Korean escapees and for returning victims of trafficking to a state known for rampant violations of human rights. The UN urges countries to protect North Korean women as victims of trafficking and their children with Chinese men in the 2014 UN Commission of Inquiry report on the human rights situation in North Korea (UN Commission of Inquiry 2014).

This study found that North Korean women in general want to move and are therefore complicit with *seon* and brokerage networks, who facilitate their movement. In fact, many North Korean women seek a third party to sell them as brides to Chinese men or agree to an arranged marriage through brokerage. Marriages involving undocumented North Korean women, however, are not legally binding; and if the women are caught by the Chinese authorities, they face deportation. Thus, smuggled or economic migrants are not quite the correct terms for North Korean female migrants in China.

These concepts fail to capture the complexity and fluidity of the North Korean migrant situations presented here. The line between *trafficking* and *smuggling* is ambiguous and does not help us to grasp the human rights violations that many North Korean women escapees face. Being voluntarily smuggled does not necessarily mean an absence of victimization, as smuggled women can end up being trapped in violent, exploitative relationships with their smugglers or their husbands. But distinguishing between *smuggling* and *trafficking* is only of use to states looking to determine whom to punish.

The immigration and asylum policies pursued by nonpariah states, along with their militarized borders, are designed to keep people out rather than lock them in. But as the North Korean escapees in my study illustrate, these policies have little to do with human rights or freedom. As Anderson and O'Connell Davidson (2003, 7) note: "If the primary concern is to locate, explain and combat the use of forced labor, slavery, servitude and the like, then there is no moral or analytical reason to distinguish between forced labor involving 'illegal immigrants' 'smuggled persons' or 'victims of trafficking.'" Some scholars argue that the boundary between smuggling and trafficking creates unnecessary confusion (Grewcock 2003). Indeed, the terms *trafficking, smuggling*, and *asylum* in antitrafficking discourse and legislation fail to understand or address the situation of the North Koreans in my study.

The *seon*, either "traffickers" or "good brokers," defied the dichotomy between altruistic or profit-oriented brokerage networks and showed the two motivations were not fixed but were on a continuum. *Seon* provide a vital service for North Korean women's migration, which is often overlooked in the literature. North Korea women in China are vulnerable to exploitation, but their vulnerability is not expressed through their journeys as ostensibly "trafficked" individuals. Rather, their vulnerability arises mostly from their illegal status in the country into which they are smuggled. As illegal migrants, North Korean women cannot carry out daily activities openly in China, and therefore must rely on someone to broker all arrangements that make their life possible, including marriage. Their brokers cannot be equated to traffickers, as the dominant discourse suggests. However, this dependency does not imply a lack of agency.

Findings from this study suggest that alternative immigration and asylum policies could be pursued to ameliorate the plights of North Koreans in China. First, China should reconsider its political agenda in favor of humanitarian needs and grant refugee status to North Koreans in China; such a move would uphold the 1951 Refugee Convention and the 1967 Refugee Protocol. Although North Korean defectors are classified as refugees under the two legislations (M. Kim 2010, 424), the Chinese government has prioritized its 1986 repatriation agreement with North Korea by categorizing North Koreans as illegal economic migrants, which opens them up to various forms of exploitations and abuses (Margesson, Chanlett-Avery, and Bruno 2007). Second, if refugee status is not possible, the Chinese government could still halt its repatriation practice, and instead send North Koreans to other countries, including South Korea, where they can receive immediate citizenship. Last, China could ratify the International Convention on Migrant Workers and Members for North Korean migrants and the UN Trafficking Protocol to protect the basic human rights of North Korean migrants.

References

Amnesty International. 2006. *Amnesty International annual report*. London: Amnesty International.

Anderson, Bridget, and Rutvica Andrijasevic. 2008. Sex, slaves and citizens: The politics of anti-trafficking. *Soundings* 40:135–45.

Anderson, Bridget, and J. O'Connell Davidson. 2003. *Is trafficking in human beings demand driven? A multi-country pilot study*. IOM Migration Research Series 15. Geneva: International Organization for Migration (IOM).

Andrijasevic, Rutvica. 2007. Problematizing trafficking for the sex sector: A Case of Eastern European women in the EU. In *Women and immigration law: New variations on classical feminist themes*, eds. Sarah van Walsung and Thomas Spijkerboer, 86–103. London: Glasshouse Press.

Bhabha, Jacqueline. 2005. *Trafficking, smuggling and human rights. Migration information source*. Available from http://www.migrationpolicy.org/article/trafficking-smuggling-and-human-rights (accessed 24 July 2017).

Bhabha, Jacqueline, and Monette Zard. 2006. Smuggled or trafficked? *Forced Migration Review* 25:6–8.

Barot, Sneha. 2012. A problem-and-solution mismatch: Son preference and sex-selective abortion bans. *Guttmacher Policy Review* 5 (2): 18–22.

Chan, Elim, and Andreas Schloenhardt. 2007. North Korean refugees and international refugee law. *International Journal of Refugee Law* 19 (2): 215–45.

Chang, Yoonok, Stephan Haggard, and Marcus Noland. 2008. Migration experiences of North Korean refugees: Survey evidence from China. Working Paper 08-04, Peterson Institute, Washington, DC.

Collins, Francis L. 2012. Organizing student mobility: Education agents and student migration to New Zealand. *Pacific Affairs* 85 (1): 137–60.

Committee for Human Rights in North Korea. 2009. *Lives for sale: Personal accounts of women fleeing North Korea to China*. Washington, DC: HRNK.

Davis, Kathleen. 2006. Brides, bruises and the border: The trafficking of North Korean women into China. *SAIS Review* 26 (1): 131–41.

de Haas, Hein. 2009. *Mobility and human development*. Human Development Research Paper No. 1. New York, NY: United Nations Development Programme, Human Development Report Office.

Derks, Annuska. 2010. Migrant labour and the politics of immobilisation: Cambodian fishermen in Thailand. *Asian Journal of Social Science* 38 (6): 915–32.

Freedman, Caren. 2005. Marrying up and marrying down: The paradoxes of marital mobility for Chosŏnjok brides in South Korea. In *Cross-border marriages: Gender and Mobility in Transnational Asia*. Philadelphia, PA: University of Pennsylvania Press.

Gallagher, Anne. 2002. Trafficking, smuggling and human rights: Tricks and treaties. *Forced Migration Review* 12 (January): 25–28.

Grewcock, Mike. 2003. Irregular migration, identity and the state—The challenge for criminology. *Current Issues in Criminal Justice* 15 (2): 114–35.

Gülçür, Leyla, and Pinar Ilkkaracan. 2002. The "Natasha experience": Migrant sex workers from former Soviet Union and Eastern Europe in Turkey. *Women's Studies International Forum* 25 (4): 411–21.

Haggard, Stephan, and Marcus Noland. 2007. *Famine in North Korea: Markets, aid and reform*. New York, NY: Columbia University Press.

Hawk, David. 2003 *The hidden gulag*. Washington, DC: U.S. Committee for Human Rights in North Korea.

Hughes, Donna M. 2005. How can I be sold like this? The trafficking of North Korean women refugees. *National Review Online*. Available from http://www.uri.edu/artsci/wms/hughes/trafficking_nk_refugees.pdf (accessed 27 January 2016).

Human Rights Watch. 2002. *The invisible exodus: North Koreans in the People's Republic of China*. Human Rights Watch Report 14 (8). New York, NY: Human Rights Watch.

International Crisis Group. 2006. *Perilous journey: The plight of the North Korean refugees in China and beyond*. Asia Report No. 122. Brussels: International Crisis Group.

Kim, Eungyoung, Minwoo Yun, Mirang Park, and Hue Williams. 2009. Cross border North Korean women trafficking and victimization between North Korea and China: An ethnographic case study. *International Journal of Law, Crime and Justice* 37 (4): 154–69.

Kim, Jane. 2010. Trafficked: Domestic violence, exploitation in marriage, and the foreign-bride industry. *Virginia Journal of International Law* 51 (2): 443–97.

Kim, Melissa M. 2010. North Korean escapees in China: Granting prima facie refugee status based on a group determination. *Journal of East Asia International Law* 3 (2): 423–49.

Kim, Sung Kyung. 2014. "I am well-cooked food": Survival strategies of North Korean female border-crossers and possibilities for empowerment. *Inter-Asia Cultural Studies* 15 (4): 553–71.

Kirkpatrick, Melanie. 2012. *Escape from North Korea: The untold story of Asia's underground railroad*. New York, NY: Encounter Books.

Kivisto, Peter, and Thomas Faist. 2000. *Beyond a border: The causes and consequences of contemporary immigration*. Thousand Oaks, CA: Sage Publications.

Lankov, Andrei. 2004. North Korean refugees in northeast China. *Asian Survey* 44 (6): 856–73.

Lee, Yoonkyung. 2009. Migration, migrants, and contested ethno-nationalism in Korea. *Critical Asian Studies* 41 (3): 363–80.

Liberty in North Korea. 2013. *Refugee stories of North Korea*. Long Beach, CA: Liberty in North Korea.

Lindquist, Johan, Biao Xiang, and Brenda S. A. Yeoh. 2012. Opening the black box of migration: Brokers, the organization of transnational mobility and the changing political economy in Asia. *Pacific Affairs* 85 (1): 7–19.

Lobasz, Jennifer K. 2009. Beyond border security: Feminist approaches to human trafficking. *Security Studies* 18 (2): 319–44.

Maluccelli, Lorenza. 2001. Tra schiavitù e servitù: biografie femminili in cerca di autonomia. In *Da Vittime a Cittadine. Percorsi di Uscita dalla Prostituzione e Buone Pratiche di Inserimento Sociale e Lavorativo*, ed. Giulianas Candia and Franca Garreffa, 37–82. Rome: Ediesse.

Margesson, Rhoda, Emma Chanlett-Avery, and Andorra Bruno. 2007. *North Korean refugees in china and human rights issues: International response and U.S. policy options*. CRS Report for Congress. Washington, DC: U.S. Congressional Research Service.

Muico, Norma Kang. 2005. *An absence of choice: The sexual exploitation of North Korean women in China*. London: Anti-Slavery International.

O'Connell Davidson, Julia. 2010. New slavery, old binaries: human trafficking and the borders of "freedom." *Global Networks: A Journal of Transnational Affairs* 10 (2): 244–61.

O'Connell Davidson, Julia. 2013. Troubling freedom: Migration, debt, and modern slavery. *Migration Studies* 1 (2): 176–95.

Office of the Under Secretary for Global Affairs (OUSGA). 2006. *Trafficking in persons report, June 2006*. Washington, DC: U.S. Department of State.

Orfano, Isabella. 2003. Country report Italy. In *Research based on case studies of victims of trafficking in human beings in 3 EU Member States, i.e. Belgium, Italy and the Netherlands*, eds. Wim Vandekerckhove, Zrinka Pari, Bruno Moens, Isabella Orfano, Ruth Hopkins, Jan Nijboer, Gert Vermeulen, and Wim Bontinck. Brussels: Commission of the European Communities, DG Justice & Home Affairs.

Priscilla, A. 1997. Feminism, sex workers, and human rights. In *Whores and other feminists*, ed. J. Nagle, 83–97. New York, NY: Psychology Press.

Refugees International. 2005. *Acts of betrayal: The challenging of protecting North Koreans in China*. Washington, DC: Refugees International.

Song, Jiyoung. 2013. Smuggled refugees: The social construction of North Korean migration. *International Migration* 51 (4): 158–73.

South Korean Ministry of Unification. 2016. *General facts of North Korean defectors in South Korea with statistics*. Available from http://www.unikorea.go.kr/ (accessed 2 April 2017).

Tucker, Catherine, and Jennifer Van Hook. 2013. Surplus Chinese men: Demographic determinants of the sex ratio at marriageable ages in China. *Population and Development Review* 39 (2): 209–29.

Turton, D. 2003. Conceptualising forced migration. *RSC* Working Paper No. 12, Refugee Studies Centre, Oxford.

UN Commission of Inquiry. 2014. *Report of the Commission of Inquiry on Human Rights in the Democratic People's Republic of Korea*. A/HRC/25/63. New York, NY: UN. Available from http://www .ohchr.org/EN/HRBodies/HRC/CoIDPRK/Pages/ReportoftheCommission ofInquiryDPRK.aspx.

U.S. Department of State. 2013. *Trafficking in persons report*. 13th ed. Washington, DC: U.S. Department of State. Available from http://www.state.gov/j/tip/rls/tiprpt/2012/index.htm (accessed 20 May 2016).

Wang, Hong-Zen, and Hong-Zen Hsiao. 2009. *Cross border marriages with Asian characteristics*. Taipei, Taiwan: Academia Sinica, Centre for Asia-Pacific Area Studies.

Rumors, Encounters, Collaborations, and Survival: The Migrant Smuggling–Drug Trafficking Nexus in the U.S. Southwest

By
GABRIELLA E. SANCHEZ
and
SHELDON X. ZHANG

The violence afflicting the Mexican migration corridor has often been explained as resulting from the brutal takeover of migrant smuggling markets by organized crime, specifically Mexican drug trafficking organizations (DTOs). Through the testimonies of twenty-eight migrants who traveled with smuggling facilitators on their journeys into the United States and who interacted with drug traffickers during their transit, we argue that the metamorphosis taking place may be even more radical, involving the proliferation of actors with little or no criminal intent to operate along the migration trails. Far from market coalescence, the increasing flattening of criminal markets along the migration trail and the proliferation of individuals struggling to survive is the result of increasingly limited paths toward mobility and is not attributable to feared cartels or *traficantes* alone. The interactions among clandestine actors are not only likely to become more common but also to reflect flexibility and adaptation that hierarchical DTOs cannot explain.

Keywords: migrant smuggling; drug trafficking; U.S.-Mexico border; cartels; organized crime

A mid the global narratives of migration as crisis, migrant smuggling facilitators have become popular, if infamous, characters. They

Gabriella E. Sanchez is a research fellow at the Migration Policy Centre at the European University Institute. A sociocultural anthropologist, she has conducted research on the internal dynamics of migrant smuggling facilitation in Latin America, the U.S.-Mexico border, North Africa, the Middle East, Australia, and Europe. She is the author of Human Smuggling and Border Crossings *(Routledge 2015).*

Sheldon X. Zhang is professor and chair at the School of Criminology and Justice Studies, University of Massachusetts, Lowell. His research primarily centers on transnational organized crime, migrant smuggling and human trafficking, and evaluation of offender reentry programs in California. He has published and lectured extensively on these topics.

Correspondence: Gabriella.Sanchez@eui.eu

DOI: 10.1177/0002716217752331

tend to be depicted as the predatory and violent men who scam, kidnap, assault, or abandon helpless and desperate migrants across Mexico, the Mediterranean, Africa, and the Middle East. Their trade is often characterized in global reports as one of the most profitable illicit activities worldwide next to drug trafficking or the sex trade (Europol-Interpol 2016; United Nations Office on Drugs and Crime [UNODC] 2017). In addition to allegedly providing high returns for its operators, smuggling organizations are described as sophisticated, evolving networks of transnational reach (Carrera and Guild 2016).

It is also common to come across references of migrant smuggling's ties to other illicit activities. The argument that two or more branches of the transnational criminal pantheon can come together is a common yet debated topic among criminologists (Zhang 2007). Some have linked smuggling to markets ranging from the weapon trade (Naim 2010) and sex trafficking (Europol-Interpol 2016) to the trafficking of nuclear material (Zaitseva and Steinhäusler 2014). Amid recent terrorist attacks in Europe, some authors have argued smuggling facilitators have helped Islamic terrorists groups infiltrate the European continent (Europol-Interpol 2016; Walt 2015), or that terrorist organizations finance their activities by funneling profits from migrant smuggling (Shelley 2014; Global Initiative against Transnational Organized Crime and Norwegian Center for Global Analysis [RHIPTO] 2015).

In the Americas, law enforcement, policy, and academic discourses have claimed Mexican drug trafficking organizations (DTOs) have now entered the migrant smuggling market, drug cartels ousting long-standing smuggling operators and forcing the few who are left to work on their behalf (Slack and Campbell 2016; Olson 2016). According to this argument, DTOs now control the routes that once were migrant smugglers' turfs, generating profits that may soon, if not already, outpace those of the drug trade (Storen Weden 2016; Donnelly and Hagan 2014).

In what follows, we challenge the takeover narrative. Instead, we propose an alternative explanation concerning these markets' contacts and their meaning. We argue that far from constituting a case of criminal convergence, interactions between drug trafficking and migrant smuggling along the U.S.-Mexico border have escalated as a result of the War on Drugs and the criminalization of mobility, leading to the proliferation not of organized crime, but of individual actors along the clandestine trail who opt, not solely defined by force or choice, to perform criminalized tasks as part of their personal attempts to survive. The testimonies collected here indicate that DTOs and migrant smuggling groups are far from being exclusive or restricted networks led by people in static positions of power. Instead, barriers to participation are not high, which has allowed for the inclusion into both markets of a growing number of ordinary, poor, and vulnerable people with no criminal background and whose actions are driven by the desire to improve their lives.

Our analysis relies on the experiences of Central American and Mexican migrant men and women who, during their journeys across the U.S.-Mexico border, traveled with smuggling facilitators and who encountered and, in many cases, partnered with drug trafficking actors with the ultimate goal of reaching their destination. Yet our analysis does not stop there. We argue that in the context of clandestine migration, migrants make collective as well as individual decisions to support, reject, or avoid the activities of actors they encounter along the way, to protect themselves and one another. Rather than indicators of market convergence we see in the interactions among drug trafficking facilitators, migrant smugglers, and migrants evidence of the development and deployment of complex processes of securitization from below (Sanchez 2018), rooted in strong notions of care and solidarity amid the increasing insecurity and precarity created by migration regimes and the "wars" against drugs and irregular migration.

While Mexican DTOs and their exploits have been well documented in popular and academic literature for decades, the Mexican War on Drugs has generated a lot of literature on the so-called Mexican cartels and their transgressions. Alongside it, there is also a corpus of research that has sought to shed light on the dramatic levels of migrant victimization along the U.S.-Mexico migration trail, which has generated widespread concern and led to international demands for an improved protection system across this corridor.[1] Many of these publications have argued that DTOs have taken over migrant smuggling, ousting long-standing operators in an attempt to extend their domain.

Less has been written about the potential reasons behind this transformation. So far, most commentators have argued that the coming together of drug trafficking and migrant smuggling is the concerted result of efforts on the part of drug trafficking actors to take advantage of migrants' vulnerability and to cash in on the allegedly limitless profits of smuggling. Many have also argued that smuggling markets are becoming increasingly sophisticated and hierarchical. Some have used examples from journalistic coverage of migrant tragedies in drug trafficking territories in Mexico as clear indicators of the transformation, claiming these instances stand as evidence that drug trafficking is relying on its own violent tactics to take over smuggling markets.

While these claims may sound reasonable, especially amid the reports of unprecedented levels of violence on the U.S.-Mexico border, they make a series of assumptions about both markets that must be unpacked—namely, that different markets would come together, attracted by the prospect of financial returns and a business model to which both can ascribe. The claim of convergence also fuels the perception that all forms of irregular migration facilitation are the domain of monolithically organized criminal structures. However, the claim appears to ignore the testimonies of migrants who have been robbed at gunpoint by gangs comprising young people or *cholos*, kidnapped from safe houses and from their smuggling facilitators by *bajadores* or rip-off crews (Martinez and Sanchez 2013; Sanchez 2016), or abandoned along migrant trails by guides they thought were reliable (O'Leary 2016)—all acts by people whose ties to DTOs are not clear, if not altogether nonexistent (Spener 2009; Sanchez 2016; Izcara Palacios 2015). Furthermore, it also dismisses the findings from scholars around the world who have documented how many clandestine migration attempts are in fact carried out among friends, family members, humanitarian organizations, or ordinary people, often for scant or no financial compensation (Carrera and Guild 2016; Ayalew, this volume; Maher, this volume).

The day-to-day experiences of the migrants who, in the course of their journeys, hear about drug traffickers, encounter them, and, on multiple occasions, even engage with them as part of their individual attempts to reduce the degree of precarity that both face are also sidelined amid the debate about the smuggling-trafficking convergence. Here we argue that the interactions between migrants and drug traffickers constitute examples of what Vogt (2016), in her work among migrants in Mexico, describes as "intimate, embodied and affective" interactions that "defy normative" and dichotomist "constructions" of criminals as predators and migrants as victims.

It is precisely because of these experiences that explanations solely focused on DTOs or smuggling organizations as coalescing agents behind the coercion, exploitation, and violence encountered by migrants should be considered suspect, as should the discourses that define migrants solely as passive entities. Analyses that unpack the smuggling–drug trafficking argument are needed. This article attempts to do so.

The Journey beyond the U.S.-Mexico Border

After the Mediterranean, the U.S.-Mexico border is the second most lethal route for migrants in the world. At least 6,915 people have died attempting to cross the U.S.-Mexico border between 1998 and 2016 (U.S. Border Patrol 2016). While there is no reliable border-wide count of the number of migrant fatalities along the U.S.-Mexico border, in the first 11 months of 2017 there were 341 migrant deaths recorded in the region (International Organization for Migration [IOM] 2017, 79). The number of dead and missing migrants has remained constant despite the dramatic decrease in border apprehensions, which by 2017 had reached 1970s levels (Washington Office for Latin America [WOLA] 2017).

Migrants are not unaware of the risks involved in the journey and, whenever possible, hire smuggling facilitators who guide them through their journeys. Smuggling services of different quality and reach are sold along the migrant trail and are purchased by migrants or their families to secure a basic level of protection and to increase their chances of crossing the U.S.-Mexico border and reaching U. S. destinations.[2]

The services of smuggling facilitators (while actors of dubious reputation) are consistently purchased with the intention of reducing the environmental, safety, and enforcement-related challenges along migrant journeys (see Martinez and Slack, this volume). In the case of the U.S.-Mexico corridor (see Guevara Gonzalez, this volume), stepped-up border enforcement and immigration controls have forced migrants and those who guide them to travel in inhospitable and remote areas. This risk is compounded by the existence of criminal actors who, aware of the unprotected nature of migratory paths, prey on those who travel along them, and engage in violence that ranges from intimidation and armed robbery to kidnapping, sexual assault, and torture (Slack and Campbell 2016). Immigration controls and the individual actions of law enforcement agents are also known to put the lives of migrants at risk. There have been reported cases of migrants sustaining injuries or dying as a result of being chased by immigration officials, or of being denied medical assistance, food, or water, which have led U.S. immigration authorities to face legal charges (see Martinez, Cantor, and Ewing 2014).

Do Mexican DTOs play a role along the migration trail within U.S. territory? Data on this are scant. There is evidence—including in this piece—that Mexican drug traffickers carry out their smuggling attempts along many of the same routes followed by migrants once they have entered the United States. Yet U.S. authorities have been careful to describe this as evidence of coalescence, even when referring to migrant smuggling facilitators as cartels. U.S. politicians' allegations of the presence of Mexican DTOs or their collusion with other markets have often been called out as lies or moral panics seeking solely to spread the distaste for irregular migration.[3]

Literature on the drug trafficking–human smuggling nexus often makes reference to the victimization that migrants face during their journeys, most often in the form of physical aggression (Slack 2015; Slack and Whiteford 2011), forced labor (Servin et al. 2015), or both (Simmons, Menjivar, and Tellez 2015). This scholarship has also argued that these acts stand as evidence of the coming together of drug trafficking and smuggling organizations, or as the takeover of the migrant smuggling business by the more powerful DTOs (Slack and Campbell 2016; Schaefer and Gonzalez 2016). Researchers have also argued that migrant smuggling has become increasingly organized and structured in response to immigration and border enforcement controls (UNODC 2017), leading to the virtual extinction of individual and independent smuggling enterprises.

We provide an alternative explanation to these interactions: that a growing number of individual actors—rather than hierarchical, network-like organizations—have entered a structurally open market (that is, characterized by low-entry or no barriers to membership) as a result of the increasing precarity they face, resulting on one hand from neoliberal economic systems, and on the other hand from migration enforcement and criminalization regimes. Globally, these actors increasingly include men and women from marginalized groups who live along the migrant trail (Stone-Cadena and Alvarez, this volume), children and young people (Derechos Humanos Integrales en Acción [DHIA] 2017; Palmer and Missbach 2017), and, most notably, migrants themselves (Achilli, this volume), whose roles do not discreetly fit the characterizations of criminal organizations. In sum, we argue that the experiences of clandestine migration facilitation must be analyzed as embedded in "a complex matrix of dependency and survival" (Vogt 2016, 367) in which actors are not merely ascribed to discrete organizations or solely seek financial profits.

When available, the data suggest that the incidence of intimidation, abuse, sexual harassment, assault, extortion, and forced recruitment along the migrant trail most often involves the interactions of migrants with their own smuggling facilitators, rip-off crews, gangs, and other migrants, rather than drug traffickers who may have other market goals (Hagan 2008; Izcara Palacios 2015; Spener 2009). A study of sixty-six migrant smuggling prosecutions in the state of Arizona—during the 2010s the main point of entry for irregular migrants and to this day one of the main points of entry for illicit drugs into the United States—also revealed the presence of nonviolent if frequent interactions between migrants and drug traffickers (Sanchez 2016). What do these encounters involve, and what do they tell us about the organization of smuggling and drug trafficking on the U.S. side of the migrant trail? In the sections that follow, we outline the interactions described by our respondents in the context of their journeys and hypothesize what they reveal.

Methods

This article is based on data collected via face-to-face qualitative, semistructured interviews conducted with four male and twenty-four female Mexican and Central American migrants who successfully crossed the U.S.-Mexico border with the assistance of smuggling facilitators along points of the U.S. southwest border (e.g., Arizona, New Mexico, and the westernmost corner of Texas). While the overall goal of the interviews was to document the gender dimensions of border crossing experiences, it soon became evident that the role of criminalized actors—particularly men involved in drug trafficking—constituted a critical element of the migratory experiences and even the survival of our respondents, leading us to explore this specific topic.

Initial interviews were carried out in spring and summer 2013 in a large city in the U.S. Southwest and relied on the critical assistance of Margarita,[4] a 33-year-old Mexican member of the local immigrant community known for her work assisting recently arrived migrants with securing goods and services. Respondents included people known to her and their acquaintances, and others recruited via snowball sampling. All respondents were working-class migrants employed in the service and hospitality industries. They had crossed the border with the assistance of a smuggling facilitator or coyote, and had at some point along their journeys heard of, encountered, or collaborated with others involved in criminal activities, namely, drug trafficking.

No deception was used, and respondents were aware of the objective of the research. All interviews were conducted in Spanish. The data collected from the initial interviews were supplemented over the following 18 months via participant observation and informal interactions and conversations with respondents, their friends, and family members. We gathered informally at churches, libraries, schools, stores, and waterparks; during weekend outings to the mountains, at casinos, and places of employment. We met with the employers, neighbors, and coworkers of respondents knowledgeable of their border crossing experiences. This prolonged contact was also the result of frequent consultations with the researchers on the part of respondents via social media and over the phone on questions ranging from immigration related procedures—how to locate relatives or friends who had been arrested or gone missing in the context of their border crossing journeys—to concerns about social services eligibility for their children and assistance with filling out medical forms and job applications. The data collected in the course of these interactions increased the trust and rapport among researchers and respondents and allowed for further data validation.

It is important to highlight that data presented here are not statistical in nature; they represent the experiences of only those who chose to be interviewed or who were interviewed through referrals and with whom contact was maintained. The data presented here, then, should not be interpreted as reflective of the experiences of all irregular migrants.

In what follows, respondents describe their encounters and collaborations with drug traffickers along their journeys. Some never came face-to-face with drug traffickers, even though they reported paying a fee to travel within the traffickers' territory. For others, their very survival depended on the intervention of people involved in drug trafficking. Still others, faced with accumulating debt emerging from failed crossing attempts, scams or robberies, opted to engage in drug trafficking activities to reach their destination. All three kinds of experiences are described below to explore what these experiences say about the smuggling and trafficking markets.

"La Mafia" and "El Piso"

The most commonly reported interaction between migrants and drug traffickers—and perhaps the only one pointing to the existence of a structured system of financial transactions connecting drug trafficking and migrant facilitators—involved the payment of *piso*, a one-time toll to access specific parts of the migrant trail under the control of a DTO. The payment of *piso* entitled migrants and their guides to, in theory, travel without fear. Margot, Leslie, and Malena described their understanding of the process:

> Margot: Along the border, the ones who govern all that are the, the … how are those called?
> Leslie: La Mafia.
> Margot: La Mafia?
> Leslie: Yes, you only pay [la mafia] when you arrive with the coyote[5] [to a specific point].
> Margot: Yes, [the smuggler] gives [the fee] to the mafia.

Malena went on to describe how the female driver who was transporting her and her husband stopped to pay the fee prior to entering a specific route:

> We were riding [in] an old van, and we took a dirt road. We were … it was a like a desert. And out there, right in the middle of nowhere, you pass by a statue of a virgin, and that was where Mrs. Martha got out of the van and left the money. It was a small structure. It looked like a small shrine. [Mrs. Martha] left the money we had already given her there … and when she got back in the van we drove off and she said, "We need to pay the quota, otherwise … many have been killed." But there was no one around. Nobody. She just left the money there and that was it.

The same way payment provided protection, lack of payment had potential implications. Testimonies suggest that the threat of violence, rather than violence itself, was sufficient motivation for guides and drivers to deposit their payment at prescribed locations. Reminders of what could happen to those who failed to follow the rules appeared to be strategically located. Margot stated:

> Right ahead, just right after we had left the little shrine behind, you could see burned cars, flipped cars, and the *coyote* said that those belonged to those who had not paid their quota, that that had been the reason that they had gotten killed. And Mrs. Martha said, "If we don't pay, that is what they will do to us." But there were no people watching. She just left the money there and that was it.

The presence of burned and flipped cars were warnings to drivers and migrants alike that there were specific guidelines for traveling the route. That smuggling facilitators had to pay a fee to use the routes suggests that they did not work for the DTOs but simply paid a fee for the use of their routes.

None of the respondents reported violence from drug traffickers upon entering their territory and having paid the fee. But they disclosed instances when segments of the routes were off-limits to migrants and their smuggling facilitators or guides. Paloma, for example, attempted to reach a location in the Arizona desert with the help of a smuggling facilitator, but the *narcos* (the term she used to described drug traffickers) did not allow her group to cross through. While they were threatened, they were never hurt:

> Paloma: So this time we did not make it [either]. We headed back [to Mexico], but they [drug traffickers] knew we would come back, that we would try some other way; [so we tried again and] the trucks of the men with the drugs were there, and they had weapons, and [they said] that they would either shoot us or send us back. So pointing at us they got us all on the back of their truck and took us back to Sasabe, Sonora. We would walk so much and the *narcos* would send us back, because we couldn't [use that route].
>
> Interviewer: All [three times] you ran into the *narcos*.
>
> Paloma: The *narcos*.
>
> Interviewer: It was not immigration.
>
> Paloma: No. It was the *narcos*. It was just *narcos* what you'd see on the hill over there, so many of them. Three times the *coyotes* tried to get us through and we couldn't make it.

Paloma's experience suggests that drug traffickers prefer to keep migrants out of drug trafficking routes, most likely to avoid unwanted attention from law enforcement. Malena's group was eventually able to cross, and nobody was hurt. Yet the repeated warnings against crossing through a specific route further suggest a degree of differentiation among two separate illicit markets.

"They gave us some suitcases"

Reports of migrants being forced by drug traffickers to carry backpacks stuffed with drugs across the border (cf. Koslowski 2011; Slack and Cambpell 2016; Burnett 2011; Leutert 2017) have been increasingly documented by researchers over the last few years. These testimonies suggest that the practice is widespread and increasing along the border, and have been used to support of the argument that drug trafficking and migrant smuggling have converged (Mendez and Sanchez Dorame 2016; Donnelly and Hagan 2014).

In our study, respondents' testimonies indicated that the decision to carry drugs often was a personal, complex choice, rather than the result of coercion. Lacking financial resources to cover basic needs like room or board, or having run out of money after traveling vast distances and no longer able to afford smuggling fees, some migrants opted to assist drug traffickers in exchange for financial compensation or transportation within the United States. During a focus group, Avelina and Claudia described the experience of one of their acquaintances, Doña Elsa, a female migrant from Mexico in her 50s, who, unable to cover her smuggling fee following her deportation, relied on informal, indentured-like work to support herself, and ultimately accepted an offer to transport drugs with the hope of reaching her final destination in the United States:

Avelina: Doña Elsa, it's been a year since she got here.

Claudia: Yes, she is the one who came with my sister. She came across carrying a suitcase.

Avelina: Oh yes, that woman did suffer a lot. Claudia's sister went back home [after being unable to cross the border] but Doña Elsa, she said she would try again. And Doña Elsa's husband told her, well, you do that but [this time] you get the money yourself, I don't have money for another [crossing attempt]. And she did, right?

Claudia: Yes, she got a job at a garlic farm [on the American side of the border] so that she could come up with the money [and then try again]; she got hired there, in Ajo.[6]

Avelina: And it was there, that a guy at the farm told her, "I'll cross you, Doña." "Really?" she asked. "Really," he said. And he did.

Claudia: And then one day I just get this message on Facebook from Doña Elsa, right, that she wanted to be friends. And I befriended her and asked her, what's up Doña Elsa, how did you cross. And she said, "At the same spot where your sister and I wanted to cross." And I told her, "But that is where the *narcos* work, so was it carrying drugs?" And she said "No, no, they just told us not to bring anything with us, that they will give us food. And they gave us some suitcases," she said, "with food." But that was when I thought, what kind of food could that be? Well yes, in my opinion they were carrying drugs. She said she walked for about a day. But I wonder, can you imagine if [she and my sister] had been caught with the drugs? That is what people do out of desperation.

Avelina: But you also have to realize, it was not like she was going to tell you, right, yes, Claudia, I did it, I was able to cross the border because I crossed drugs. No way.

Claudia: Who knows … perhaps she was just very lucky, or maybe, maybe when [migrants] carry [drugs] you are cared for better than when you are only a migrant, but by the time I spoke with her she was doing very well. [People who cross drugs] are cared for better, not like the *coyotes* who just throw you out so that they can distract [law enforcement] while they get another group across.

There was consensus among respondents that traveling with drug trafficking actors on occasion could translate into improved travel conditions, and even better treatment than with smuggling facilitators, since drug traffickers relied on specific, faster routes inaccessible to smugglers. Traveling that way, however, implied different risks.

An 18-year-old male migrant from Mexico, Alfredo was apprehended while attempting to enter the United States with a smuggling facilitator. While held in immigration detention, he met two other young men who had heard about a pilot in the town of Nogales, Sonora, who flew migrants into Phoenix, Arizona, in the same light aircraft that he used to transport drugs. Alfredo considered traveling this way with the hope of arriving quicker to his sister's home in Salt Lake City. He explained:

> Before we went there I called my sister and I asked her, "What do you think, should I go with him? He charges US$4,000 to travel on a Cessna. You only have to jump [across the border] and run into a house and the owner of the house flies you. But he says he lands in Phoenix."

Alfredo and his sister considered the option, knowing he had already attempted to cross the border several times with no success. The journey appeared to be, in theory, fast and uneventful, and Alfredo wanted to arrive and start working, as the debt arising from unfulfilled border crossing attempts had increased with every try. Alfredo met with the pilot and discussed the conditions of the flight—it was then that he realized he would be flying next to a cocaine load that was to be delivered on a clandestine landing strip in the outskirts of Phoenix. Fearing the repercussions of a journey of this nature, he ultimately opted not to cross the border that way:

> I called my sister back and I told her: "Nah, they have explained us now how it works. It involves a lot of risk. It sounds good but can you imagine, if I fly and when I get off right there [law enforcement] arrests me? Can you imagine how many years [in prison] I would get?" And so my sister said, "No, forget it, just stay [in Nogales]. I will wire you money and you go back home."

Alfredo's story indicates how individual drug traffickers—rather than organizations—may rely on the same resources they use for drug trafficking for the facilitation of migrant smuggling. Yet again, these efforts appear to be made independent of any organizational or leadership demands. While it could be argued that the pilot was operating in secret, there was no indication that the services he provided were, as his name and address were of common knowledge among migrants.

The race for survival

It was not uncommon for respondents to narrate instances in which their lives were at risk. All reported sustaining injuries ranging from scratches and cuts to sprains and broken bones. One drank stagnant water, ingesting in the process a life-threatening parasite that led to the loss of half of his liver. Mothers described tying their children to their bodies to avoid them being pulled by water currents. Some respondents also disclosed witnessing times when migrants decided they were unable to continue; when friends and relatives opted to abandon someone unable to keep up; or the deaths of migrants as a result of falls, dehydration, or heatstroke.

In these narratives, smuggling facilitators played varying roles. While the actions of many did in fact match the dominant discourses that depict them as disregarding human life, many other times they appeared to be as vulnerable as the migrants they guided. Yet even more common were the references to the provision of care and support.

To think of smuggling facilitators along these lines may sound contradictory (Sanchez 2016, Vogt 2016), especially amid the narratives that systematically depict them as cruel and predatory. Yet smuggling, despite its labels, is at its core a primal attempt to preserve life; and in that sense, it should not come as a surprise that alongside death and violence, acts of solidarity, friendship, and even love emerge among those who experience extraordinary vulnerability. People spoke of the times they had come together to support and care for each other. There were examples of young men whose wounds were nursed by other men and of women who carried the children of other women too weak to walk. One woman described how the men in her group would form a circle around her so that she could sleep during a stop (she was the only woman in the group of migrants). Middle-age or elderly women often pretended to be the mothers of younger women traveling alone so that they would not be harassed by other migrants or separated from the group in the event they were apprehended by U.S. immigration.

It was in these extreme conditions that many migrants reported encountering drug traffickers, some of whom had scant if any advantage over migrants and whose very survival was also compromised by enforcement and the environment. Respondents identified multiple instances in which even under this high level of stress they were able to provide and receive assistance from others, including people involved in drug trafficking.

Cynthia narrated a time when the group of migrants with which she was traveling encountered men carrying drugs who were being chased by law enforcement:

> [We saw] the drug people trying to escape and the helicopters [flying] on top. The next day we were asleep in a cave and the drug people walked in and they asked us to give them food, and the people [sleeping] at the mouth of the cave said, "We don't have any" [and they said] "Yes you do, how would you be able to walk otherwise, we want you to give us what you have. We are asking nicely, or do you want us to do otherwise," and they took out the guns and the knives. One [of the men] said, "All of you ... open your bags and give us some of the food you have." But the helicopter was still searching for them outside and one of the [drug traffickers] came and told [the one threatening the group]: "Let's go. They still have a ways to go and we are on our way out. Leave them their food."

The actions of the people transporting drugs can be understood as a desperate attempt to secure food and water in the desert after having been chased for days. Ultimately, they left the cave emptyhanded; Cynthia's group did not see them again. The encounter was also another indicator of how, rather than working together, smugglers and drug traffickers merely use the same routes. They frequently face similar challenges and threats to survival, but this is not an indication of their markets merging.

Rosa also had an encounter with *narcos* during one of her crossings. Her words again reflect how defenseless people traversing the desert clandestinely can be, regardless of who they are:

> Interviewer: So you did get to see the *narcos*.
>
> Rosa: From quite up close! Too close. Too much. Some … there are some who are like the [smuggling] guides. They are good people. That one time when we were hiding, they were too; they come to you; if they have food they share it, and if not, they ask that you share and you do. All the food we had left was a tiny can of tuna. One of those really little ones. And they had water. Well, guess what: all of us ate from that can, and we shared the water. That was how we survived.

Analysis: Crowded Illicit Marketspace on the Border

Our field data do not support the claim that migrant smuggling and drug trafficking have converged into a single market. Such a hypothesis fails to reflect the rich range of interactions that take place among people—whether migrants, drug traffickers, or smugglers—once they have entered the United States. Most importantly, such a hypothesis makes assumptions about the structure of both practices as monolithically organized and inherently prone to violence.

The data presented here confirm that on the U.S.-Mexico border, migrant smugglers and drug traffickers—most often, ordinary, working-class people operating independently, with no criminal background and no particular affiliation—do engage in transactional interactions of varying range, but do so mainly as a result of enforcement policies that have forced them into the most inhospitable and remote corridors of the border where their personal safety is often compromised. As a result, what we most often identified was a landscape where negotiation, trade, and partnerships—even if among unequal parties—often take place among actors who share the common goal of crossing the border undetected in order to survive; they share limited structural similarities or common goals beyond that.

Interactions between drug traffickers and migrant smugglers vary in range and nature, yet they are not solely exploitative or victimizing. While we do not suggest that no migrant has ever been the victim of these actors, our data serve as examples of the ways in which migrants and those who facilitate their journeys interact with other criminalized actors to better navigate the spaces where they coincide, and in so doing improve their chances of completing their journeys safely. This finding is of critical importance, as it suggests that despite the precarious conditions they face, migrants in the U.S. migration corridor and elsewhere can devise, negotiate, and mobilize strategies and mechanisms to improve their condition as irregular migrants in transit. As shown in our data, we also acknowledge that some migrants do find themselves in more vulnerable positions than others, and that they are often at a disadvantage in relation to other actors along the trail. Yet by looking into the largely ignored cases when smuggling journeys are completed successfully and relatively uneventfully, as we did here, we found that coercion or intimidation were not as frequent or widespread as previously thought, and there were constant acts of care and solidarity taking place along the migrant trail. Here again, we do not intend to minimize the abuses experienced by migrants, but argue that embedded in their precarity, migrants consistently deploy individual and collective strategies to increase the protection of life, albeit with varying results.[7]

Our data also show that migrants were able to decline, along some corridors and in some instances, collaborations with criminal actors with no repercussion. Among our respondents, for example, no one reported having faced retaliation as a result of his or her unwillingness to work or travel with drug traffickers. Many, however, did complain about the treatment that they received during their migration at the hands of their smuggling facilitators.

This was however not an option that all could take, which further demonstrates the need to deconstruct the dynamics of clandestine journeys. Our respondents' testimonies, and those collected by other researchers along the U.S.-Mexico migratory trail, suggest that not all migrants' experiences can be discreetly categorized. Yet it is precisely this diverse range of experiences along different migratory corridors that may hold the clue to identify strategies of security from below that can reduce risks associated with clandestine migration.

Research has shown that it is not uncommon for men's and women's involvement in the migrant smuggling and drug trafficking markets to be rooted in their initial experiences as irregular migrants (see Achilli, this volume; Ayalew, this volume). While in some cases these experiences stay at the level of occasional supplemental income-generating opportunities (see Sanchez 2016, 80), there are also worrisome examples of how they may open paths to the professionalization of violence targeting migrants (see Slack and Whiteford 2011). Neither one, however, can or should be solely explained under criminological frameworks, and even less so under the often myopic lens of transnational crime, in which discourses often favor the criminalization of the practices of the poor—including migrants—while allowing for the establishment of enduring legacies of injustice. The analysis of the data solidifies the notion articulated by many others that the feared traffickers of migrants and drugs mobilized in state narratives of crime and crime control are most often ordinary citizens—including migrants themselves—whose choices and decision-making processes are far from driven by nefarious motives alone (see Zhang 2008; Chu 2010).

It is important to remember that it is in the context of their heightened vulnerability that people make decisions to enter into specific kinds of partnerships along their migration journeys, decisions that lead to varying levels of criminal involvement. Most often, these decisions are made with the goal of reducing the risks associated with irregular journeys and, in so doing, improving the possibility of crossing the border successfully. In the words of migrants, such partnerships are more a response to a logic of survival than to criminal motivations, even, and perhaps particularly, when violence is involved. These partnerships, however, do not constitute evidence of market convergence, but instead point to collective and individual survival strategies deployed to reduce risk.

The testimonies discussed in this article are only a sample of experiences amid a wide range of interactions that emerge among those who transit and traffic on the border and, as such, should be interpreted with caution. They do suggest that the relationship between human smuggling and criminal/ized actors exists, but is often not necessarily structural or even criminal in nature. Instead, our analysis of the interactions—what Vogt refers to as "micro-level interpersonal dynamics" (2016, 368)—suggests that they are rooted in a complex system where reciprocity, care, and solidarity take place alongside the potential for violence.

Criminologically, the data amount to contacts among individuals who independently work and navigate the space of the border, and who most often do not claim or recognize a particular membership or association. In other words, they indicate that membership to specific groups is blurry if not altogether nonexistent. Collaboration among groups—of migrants, coyotes, or narcos—is fluid, adaptable, and organized in different ways, some better orchestrated than others. At the same time, the relationships that allow for human smuggling occur alongside drug trafficking. Our data indicate that all actors are aware that they share the same geographic landscape and that unwritten rules, often grounded in fear, give priority to drug trafficking groups along specific routes. The data also reveal that these implicit arrangements often generate disputes and disagreements among migrant smugglers and their clients, the latter often opting to find alternative means of crossing—a decision that may lead to interactions or collusions with members of other illicit groups, including drug traffickers.

In all our cases, it appears that human smugglers and drug traffickers are part of the growing groups of ordinary people who, around the world, have opted to enter illicit markets that pose scant membership restrictions amid the ever-decreasing prospects of late modernity. The stories of human traders and narco-traffickers on the loose galvanize support among the public for greater enforcement, but draconian immigration laws and the building of "big, beautiful, border walls" (Trump 2015) far from address or even shed light on the complexity of the experiences of those who seek their futures along clandestine paths. In sum, our data suggest that all actors on the migrant trail seek not only to avoid detection from law enforcement but also to survive.

Conclusion

The interactions between human smuggling facilitators and members of other criminal/ized groups along the U.S.-Mexico border (often referred to collectively as *La Mafia*) are common elements of a little-understood but thriving economic ecosystem and tend to vary greatly in nature. The relationships that emerge among people of the border (and specifically those who reside in communities along the drug trafficking and migrant smuggling routes) are often monolithically referred to as criminal, but our data suggest that this characterization is narrow and simplistic. We find that most interactions lack criminal intention. The nature of the U.S.-Mexico border as a liminal, marginal/ized space makes it hard to establish a line where the licit economy ends and the illicit starts. Both are inextricably connected in a region with limited employment options where even "law-abiding" activities are often intertwined with the "illicit" enterprise of border crossings and drug trafficking.

The emphasis on the part of law enforcement, policy-makers, and scholars to define markets such as human smuggling and drug trafficking as controlled by or organized in networks has often obscured the variety of interactions among the people who share the migrant trail, by applying blanket terms or designations that simplify and narrowly define community-grounded practices and, by extension, the people who participate in them. The testimonies of those who cross the border extralegally point to a misunderstanding of human smuggling along the U.S.-Mexico border as being under the control of DTOs. Beyond the collection of land tax or *piso*, the "connection" between drug trafficking and human smuggling is often blurry. What is clear is that participants in both markets acknowledge their mutual existence, and have over time devised arrangements for coexistence. Interactions between drug trafficking and human smuggling groups are hardly the result of networks coming together. Instead, they reveal the growing number of people from the margins striving to survive.

Notes

1. Refer to the annual reports from Mexico's National Human Rights Commission, WOLA, Amnesty International, and the United Nations High Commissioner for Refugees (UNHCR).

2. While there are no official numbers on the people who are smuggled along the U.S.-Mexico border each year, some numbers have been used as proxies. It is, for example, estimated that about 200,000 people travel through Mexico each year in an attempt to reach the United States (IOM COLEF 2016). U.S. Immigration and Custom Enforcement reported 303,916 people had been apprehended along ports of entry along the southwest border (WOLA 2017).

3. To mind come the statement of then–Arizona governor Jane Hull that the finding of "headless bodies" in the desert—a claim denied by local law enforcement—pointed to the presence of Mexican DTOs and the unfortunate remarks of then-Sheriff Babeau, who attributed it to Mexican migrant smugglers.

4. All names used in this article are pseudonyms.

5. *Coyote* is the colloquial term used in reference to smuggling facilitators on the U.S.-Mexico border. In this article, we opt for the terms *smuggling facilitators* or *smugglers* as they are more inclusive of the actors who participate in the market and who do not define their activities as those of a coyote, a term that may carry derogatory connotations.

6. Ajo Arizona is a community on the U.S. side of the border where organic farms abound. Elsa's testimony is indicative of the experiences of migrants who having crossed the U.S. border, manage to avoid detection and gain employment in small, local farms.

7. See the excellent analyses of Slack and Whiteford (2011) and Izcara Palacios (2015) of poststructural violence, documenting the involvement of migrants in the victimization of other migrants.

References

Burnett, John. 4 December 2011. Migrants say they are unwilling mules for cartels. *Around the Nation*. National Public Radio. Available from http://www.npr.org.

Carrera, Sergio, and Elspeth Guild. 2016. *Irregular migration, trafficking and smuggling of human beings: Policy dilemmas in the EU*. Brussels: Centre for European Policy Studies.

Casillas, Rodolfo. 2010. Masacre de transmigrantes. Reflexiones e interrogantes sobre el asesinato de 72 migrantes. *Foreign Affairs Latin America* 10 (4): 52–59.

Chu, Julie. 2010. *Cosmologies of credit: Transnational mobility and the politics of destination in China*. Durham, NC: Duke University Press.

Derechos Humanos Integrales en Acción (DHIA) 2017. *Neither criminals nor illegals: Children and adolescents in the smuggling market on the U.S. Mexico border*. Ciudad Juarez, Chihuahua: DHIA.

Donnelly, Robert, and Jacqueline Hagan. 2014. The dangerous journey: Migrant smuggling from Mexico and Central America, Asia, and the Caribbean. In *Hidden lives and human rights in the United States: Understanding the controversies and tragedies of undocumented immigration*, ed. Lois A. Lorentzen, 71–106. Hartford, CT: Praeger

Europol-Interpol. 2016. *Migrant smuggling networks: Joint Europol-Interpol report*. Executive Summary. Brussels: Europol-Interpol. Available from https://www.europol. europa.eu.

Global Initiative against Transnational Organized Crime and Norwegian Center for Global Analysis (RHIPTO). 2015. *Libya: A growing hub for criminal economies and terrorist financing in the trans-Sahara*. Policy Brief. Geneva, Switzerland: Global Initiative. Available from http://globalinitiative.net/wp-content/uploads/2017/02/2015-1.pdf.

Hagan, Jacqueline. 2008. *Migration miracle: Faith, hope and meaning on the undocumented journey*. Cambridge, MA: Harvard University Press.

International Organization for Migration (IOM). 2017. *Missing migrants project*. Berlin, Germany: GMDAC. Available from https://missingmigrants.iom.int/.

International Organization for Migration-Colegio de la Frontera Norte (IOM COLEF). 2016. *Migrantes en Mexico: Vulnerabilidad y Riesgos*. Ginebra, Switzerland: IOM.

Izcara Palacios, Simon P. 2015. Violencia post-estructural: migrantes centroamericanos y cárteles de la droga en México. *Revista de Estudios Sociales* 56:12–25.

Koslowski, Rey. 2011. Economic globalization, human smuggling and global governance. In *Global human smuggling: Comparative perspectives*, eds. David Kyle, David and Rey Koslowski, 60–86. Baltimore, MD: Johns Hopkins University Press.

Leutert, Stephanie. 14 July 2017. When drug trafficking is your only option. *Foreign Policy*. Available from http://foreignpolicy.com.

Martínez, Daniel, Guillermo Cantor, and Walter Ewing. 2014. *No action taken: Lack of accountability in responding to complaints of abuse*. Special Report. Washington, DC: American Immigration Council.

Martinez, Daniel, and Jeremy Slack. 2013. What part of "illegal" don't you understand? The social consequences of criminalizing unauthorized Mexican migrants in the United States. *Social and Legal Studies* 22 (4): 1–17.

Mendez, Ernesto, and Daniel Sanchez Dorame. 7 July 2016. Ninos polleros en la frontera trasiegan droga y burlan balaceras. *Excelsior*. Available from http://www.excelsior.com.mx/nacional/2016/06/07/1097283.

Naim, Moises. 2010. *Illicit: How smugglers, traffickers and copycats are hijacking the global economy*. New York, NY: Random House.

O'Leary, Anna Ochoa. 2016 Con El Peso Peso En La Frente: A gendered look at the human and economic costs of migration on the U.S.-Mexico border. In *Migrant deaths in the Arizona Desert: La Vida No Vale Nada*, eds. Raquel Rubio-Goldsmith Celestino Fernández, Jessie K. Finch, and Araceli Masterson-Algar, 69–96. Tucson, AZ: University of Arizona Press.

Olson, Eric. 2016. *Migrant smuggling and trafficking at the Rio Grande Valley*. Washington, DC: Latin American Program at the Wilson Center. Available from https://www.wilsoncenter.org/article/migrant-smuggling-and-trafficking-the-rio-grande- valley.

Palmer, Wayne, and Antje Missbach. 2017. Trafficking within migrant smuggling operations: Underaged transporters as "victims" or "perpetrators"? *Asian and Pacific Migration Journal* 26 (3): 287–307.

Sanchez, Gabriella. 2016. *Human smuggling and border crossings*. London: Routledge.

Sanchez, Gabriella. 2018. Portrait of a human smuggler: Race, class and gender among facilitators of irregular migration on the U.S.-Mexico border. In *Race, criminal justice and migration control: Enforcing the boundaries of belonging*, eds. M. Bosworth, A. Parmar, and Y. Vazquez, 29–42. London: Oxford University Press.

Schaefer, Richard, and Caroline Gonzalez. 2016. Human trafficking through Mexico and the southwest border: Accounts from Hidalgo and Cochise counties. In *Borderline slavery: Mexico, United States, and the human trade*, eds. Susan Tiano and Moira Murphy-Aguilar, 173–96. New York, NY: Routledge.

Servin, Argentina, Kimberly Brouwer, Leah Gordon, Teresita Rocha-Jimenez, Hugo Staines, Ricardo Vera-Monroy, Steffanie Strathdee, and Jay Silverman. 2015. Vulnerability factors and pathways leading to underage entry into sex work in two Mexican-US border cities. *Journal of Applied Research on Children* 6 (1): 1–17.

Shelley, Louise. 2014. *Human smuggling and trafficking into Europe: A comparative perspective*. Washington, DC: Migration Policy Institute.

Simmons, William, Cecilia Menjivar, and Michelle Tellez. 2015. Violence and vulnerability of female migrants in drop houses in Arizona: The predictable outcome of a chain reaction of violence. *Violence against Women* 21 (5): 551–70.

Slack, Jeremy. 2015. Captive bodies: Migrant kidnapping and deportation in Mexico. *Area* 48 (3): 271–77.

Slack, Jeremy, and Howard Campbell. 2016. On narco-coyotaje: Illicit regimes and their impacts on the US–Mexico border. *Antipode* 48 (5): 1380–99.

Slack, Jeremy, and Scott Whiteford. 2011. Violence and migration on the Arizona-Sonora border. *Human Organization* 70 (1): 11–21.

Spener, David. 2009. *Clandestine crossings: Migrants and coyotes on the Texas-Mexico border*. Ithaca, NY: Cornell University Press.

Storen Weden, Axel. 24 January 2016. Deadly human trafficking business on the U.S.-Mexico border. *Al Jazeera*. Available from http://www.aljazeera.com.

Trump, Donald. 18 August 2015. Trump on immigration plan: "Start by building a big, beautiful, powerful wall." *Fox News Insider*. Available from https://www.youtube.com/watch?v=YM7mPl20GhQ.

United Nations Office on Drugs and Crime (UNODC). 2017. *The concept of financial or other material benefit in the smuggling of migrants protocol*. Vienna, Austria: United Nations Office on Drugs and Crime.

U.S. Border Patrol. 2016. U.S. Border Patrol fiscal year southwest border sector deaths (FY 1998 - FY 2016). Available from https://www.cbp.gov/newsroom/media-resources/stats (accessed 4 July 2017).

Vogt, Wendy. 2016. Stuck in the middle with you: The intimate labors of mobility and smuggling along Mexico's migrant route. *Geopolitics* 21 (2): 366–86.

Walt, Vivienne. 13 May 2015. ISIS makes a fortune from smuggling migrant says report. *Time Magazine*. Available from http://time.com/3857121/isis-smuggling/.

Washington Office for Latin America. 2017. *WOLA's response to February CBP southwest border migration numbers*. Washington DC: Washington Office for Latin America. Available from https://www.wola .org.

Zaitseva, Lyudmila, and Friedrich Steinhäusler. 2014. *Nuclear trafficking issues in the Black Sea region*. Non-Proliferation Papers no. 39. Geneva, Switzerland: Non-Proliferation Consortium.

Zhang, Sheldon X. 2007. *Smuggling and trafficking in human beings: All roads lead to America*. Westport, CT: Praeger/Greenwood.

Zhang, Sheldon X. 2008. *Chinese human smuggling organizations: Families, social networks and cultural imperatives*. Stanford, CA: Stanford University Press.

What Makes a Good Human Smuggler? The Differences between Satisfaction with and Recommendation of Coyotes on the U.S.-Mexico Border

By
JEREMY SLACK
and
DANIEL E. MARTÍNEZ

This article draws on a unique dataset of more than eleven hundred postdeportation surveys to examine migrants' experiences with coyotes (human smugglers) along the U.S.-Mexico border. Our focus is on migrants' satisfaction with the services provided by their most recent smuggler and whether they would be willing to put family or friends in contact with that person. We find a distinct difference between people's expectations for their own migratory experience compared to what they would be willing to subject loved ones to. Expectations of comfort and safety are decidedly low for oneself; but for loved ones, a more expressive, qualitative assessment shapes their willingness to recommend a coyote: qualities such as trustworthiness, honesty, comportment, and treatment come to the fore. News coverage focusing on the deaths of smuggled migrants often portrays coyotes as nefarious and exploitative, but the migrant-smuggler relationship is much more complex than suggested by these media accounts. We provide empirical insight into the factors associated with successful, satisfactory, and safe relationships between migrants and their guides.

Keywords: U.S.-Mexico border; human smuggling; unauthorized migration; clandestine migration; border crossing; coyotes; *coyotaje*

The social scientific study of informal economies and illicit service providers is a complex and challenging task. This is the case not only because the very nature of these activities is intended to prevent them from being observed,

Jeremy Slack is an assistant professor of geography in the Department of Sociology and Anthropology at the University of Texas, El Paso. His research interests include state theory, illegal and illicit activity, the U.S.-Mexico border, drug trafficking, violence, participatory/activist-oriented research methodology, and public scholarship.

Daniel E. Martínez is an assistant professor in the School of Sociology at the University of Arizona. His research interests include unauthorized migration, migrant deaths, and the criminalization of immigration.

Correspondence: jmslack@utep.edu

DOI: 10.1177/0002716217750562

measured, and analyzed, but also because the norms, treatment, and acceptable practices vary widely. Human smuggling along the U.S.-Mexico border is just one example of such activities. In this article we examine the smuggler-migrant relationship by drawing on more than eleven hundred surveys with recent deportees in six different Mexican cities. Specifically, we identify the factors associated with undocumented Mexican migrants' self-reported satisfaction with the services they received from their guides, known colloquially as *coyotes*.[1] This provides greater insight into the ways in which consumers of illegal services conceptualize the positive and negative qualities of the interactions, exchanges, and relationships with their service providers. Furthermore, we examine the disjuncture between "satisfaction" with one's coyote and their "willingness to recommend" them to a family member or friend. While 75 percent of deportees who used a coyote reported being satisfied with the services, only 45 percent indicated that they would recommend them to a loved one. What accounts for this difference? Why are people generally satisfied with their guides but unwilling to subject their family and friends to the same treatment and experiences?

These questions provide the first empirical test of one particular aspect of the growing literature on Mexican coyotes, which asserts that word-of-mouth referrals lead to better treatment, and that smugglers are essentially good-faith actors providing a service (Spener 2009; Sanchez 2014; Izcara Palacios 2014, 2012a, 2012b, 2012c). This contrasts with law enforcement narratives that often demonize coyotes for migrant deaths in the desert and cases of kidnapping and rape (see Spener 2009).

We aim to contribute to the creation of a more fully formed understanding of smugglers that neither demonizes nor romanticizes them. Doing so will help scholars to better understand some of the consequences of increased border enforcement by exploring how and why relationships between migrants and their guides may break down, leading to violence and dangerous situations. With controversies surrounding unauthorized immigration, including fears of smugglers as abusive victimizers as well as the deaths of migrants while being smuggled into the United States, our findings offer a new understanding of the factors contributing to successful, satisfactory, and safe relationships between migrants and smugglers. This article also provides key insights into the policies that cause these relationships to deteriorate and, in turn, increase the danger for migrants.

Our unique postdeportation survey offers insight on a broad range of situations and experiences that occur between smuggled migrants and their guides. For instance, we have documented forty-two instances of people being held captive by their coyotes,[2] which often involved coyotes charging exorbitant fees, much higher than the ones initially agreed upon (Slack 2015). We were also informed of several eyewitness accounts of rape or sexual assault committed by coyotes. However, we also have documented cases of migrants escaping from their guides and refusing to pay. We heard stories of violence committed against coyotes, including one murder where the migrants decapitated their coyote with a machete. This is obviously an extreme example, but it shows that neither coyotes nor smuggled migrants lack the capacity to commit violence or act outside of the normal parameters of the smuggling relationship.

In the following section, we discuss our theoretical approach to unpacking the migrant-smuggler relationship. We ask how, if at all, traditional modes of reciprocity and trust operate within the illegal milieu. We proceed with an overview of our data, sample, and research methodology before moving on to our findings, which identify the factors associated with satisfaction with one's coyote or guide. We then compare and contrast migrants' "satisfaction" with their coyotes with their "willingness to recommend" their guide to family or friends. We find that while satisfaction is based on instrumental outcomes or factors (e.g., "success"), a recommendation is far more complicated and subjective, often tied to expressive or affective factors or experiences. We conclude by discussing future needs for research and by addressing the limitations of our data.

Theoretical Orientation

There is a need for a robust theoretical framework that accounts for interactions that take place outside of a state's regulatory control. Without the legal apparatus of the state, violence can easily become the main leveling mechanism (Gibler 2011; Boyce, Banister, and Slack 2015). This seems to be less true (at least in terms of murder) in less violent contexts, as evidenced by Colombian drug dealers in the Netherlands (Zaitch 2002). However, within highly unequal power relations, one party tends to control the violence. While there are certainly variations and exceptions (for example, when coyotes are isolated in the desert with a group of twenty or more migrants), smuggled people are less likely to use force to ensure that the deal they struck is kept. Adapting sociological understandings of trust and cooperation to the illegal economy are essential for developing a better understanding of what leads to a successful transaction between an undocumented migrant and his or her smuggler.

The coyote-migrant relationship is unique when compared to other cases of illegal transactions because people seldom entrust their physical safety to a clandestine actor. The coyote is responsible not only for taking migrants to their final destination but also ensuring that they survive the journey. The process of choosing a coyote therefore requires a great deal of trust given the well-known life-and-death nature of the journey. This type of trust prioritizes the life-and-death nature of migration, over issues of treatment, courtesy, respect, and other factors that we normally would consider essential to customer satisfaction. When compared to Damien Zaitch's (2002) work on trust among Colombian drug dealers, trust, or, more frequently, distrust, is a commodity used for safety purposes. Not allowing people access to information about oneself is an important part of those clandestine relationships. However, the migrant-coyote relationship is distinct.

In this article, we do not analyze how migrants evaluate their guides before the journey but, rather, examine how they characterize this relationship after the fact, contrasting this with the prospect of a loved one placing her or his trust in that same guide. We find that there is a notable disjuncture between self-reported satisfaction with a guide and the willingness to subject a loved one to this treatment. We hypothesize that this stems from the desperation that drives undocumented migration, which results in a utilitarian assessment of one's own experience, as opposed to deeper concerns for the treatment, well-being, and safety that shape people's willingness to recommend their guide to loved ones.

To test this hypothesis, we must first have an operational conception of *trust*. We draw from Hardin's (1991, 2001, 2002) discussion of "encapsulated interest" to expand upon how trust occurs outside of the regulatory mechanisms of the state. This conceptualization of trust is essentially contractual, defined as actor *A* entrusting *B* to effectively execute action *X* and not *Y*. In this case, the coyote must facilitate a successful crossing and not abandon, kidnap, extort, or expose the migrant to unnecessary risk. As Cook, Hardin, and Levi (2005) note, "We suppose you are competent to perform what we trust you to do and that we suppose your reason for doing so is not merely your immediate interest but also your concern with our interests and well-being" (p. 7). This trust requires some sort of consequence for poor performance. Other scholars have asserted that failing to recommend a guide would harm the guide's business, and therefore it is in the coyote's interest to perform well (Spener 2009; Sanchez 2014). The importance of word-of-mouth business relates to the need for some sort of built-in social consequence for failing to deliver on the bargain. Studies of criminal organizations such as the mafia have found that familial ties are prevalent within organized crime groups because such ties reinforce trust by increasing the social consequences for betrayal (Campana and Varese 2013; Zaitch 2005, 2002). However, it is impossible to have family ties that could ensure trust between the hundreds of thousands of migrants who cross the U.S.-Mexico border with coyotes each year. The important thing to note in both these scenarios is the need for some sort of social mechanism that takes the place of state regulations.

Scholars have noted that society has largely attempted to lessen the need for trust on a large scale. State regulation and coordination, third-party enforcers, contracts, and legal stipulations all serve to decrease the importance of trust, or trustworthiness in our day-to-day interactions (Cook, Hardin, and Levi 2005). We are generally assured that a third party will step in to rectify the situation, should a problem develop. This, however, does not hold true for the clandestine world. Outside of the purview of state regulation there are no, or at the least, a very limited version, of third-party enforcers. As Randall Collins asserts, "we should see individuals as transient fluxes charged up by situations" (2014, 6). Interpersonal relations are situational, and therefore we must start with the social field, rather than the person involved (Collins 2014). We should approach questions of interaction based on the situation in which people are interacting, and how people decide to classify that interaction, in this case, the migrant-coyote relationship. There are many nuances to the types of guides and settings in which people interact with their guides, ranging from someone in their hometown, to an unknown stranger in the plaza or running a convenience store as a cover business. From the encapsulated interest perspective, we have to assume that (1) there is some sort of ongoing relationship between the two, and (2) that there are some sort of mutual benefits at work. For the ongoing relationship stipulation to be true, migrants must assume that they may try to cross the border multiple times, and the coyote also assumes that the migrant or other acquaintances will employ their services to cross with them in the future. However, this formation does not apply to everyone. Many migrants try to learn the trail so that they can travel alone in the future. Others have no intention of ever returning to Mexico. Further, some coyotes are only tangentially involved in smuggling, spending the majority of their time involved with other economic activities (Izcara Palacios 2014). Therefore, the lack in continuity of relationships between coyotes and migrants means that it is difficult to ensure that encapsulated interests balance cooperation and trust. This is especially true given our finding that the bar for recommending a coyote appears to be set much higher than for reporting satisfaction with their services.

Moreover, "unequal power may make it nearly impossible for the more powerful to convince the less powerful of their credibility of their trustworthiness" (Cook, Hardin, and Levi 2005, 4). This highlights how diverging interests between smuggler and migrant create many of the potential problems, whereupon a guide may abandon the migrant or attempt to extort payment without delivering them to their destination. Cook and colleagues state that "a violation of trust is especially likely to happen when there is a systematic conflict of interest between us, as when I could profit at your expense while seeming to act as your agent" (2005, 5). Demanding early payment, guiding migrants by phone, and deceiving people to believe that they have crossed into the United States despite still being in Mexico are possible scenarios in which coyotes can profit without the risk involved in undocumented migration. Placing these interactions outside of the regulatory control of the state, with essentially no third-party enforcers, further exacerbates these divergences in interests. To understand when these interests diverge we briefly discuss the literature on human smugglers and *coyotaje*, and the different processes by which people are smuggled, before proceeding to our research methodology and discussion.

Literature Review

Baird and van Liempt (2015) outline the different approaches to understanding human smuggling. Is it a business? Should it be understood in purely criminal terms or as a network analysis? Or is human smuggling part of a larger human rights discussion? While these debates will likely continue, this article provides a new methodology to examine how clients of human smugglers perceive their relationship with the smuggler. While scholars have speculated that smugglers treat migrants well in an attempt to garner repeat business and referrals (Spener 2009; Sanchez 2014), this is a challenge to test. Lopez-Castro's (1998) early study on coyotes indirectly addressed this question by creating a unique typology of guides based on in-depth interviews with coyotes in northeastern Mexico. Lopez-Castro identified at least three different types of guides: "local-interior" coyotes, who largely cross friends and family members from their communities of origin; "local and border" coyotes, who are from the same place in the interior of Mexico as their clientele, but live and work at the border; and "border business" coyotes, who are full-time clandestine entrepreneurs and seldom personally know their clients (Lopez-Castro 1998, 967–68). Qualitative work by Spener (2009) and Sanchez (2014) found greater reliance on local-interior coyotes among their respondents, which helps to bolster the argument that word-of-mouth referrals, and the need to maintain a good reputation in small, rural towns, are of the utmost importance.

However, our survey research has demonstrated an increasing shift in the reliance on "border business" coyotes over "interior coyotes" (broadly conceived) since at least the mid-2000s (Martínez 2016). For instance, 45 percent of unauthorized Mexican migrants used border business coyotes on their most recent border crossing attempt compared to 30 percent who used someone from the interior (Martínez 2016). This, along with the rise in tolls being charged for *derecho de piso*, "right to use an area" (Izcara Palacios 2014), suggests that there are some changes happening that may have been affecting current migration, such as a monopolization of migrant smuggling and the impact of other illicit businesses such as drug smuggling on the use of clandestine spaces along the border (Slack and Campbell 2016). These notable changes have further complicated the narrative surrounding the migrant-coyote relationship.

The difference between these interpretations may be a result of variations in methodologies, geographic region, or the period in which each study was conducted, but it nonetheless causes us to question which factors improve the migrant/coyote experience. There are numerous factors outside the control of the coyote, and preconceived notions people have about the crossing experience can also alter people's evaluations of their guides. What is considered acceptable or unacceptable treatment? How long and how far and how hard must people walk in the harsh desert climate, before it is considered mistreatment? When do words of encouragement become insults or harsh admonitions? How much food or freedom is deemed acceptable when people wait in a safe house upon arrival to the United States?

These questions open an obvious, yet sometimes overlooked, reality of clandestine migration: it is not a pleasant experience. It is born out of necessity (see Rodríguez 1996). People expect to undergo some level of hardship. While the level of hardship people expect and are prepared for most likely varies by age, gender, and previous experiences, the primary concern is survival. With the changes to immigration enforcement on the U.S.-Mexico border in the mid-1990s, the number of fatalities increased exponentially (Eschbach et al. 1999; Cornelius 2001; Nevins and Aizeki 2008). The dangers of the desert are well known among potential migrants, and scholars have pointed out that knowing someone who has died actually increases the likelihood that a person will attempt a border crossing (Cornelius and Lewis 2007). The fear of being abandoned, of having a guide who does not know the way, or knowing how to find additional food and water along the trail are of the utmost importance for success, as well as survival. Despite a decrease in undocumented migration border-wide, the rate of death has remained high, suggesting that migration has become more dangerous and deadly since increased border enforcement in the 1990s and 2000s (Martínez et al. 2014; Slack et al. 2016).

Moreover, migrants constantly battle with the challenge of being deceived or extorted. Instances of phone calls extorting family members, either by lying about a kidnapping or claiming to have successfully crossed the border, are common (Slack 2015) and demonstrate that many would-be guides prefer to extort money without providing the service of a clandestine border crossing. For guides, not only is the border crossing dangerous, difficult, and unpleasant, but efforts from law enforcement on both sides of the border have attempted to clamp down on them, leading to harsher sentences. The most notable effort is the Operation against Smugglers. Initiative on Safety and Security (OASISS) that uses confessions extracted by law enforcement in the United States to incarcerate alleged smugglers once they are deported to Mexico (U.S. Government Accountability Office [GAO] 2013). This takes advantage of the uneven legal geography of the two countries whereupon, in Mexico, a police report known as a "demanda" is sufficient evidence to incarcerate an individual, often for years. Once migrants have formally accused their guides, they are deported directly to the Procurador General de la República (PGR; Federal Prosecutor's Office) to sign the statement of admission, at which point the accused is also deported and sent straight to prison in Mexico.

OASISS stretches the limits of acceptable international cooperation between law enforcement and marks a new and extreme form of punishment. Because prosecuting coyotes has been challenging and has led to few arrests (Spener 2009), taking advantage of Mexico's legal system would be useful from the United States' perspective. However, this also serves to drive a wedge between migrants and their guides. The potential for someone to accuse a guide, while always a threat, must be met with either more convincing threats of violence upon removal, or preemptive accusations of their own, fingering one of their clients as the true guide. Moreover, according to our research, the fear of incarceration also leads many coyotes to preemptively abandon their clients in the desert. Migrants frequently complain about being left in the desert when authorities approach. Trust, therefore, has to work both ways, as guides are fearful of being accused by migrants and sentenced to jail in the United States or Mexico.

This raises one of the most important questions within the smuggling literature. Are the people who extort migrants or abandon them after getting money from family members actually coyotes; in other words, do they sometimes extort and other times comply with the full terms of the agreed-upon service? Scholars such as David Spener, Gabriella Sanchez, and Simón Izcara Palacios have asserted that *coyotaje* only involves the legitimate act of facilitating a border crossing (Spener 2009; Sanchez 2014; Izcara Palacios 2012a, 2012b, 2012c). Sanchez states that even *enganchadores*, people who recruit migrants, are also good-faith actors (2014). However, these claims are difficult, if not impossible, to verify.

While the rise of kidnapping on the border has attracted new types of organized crime, focused explicitly on kidnapping a large number of relatively poor people (Izcara Palacios 2014; Slack 2015), it is unclear how this relates to human smugglers. Izcara Palacios (2014) has discussed how organized crime groups have attempted to recruit coyotes, indicating that coyotes know which migrants have money and would therefore be good targets for extortion. It is difficult to ascertain whether all coyotes only engage in facilitating a crossing, or if, depending on the situation, they take advantage of a particularly vulnerable, wealthy, careless, or naïve migrant. Simply relying on interviews with coyotes leads to the same authenticity trap, whereupon a highly persecuted group of people seeks to engage in boundary policing, defining what is and is not considered part of their profession.

On the other side of the methodological spectrum, interviews with migrants can shed light on the vast array of experiences associated with crossing the border but are unable to tie those experiences to a specific smuggler. The fact that coyotes are a heterogeneous group of people behaving in a variety of ways is not surprising, but it does raise challenges that must be addressed through careful research design. For example, our quantitative data explore the most recent interaction between a migrant and their guide. This includes people who successfully arrived at their destination (37 percent), only to be deported later, as well as those who were apprehended during a failed crossing attempt. This allows us to evaluate the factors that influenced migrants' perceptions of their guides, but it does not give us an understanding of the guides' perspectives, or a background on the intentions, level of experience, or sophistication of the guides migrants chose (i.e., problems may be caused by incompetence rather than maliciousness). Therefore, we hope to answer what influences migrants' perceptions of a successful guide-migrant relationship, and why a migrant may or may not recommend their guide to others, particularly loved ones.

Data and Sample

We examine migrants' satisfaction with their coyotes and their willingness to recommend them to a family member or friend by drawing on a subsample of the second wave of the Migrant Border Crossing Study (MBCS). The subsample consists of recent border-crossers (i.e., people who most recently crossed the border within five years of being surveyed) and who relied on the services of a coyote to facilitate their most recent border crossing attempt ($N = 655$).

To the best of our knowledge, the second wave of the MBCS is the first quantitative study of Mexican border-crossers to ask respondents questions pertaining to the satisfaction with their coyotes as well as their willingness to recommend them to others. Specifically, we ask: (1) "Were you satisfied with the services of your coyote?" and (2) "Would you be willing to recommend your coyote to family members or friends?"

The MBCS is an unprecedented cross-sectional survey of Mexican migrants who attempted an unauthorized border crossing, were apprehended by any U.S. authority (either while crossing the border or once at their destination in the U.S. interior), and ultimately returned to Mexico. Interviews were completed with migrants in person at ports of entry and in migrant shelters immediately following respondents' most recent deportation experience. We selected shelters that work directly with the Mexican government (although none were government-operated)

FIGURE 1
Research Site

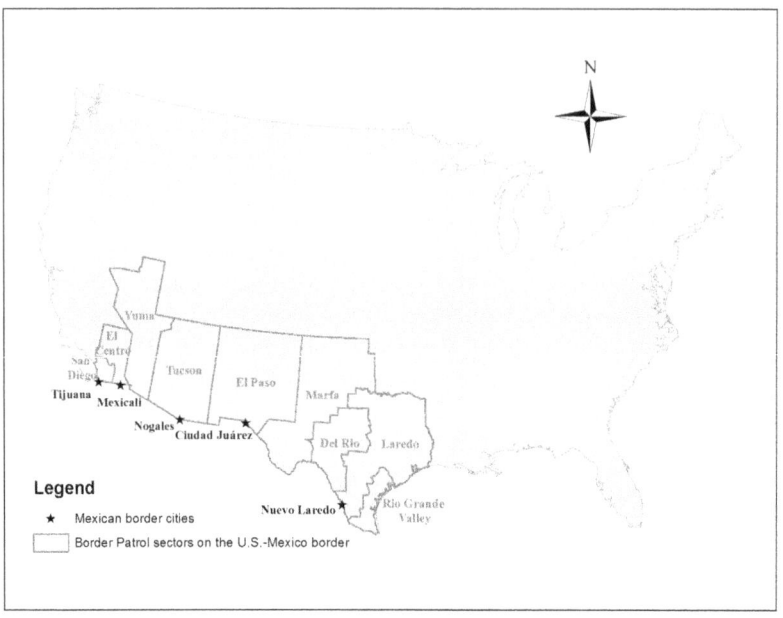

SOURCE: Rolando Díaz Caravantes, El Colegio de Sonora.

because Mexican authorities directly transport migrants to these shelters from ports of entry upon repatriation, thus providing the most representative sample. The MBCS limits its sample frame to individuals 18 years of age or older, who had not previously been interviewed for the study, who crossed the U.S.-Mexico border post–September 11, 2001, and who had been repatriated to Mexico within one month of the interview. Potential study participants were randomly selected using a spatial sampling technique, screened for eligibility, and then invited to participate if they met the eligibility requirements. These criteria were established to allow for reasonable comparison between cases within a specific timeframe, most notably during an era of increased border and immigration enforcement. Interviews lasted about 45 minutes and were completed in Spanish by the authors, graduate students, and professional interviewers. The response rate for the survey was approximately 94 percent.

The surveys were completed in Tijuana and Mexicali, Baja California; Nogales, Sonora; Ciudad Juárez, Chihuahua; Nuevo Laredo, Tamaulipas; and Mexico City (see Figure 1) between 2010 and 2012, with the overwhelming majority (90 percent) of interviews being completed in 2011. All respondents surveyed in Mexico City had participated in the Mexican Interior Repatriation Program (MIRP), which provides flights to Mexico City among an eligible subsample of people apprehended in the Tucson Sector during summer months. Sixty-six percent of all migrants repatriated to Mexico in 2011 were returned to one of these six cities (Slack et al. 2015). And although surveys were only carried out in five of the nine border patrol sectors along the border, all sectors are represented in terms of where deportees/returnees had attempted their most recent crossing. In terms of place of origin, all thirty-one Mexican states and the federal district are represented in the wave II sample of the MBCS. The MBCS is therefore generalizable to Mexican deportees from the six study cities during the study period.

Variables Used in the Analysis

Dependent variables

Table 1 provides the descriptions, proportions, and standard errors for the dependent variables examined in our analyses. As noted, 75 percent of the analytic sample indicated that they were satisfied with the services of their coyote (1 = yes; 0 = no). On the other hand, only 45 percent suggested that they would recommend their coyote to a family member or friend (1 = yes; 0 = no).

Focal independent variables: Most recent crossing

Table 1 also illustrates the descriptions, proportions, and standard errors for the focal independent variables used in the analyses, which consist of factors associated with migrants' most recent border crossing attempt.

We included a measure representing the border patrol sector in which each respondent had attempted their most recent border crossing (*sector of crossing*). There are a total of nine border patrol sectors along the U.S.-Mexico border, which are listed in Table 1 from the most western (i.e., San Diego) to the most eastern sector (i.e., Rio Grande Valley). Each sector was dichotomized for our analyses. Thirty-one percent crossed through the Tucson sector, 31 percent through the Laredo sector, 13 percent through the Rio Grande Valley sector, 12 percent through the San Diego sector, and 7 percent through the El Centro sector.

This analysis operationalizes a *coyote* as an individual who guided or physically accompanied a migrant across the border. Prior research has highlighted the diversity and complexity of *coyojate* (Spener 2009). We contend that what truly matters, especially when it comes to whether "enforceable trust" serves as a form of informal social control against mistreatment, exploitation, or abandonment—and ultimately "satisfaction" and "willingness to recommend"—is the nature of one's social tie to his or her coyote. In other words, we have moved away from differentiating between *coyote types* and focus instead on the *types of ties* migrants have to their coyotes. In doing so, we identified three types of ties: "no tie," an "indirect tie," and a "direct tie." No tie indicates that the respondent did not know the coyote prior to their most recent crossing attempt; nor was he or she put into contact with the coyote by family or a friend, but rather met the coyote for the first time near the border while preparing to cross the border. An indirect tie indicates that someone referred the respondent to his or her coyote, but that he or she did not know the coyote before his or her most recent crossing

TABLE 1
Proportions and Descriptions of Dependent and Independent Variables Used
in the Analysis (Multiply Imputed Data)

	Mean	Std. Err.
Dependent variables		
Satisfied?	0.75	0.02
Recommend?	0.45	0.03
Focal independent variables: Most recent crossing		
Sector of crossing		
San Diego (Ref.)	0.12	0.01
El Centro	0.07	0.01
Yuma	0.00	0.00
Tucson	0.31	0.02
El Paso	0.02	0.00
Big Bend (formerly Marfa)	0.00	0.00
Del Rio	0.03	0.01
Laredo	0.31	0.02
Rio Grande Valley	0.13	0.02
Tie to coyote		
No tie (Ref.)	0.36	0.02
Indirect tie	0.53	0.02
Direct tie	0.11	0.02
Smuggling fee (in $US)	2,357.10	50.21
Days traveled	2.19	0.10
Group size	10.38	0.37
Bajadores (i.e., "border bandits")	0.12	0.02
Witnessed abuse of group members?	0.06	0.01
Abused by group members?	0.03	0.01
Abandoned by coyote?	0.16	0.02
Abandoned group members?	0.15	0.02
Successfully reached destination?	0.37	0.02
Control variables: Demographic characteristics		
Male	0.89	0.01
Age		
18–24 years old	0.23	0.02
25–34 years old	0.41	0.02
35–44 years old	0.28	0.02
45 years or older	0.07	0.01
Years of education	8.29	0.12
Monthly household income (in $US)	341.97	16.88
Indigenous	0.07	0.01
Region of origin		
North	0.17	0.02
Traditional (west-central)	0.37	0.02
Central	0.17	0.02
South-southeast	0.28	0.02
Number of lifetime crossings	4.29	0.21
$M = 20$		
$N = 655$		

SOURCE: MBCS, wave II (weighted data).
NOTE: Analytic sample limited to people who had used the services of a guide and had crossed the border within five years of being surveyed.

attempt. Finally, a direct tie denotes that the respondent personally knew his or her coyote prior to his or her most recent crossing attempt. These types of ties were dichotomized for inclusion in the analysis. As noted in Table 1, 36 percent of respondents did not have a tie to their coyote, while 53 percent had an indirect tie and 11 percent had a direct tie to their coyote.

We also controlled for the smuggling fee one paid (or agreed to pay) their coyote, the number of days one traveled during their most recent crossing before either being apprehended by U.S. authorities or being picked up by a *raitero* (i.e., driver) and transported to a drop house, and the size of the group in which one traveled while crossing the border. On average, the typical migrant paid or agreed to pay $2,357 to her or his coyote, walked for just over two days, and traveled in a group of about ten other individuals, not including the respondent or coyote. During the most recent crossing attempt, 12 percent encountered *bajadores* (i.e., stick-up crews), 6 percent witnessed physical abuse of fellow group members, 3 percent experienced physical abuse by someone in their group, 16 percent were abandoned by their coyote, and 15 percent were abandoned by at least some of their group members. Finally, 37 percent successfully reached their desired U.S. destination.

Control variables: Demographic characteristics

We also controlled for a series of demographic factors, including gender, age, years of formal education, monthly household income (in hundreds of $US), whether the respondent was an indigenous language speaker, Mexican region of origin, and number of lifetime unauthorized crossing attempts. Overall, the typical respondent in the analytic sample can be described as a male (89 percent), between 18 and 34 years of age (64 percent; 18–24 years old and 25–34 years old categories combined), with just over eight years of formal education, earning about $342 before his most recent crossing attempt. Seven percent spoke an indigenous language in addition to Spanish. Seventeen percent were from northern Mexico, 37 percent from west-central Mexico, 17 percent from central Mexico, and 28 percent from the south-southeastern part of the country. The typical migrant, on average, had just over four lifetime unauthorized crossing attempts before his most recent journey across the border.

Methods

Our analytic plan consisted of two approaches. First, we utilized logistic regression to identify the factors associated with "satisfaction" with the services of one's coyote. Second, we employed a bivariate (chi-squared) analysis to examine the association between "willingness to recommend" one's coyotes and "satisfaction" as well as the association between "willingness to recommend" and successfully reaching one's desired destination.

The methodological challenges associated with missing data were addressed by using multiple imputation (MI) to deal with missing observations (Rubin

1987; Schafer 1997). We also used qualitative responses to why people decide to recommend or not to recommend their coyote to differentiate between those who are satisfied and yet decline to give a recommendation.

Results

Logistic regression results for "satisfaction"

Table 2 illustrates the coefficients, standard errors, and significance levels for the logistic regression predicting satisfaction with one's coyote. Odds ratios can be obtained by exponentiating the statistically significant coefficients associated with each predictor variable. As noted, several factors are associated with satisfaction, including the strength of one's tie to his or her coyote, encountering *bajadores*, and having successfully reached one's desired destination in the United States. Specifically, the odds of "satisfaction" are 1.5 times larger for respondents with an indirect tie to their coyote compared to those without a tie (exp [0.42] = 1.52). In a similar vein, the odds of "satisfaction" are nearly two times larger for respondents with a direct tie to their coyote relative to those without a tie. This supports the findings from the extant qualitative literature on coyotes (Spener 2009; Sanchez 2014; Izcara Palacios 2012d). We also find that the odds of a respondent who encountered *bajadores* on their most recent crossing attempt noting that they were satisfied with their coyote are about 1.5 times larger than the odds of a respondent who did not encounter *bajadores*. Perhaps migrants thought that the guide protected them from harm, which often happens if the guide has paid the correct tolls to organized crime (Slack and Campbell 2016). More research is needed to expand upon this finding. However, unsurprisingly, the strongest predictor of satisfaction is having successfully reached one's desired U.S. destination during their most recent crossing: the odds of satisfaction are 3.6 times larger among those who successfully made it relative to those who did not. This suggests that satisfaction is highly dependent upon utilitarian factors, as the goal of migration is paramount for predicting a positive experience between migrant and coyote.

On the other hand, several factors appear to decrease one's odds of satisfaction with his or her coyote. There appear to be important regional differences, such as being from the north of Mexico and crossing through the El Paso sector. For instance, migrants who crossed through the El Paso sector have 80 percent lower odds of satisfaction when compared to those who crossed through the San Diego sector. The El Paso sector has been subject to increased enforcement, as well as a drastic drop in apprehensions since the mid-1990s. It also had high rates of incarceration of migrants (due to the reduced flow) for longer periods and higher instances of people's possessions being taken away and not returned (Martínez, Slack, and Heyman 2013). These factors, more attributable to migration enforcement policies than to the guides themselves, may contribute to lower satisfaction with coyotes.

We also find that higher coyote fees are associated with lower odds of satisfaction. The treatment that one experiences during his or her crossing attempt also influences the odds of satisfaction. Specifically, migrants who were physically

TABLE 2
Logistic Regression Results for Coyote Satisfaction and Recommendation
(Multiply Imputed Data)

Variable	"Coyote Satisfaction: Yes"	
	Coefficient	Std. Err.
Focal independent variables: Most recent crossing		
Sector of crossing		
San Diego (Ref.)		
El Centro	−0.54	(0.38)
Yuma	−1.95	(1.47)
Tucson	−0.67	(0.45)
El Paso	−1.57°°°°	(0.37)
Big Bend (formerly known as Marfa)	−1.54	(1.20)
Del Rio	0.25	(1.02)
Laredo	0.18	(0.47)
Rio Grande Valley	−0.66	(0.48)
Tie to coyote		
No tie (Ref.)		
Indirect tie	0.42°°	(0.17)
Direct tie	0.68°°°	(0.23)
Smuggling fee (in $US)	−0.00°°	(0.00)
Days traveled	−0.02	(0.03)
Group size	−0.02	(0.02)
Bajadores (i.e., "border bandits")	0.41°°	(0.18)
Witnessed abuse of group members?	−1.16°	(0.60)
Abused by group members?	−0.90°°	(0.41)
Abandoned by coyote?	−1.31°°°°	(0.21)
Abandoned group members?	−0.54	(0.46)
Successfully reached destination?	1.30°°°°	(0.34)
Control variables: Demographic characteristics		
Male	0.11	(0.27)
Age		
18–24 years old (Ref.)		
25–34 years old	0.47°	(0.28)
35–44 years old	0.08	(0.39)
45 years or older	0.22	(0.14)
Years of education	−0.05	(0.03)
Monthly household income (in $US)	−0.00	(0.00)
Indigenous	0.03	(0.25)
Region of origin		
North	−0.49°°°°	(0.11)
Traditional (Ref.)		
Central	0.07	(0.27)
South-southeast	0.29	(0.27)
Number of lifetime crossings	−0.01	(0.01)
M = 20		
N = 655		
Pseudo-R^2 = .1949		

SOURCE: MBCS, wave II (unweighted data).
NOTE: Analytic sample limited to people who used the services of a guide and had crossed the border within five years of being surveyed.
°$p < .10$. °°$p < .05$. °°°$p < .01$. °°°°$p < .001$.

TABLE 3
Adjusted Predictions at Representative Values, all Other Variables Set at Means

	"Satisfied"
Succeeded	.88
Direct tie to coyote	.84
Indirect tie to coyote	.78
Not abandoned	.78
No tie to coyote	.69
Did not succeed	.67
Abandoned	.49

SOURCE: MBCS, wave II (unweighted data).
NOTE: All adjusted predictions are statistically significant beyond $p < .01$. $M = 20$. $N = 655$.

abused by fellow group members and those who were abandoned by coyotes have 60 percent and 73 percent lower odds of satisfaction, respectively, when compared to migrants who did not experience these events.

Table 3 illustrates the adjusted predictions of "satisfaction" for having succeeded in reaching one's U.S. destination, having been abandoned by one's coyote, and the strength of one's tie to his or her coyote, with all other factors set at their means. These adjusted predictions help to provide a more substantive illustration of our findings.

Overall, we find that "success" appears to be the strongest predictor of satisfaction with one's coyote, followed by having a direct tie to one's coyotes, and an indirect tie to one's coyote. For example, respondents who successfully reached their desired U.S. destination on their most recent crossing attempt have an 88 percent likelihood of satisfaction, while those with a direct tie to their coyote have an 84 percent likelihood of satisfaction, and those with an indirect tie have a 78 percent likelihood of satisfaction. In other words, "success" and the strength of one's tie to their coyote appear to matter most when predicting satisfaction. Interestingly, we also find that people who did not succeed in reaching their desired destination still have a 67 percent likelihood of satisfaction, while those who were abandoned have a 49 percent probability of satisfaction. In other words, it appears that the bar for "satisfaction" with one's coyote is set relatively low. Indeed, a full 75 percent of our respondents indicated that they were satisfied with their coyote. However, it seems that satisfaction is ultimately shaped by instrumental factors—namely, "success" or staying out of harm's way (e.g., not being abandoned). We return to the implications of these results below.

Bivariate results: "Recommend" and "satisfaction"

While the rather obvious conclusion is that satisfaction is correlated to the material outcomes of the migrant/guide relationship (successfully crossing the border), this contrasts with the more complex question of whether the migrant

TABLE 4

Willingness to Recommend Coyote to a Family Member or Friend, by
Satisfaction with Coyote

		Were you satisfied with your coyote?		
		No	Yes	Total
Would you put a family member or friend in contact with your coyote?	No	91%	32%	48%
	Yes	7%	57%	44%
	Don't know	2%	11%	8%
	Total	100%	100%	100%

NOTE: Column percentages reported. N = 632 (weighted data). Pearson's chi-squared = 167.12. p = .000.

would recommend a guide to others. What, if any, is the association between "willingness to recommend" one's coyote to his or her family members or friends? Table 4 provides greater insight into the relationship between these two outcomes.

Table 4 provides the column percentages for "willingness to recommend" by "satisfaction" among the weighted analytic subsample. As illustrated in this table, there appears to be a notable association between *not* being satisfied and *not* being willing to recommend. In fact, only 7 percent of people who were not satisfied with their coyote indicated that they would put a family member or friend in contact with them. In other words, it appears that "satisfaction" approaches what could be described as a necessary condition for a recommendation. However, "satisfaction" is by no means a sufficient condition for a recommendation. Among those who were satisfied, only 57 percent indicated that they would put a family member or friend in contact with their coyote.

Bivariate results: "Recommend" and "success"

While success is the strongest predictor of satisfaction, it does not fully explain willingness to make a recommendation. What is the relationship between "success" and "willingness to recommend" one's coyote? Table 5 offers greater insight into the association between these two outcomes.

Recall that 37 percent of our subsample successfully arrived at their desired destination after their most recent crossing attempt. Successfully reaching one's destination certainly helps to influence a recommendation, but it is not the only factor that matters, as 36 percent of respondents who *did not* reach their destination indicated that they would still recommend their coyote to a family member or friend. In other words, unlike *satisfaction, success* does not nearly come close to being a necessary condition for a recommendation. In our discussion, we draw on direct quotes from our respondents to help contextualize the complex

TABLE 5
Willingness to Recommend, by Successful Crossing

		Did you successfully arrive to your desired destination?		
		No	Yes	Total
Would you put a family member or friend in contact with your coyote?	No	59%	30%	48%
	Yes	36%	56%	44%
	Don't know	5%	14%	8%
	Total	100%	100%	100%

NOTE: Column percentages reported. N = 627 (weighted data). Pearson's chi-squared = 50.93. p = .000.

relationship between coyote satisfaction and willingness to recommend one's coyote to a family member or friend.

Discussion

We hypothesized that trust was significantly more important when related to the safety of others than with one's own well-being. Encapsulated interest (Hardin 2001, 2002, 1991) is no longer such a simple formula, as people must worry about poor treatment and the possibility that negative events occurring during migration will affect their own social capital. Moreover, a better understanding of the true dangers of crossing may discourage a migrant to involve himself or herself in the migration experiences of others. This finding, however, does raise important questions for other research on human smuggling and migration in general. Namely, if we are to accept the premise that human smugglers rely almost entirely on word-of-mouth recommendations (and the social networks involved in the cumulative causation of migration for that matter), why are people so hesitant to provide a recommendation post migration?

We argue that while satisfaction is largely based on instrumental outcomes (i.e., success), a recommendation is expressive, relying on subjective classifications such as treatment, competence, temperament, and courtesy. Open-ended responses give us some insight into this thought process. For people who were satisfied and would recommend, we hear stories of intense loyalty and help. Eighteen-year-old Amado, from Veracruz, who paid a $2,700 fee, and had an indirect tie to his smuggler, described his experience. "Really, it's luck—it's a game if you make it [across the border] or not. But my guy crossed my father before. He's not like these other guys that will leave you. I was vomiting blood [while crossing] and he stayed with me." Another migrant asserted: "He's a good person. There were women in our group and he treated them all well. We made it safe and sound" (Andres, 32, Jalisco; $1,300 fee, no tie). Sometimes assertions made as to why their guide was satisfactory give us reason to assert that standards for treatment are, in fact, extremely low: "He doesn't mistreat people and is honest. He didn't abandon anyone along the way. And he got me out of where I was (in Mexico)!" (Ricardo, 22, Michoacán; $1,500 fee, direct tie). Not abandoning people can be seen as a low bar, but considering the realities of the southwest border crossing experience, it is a constant threat.

For people who report being satisfied, but would not recommend their coyote, lack of trust and fear of the uncertainty in crossing are important themes.[3] "He lied and the passage isn't safe" (Jose, 34, Tabasco; $3,300 fee, indirect tie). "He left a 16-year-old girl by herself [in the desert] who couldn't cross. That's why I didn't make it [across], because I didn't want to leave the girl alone" (Juana, 30, Morelos, indirect tie). Others were concerned about treatment: "He's not a responsible person, he didn't help us. He said he was going to support us along the way and he didn't, instead he insulted us" (Yesenia, 36, Oaxaca; $3,000 fee, indirect tie).

However, the potential for extortion or dishonesty stood out as well. Even those who were satisfied with their guides expressed doubt about the honesty of their coyotes. "They asked for my family's phone number back home. They also kept sending me to other people and I got the run-around" (Gloria, 41, Guerrero; $3,000 fee, direct tie). "They called my sister and asked her for money" (Pancho, 24, Guerrero; $3,600, indirect tie).

We should also note that during this research the prevalence of cyber coyotes, guides who do not walk with the migrants, but guide them over cell phones, increased. We did not have questions directly about this change but noted that migrants universally disliked this trend. They felt unsafe, abandoned, and scared of being alone in the desert. Coyotes, however, were understandably concerned about efforts to arrest and prosecute them should they get caught in the United States.

One migrant in particular noted that recommendations create a lot of responsibility, which is a scary proposition considering the unpredictability of the crossing. "If I recommend him to someone and then something happens to that person—they'll blame me! No, it's not good to recommend" (Eduardo, 50, Oaxaca; $600 fee, no tie). Many people who were shocked at the danger and difficulty of the crossing simply stated that they would not do anything to encourage another person to undertake the journey. The risk of death or harm is too great to have on one's conscious. This poses a significant challenge to previous understandings of *coyotaje*. If word of mouth was the primary driver of coyotes as a business model, then we can see why hesitance to recommend may lead to greater monopolization of human smuggling at the border and the rise of border business coyotes (Martínez 2016). Fewer recommendations do seem to lead to less satisfaction, although it is unclear which way the causal arrow points in this case. Does a recommendation improve treatment, or does it increase the likelihood of finding a good guide?

When trying to understand issues related to organized crime such as coyote involvement with drug cartels, scholars must seriously confront these questions.

How has the border milieu changed? Has it changed in such a way that promotes greater specialization (i.e. full-time, professional coyotes with ties to organized crime that can protect them) and, therefore, monopolization, excluding guides who may have closer social ties to the migrants but less knowledge of the rules of the border (Slack and Campbell 2016)?

It is also clear that enforcement measures play a part in these challenges. Scholars have already noted that increased enforcement has led to more expensive coyote fees (Durand and Massey 2004); however, does it also cause a worse experience for migrants? As crossing the border continues to receive greater scrutiny and significantly more intense criminal charges, changes such as cyber coyotes may lead to greater lethality and an increase in migrant deaths. Do criminalization and enforcement also lead to a lower standard of treatment for migrants and the possibility for more exploitation? More research is needed to fully answer these questions.

Conclusion

Migrants' satisfaction with coyote services appears to be driven by utilitarian factors; however, the prospect that a migrant will recommend his or her coyote appears to be more complex. Scholars who support a business model of smuggling, as well as those highlighting the human rights aspects of smuggling, are likely to disagree on how to interpret these results. The disconnect between personal satisfaction and the desire to give a recommendation hints that people may have lower standards for treatment throughout the harsh journey for themselves than for their loved ones. This suggests that their conceptions of trust change when projected onto others. Migration, particularly undocumented migration, is an act of desperation that people do not enter into lightly; therefore, they are willing to accept many of the risks. However, when asked about their willingness to subject other people to those same risks, after having immediately gone through this experience, people hesitate. Affective issues such as treatment, demeanor, and trustworthiness are key in determining whether people will make a recommendation, whereas satisfaction is much more dependent on utilitarian factors of survival and success. More work should be done to analyze how people go about deciding whom to trust as well as constructing an understanding of what characteristics are more highly valued than others. Since the border is highly dynamic and can change significantly from one year to the next, additional studies are necessary.

Moreover, it is important to recognize that smugglers and migrants are a complex, heterogeneous group of people, with varying levels of skill, honesty, and incentives to fulfill their responsibilities. The debate about coyotes as evil criminals or noble facilitators, while helpful in combating the straw man smuggler portrayed by law enforcement, is highly limited in intellectual merit. Generally, defining people in such value-laden terms as good or bad is far too simplistic for social science and should be avoided. More attention should be focused on how the relationships produced within these clandestine situations leads to unique bonds and mechanisms for trust. While human smugglers represent a special case, other situations could also be studied, such as relationships between addicts and drug dealers, for example.

From a policy perspective, we should take a closer look at programs designed to arrest smugglers and curtail undocumented migration, because these programs exacerbate the danger faced by migrants and lead to increased death on the border. This has been the major criticism of all border enforcement strategies to date. They are essentially predicated on making it more dangerous and more deadly to cross the border, leading to a loss of life. Attempts to arrest human smugglers are one of the main reasons that the relationships between migrants and their guides break down. Programs to arrest and incarcerate migrants have led to cyber coyotes, which means that no one is walking with the group of migrants, and the migrants are more likely to get lost and die in the treacherous terrain. Forcing migrants to testify against their guides not only can put them in danger for reprisals upon return to Mexico, but it also makes it more likely for guides to abandon migrants in the desert if they expect that they will be caught. Programs like OASISS as well as most antitrafficking initiatives that are aimed at smugglers should be ended, not only because they rely on a dubious bending of the law, and have failed to stop human smuggling, but also because they continue the politics of death and danger as a deterrence. It is firmly established that this does not work.

Moreover, we should note that the factor most related to migrants' dissatisfaction with their guide is not mistreatment or kidnapping or violence; rather, it is abandonment. Being left behind, and witnessing others left behind, is a reminder about what is at stake here: people's lives. Guides are there to help people cross, but more importantly they are hired to make sure people do not die. The move to demonize smugglers, often blaming them for migrant deaths, comes after decades of policies designed to make it more dangerous to cross the border.

To prevent these breakdowns between migrants and their guides, we must fully understand the incentives for coyotes to behave in different ways. While most of the research with coyotes has helped to demystify stereotypes of coyotes, it is difficult to provide a fully formed picture of their activities. The activities we see represented in our survey are not fully accounted for in the qualitative research with coyotes. Part of this is due to the very nature of clandestine industries; another aspect of this stems from the long-standing demonization of coyotes. While it is important to document these voices, we must be wary of reproducing an authenticity narrative.

Finding the points where the goals and intentions of migrants and coyotes diverge is the key. What are the incentives to successfully cross a group of migrants (paying up-front versus upon arrival)? What are the incentives to build trust, or treat people well? The motives of migrants (successful international migration without detection) and coyotes (payment) do not always coincide. Creating a fully formed understanding of the motivating factors that drive positive and negative relationships between migrants and guides is paramount for a full understanding of the negative consequences of enforcement, criminalization, and even the thousands of deaths that occur every year along our world's borders.

Notes

1. For the purposes of this article, we use the terms *coyote, guide*, and *smuggler* interchangeably. There are a great many terms used along the U.S.-Mexico border for guides, such as *patero*, or *polleros*; however, *coyote* is by far the most common. In our survey, we asked migrants if they used a coyote and if they used a guide, which is a more benign term. Sometimes migrants would differentiate the two, stating that the coyote is akin to a manager, the person who organizes the different groups of crossers, while other times they are considered one and the same. Some people responded in the negative when asked whether they used a coyote, but in the positive to a guide, although there appears to be no significant difference in treatment. To standardize our questionnaire for people who may have had multiple people involved in their crossing (not including the *raiteros* who pick them up in vehicles once they leave the desert), we focused strictly on the individual who spent the most time walking with them. We considered the desert crossing to be the most risky (e.g., possibility of apprehension; risk of death) part of the journey and, therefore, the most important context to analyze for the purposes of this study.

2. The respondents self-identified the kidnapper as their coyote. Whether these persons intended to provide legitimate services is difficult to determine.

3. All quotes from people who are satisfied but would not recommend.

References

Baird, Theodore, and Ilse van Liempt. 2015. Scrutinising the double disadvantage: Knowledge production in the messy field of migrant smuggling. *Journal of Ethnic and Migration Studies* 42 (3): 400–17.

Boyce, Geoffrey A., Jeffrey M. Banister, and Jeremy Slack. 2015. You and what army? Violence, the state, and Mexico's war on drugs. *Territory, Politics, Governance* 3 (4): 446–68.

Campana, Paolo, and Federico Varese. 2013. Cooperation in criminal organizations: Kinship and violence as credible commitments. *Rationality and Society* 25 (3): 263–89.

Collins, Randall. 2014. *Interaction ritual chains*. Princeton, NJ: Princeton University Press.

Cook, Karen S., Russell Hardin, and Margaret Levi. 2005. *Cooperation without trust?* New York, NY: Russell Sage Foundation.

Cornelius, Wayne A. 2001. Death at the border: Efficacy and unintended consequences of U.S. immigration control policy. *Population and Development Review* 27 (4): 661–85.

Cornelius, Wayne A., and Jessa M. Lewis. 2007. *Impacts of border enforcement on Mexican migration: The view from sending communities*. La Jolla, CA: Center for Comparative Immigration Studies.

Durand, Jorge, and Dougals S. Massey, eds. 2004. *Crossing the border: Research from the Mexican Migration Project*. New York, NY: Russell Sage Foundation.

Eschbach, Karl, Jacqueline Hagan, Nestor Rodriguez, Ruben Hernandez-Leon, and Stanley Bailey. 1999. Death at the border. *International Migration Review* 33 (2): 430–54.

Gibler, John. 2011. *To die in Mexico: Dispatches from inside the drug war*. San Francisco, CA: City Lights Books.

Hardin, Russell. 1991. Trusting persons, trusting institutions. *Strategy and Choice* 185:185–209.

Hardin, Russell. 2001. Conceptions and explanations of trust. Russell Sage Foundation Working Paper, New York, NY.

Hardin, Russell. 2002. *Trust and trustworthiness*. New York, NY: Russell Sage Foundation.

Izcara Palacios, Simón Pedro. 2012a. Coyotaje y grupos delictivos en Tamaulipas. *Latin American Research Review* 47 (3): 41–61.

Izcara Palacios, Simón Pedro. 2012b. El declive del contrabando de indocumentados en México. *Mexican Studies/Estudios Mexicanos* 28 (2): 351–76.

Izcara Palacios, Simón Pedro. 2012c. Opinión de los polleros tamaulipecos sobre la política migratoria estadounidens. *Migraciones Internacionales* 6 (3): 173–204.

Izcara Palacios, Simón Pedro. 2012d. Violencia contra inmigrantes en Tamaulipas. *European Review of Latin American and Caribbean Studies/Revista Europea de Estudios Latinoamericanos y del Caribe* 93:3–24.

Izcara Palacios, Simón Pedro. 2014. Coyotaje and drugs: Two different businesses. *Bulletin of Latin American Research: Journal of the Society for Latin American Studies* 34 (3): 324–39.

Lopez-Castro, Gustavo. 1998. Coyotes and alien smuggling. In *Binational study of migration between Mexico and the United States*, vol. 2, 965–74. Washington, DC: U.S. Commission of Immigration Reform.

Martínez, Daniel E. 2016. Coyote use in an era of heightened border enforcement: New evidence from the Arizona-Sonora border. *Journal of Ethnic and Migration Studies* 42 (1): 103–19.

Martínez, Daniel E., Robin C. Reineke, Raquel Rubio-Goldsmith, and Bruce O. Parks. 2014. Structural violence and migrant deaths in southern Arizona: Data from the Pima County Office of the Medical Examiner, 1990–2013. *Journal on Migration and Human Security* 2 (4): 257–86.

Martínez, Daniel E., Jeremy Slack, and Josiah Heyman. 2013. *Bordering on criminal: The routine abuse of migrants in the removal system*. Washingotn DC: American Immigration Council.

Nevins, Joseph, and Mizue Aizeki. 2008. *Dying to live: A story of U.S. immigration in an age of global apartheid*. San Francisco: Open Media/City Lights Books.

Rodríguez, Néstor. 1996. The battle for the border: notes on autonomous migration, transnational communities, and the state. *Social Justice* 23 (3, 65): 21–37.

Rubin, D. B. 1987. The calculation of posterior distributions by data augmentation. *Journal of the American Statistical Association* 82 (398): 543–46.

Sanchez, Gabriella. 2014. *Human smuggling and border crossings*. New York, NY: Routledge.

Schafer, J. L. 1997. *Analysis of incomplete multivariate data*. Boca Raton, FL: CRC Press.

Scott, James C. 2009. *The art of not being governed: An anarchist history of upland Southeast Asia*. New Haven, CT: Yale University Press.

Slack, Jeremy. 2015. Captive bodies: Migrant kidnapping and deportation in Mexico. *Area*. doi:10.1111/area.12151.

Slack, Jeremy, and Howard Campbell. 2016. On Narco-coyotaje: Illicit regimes and their impacts on the US-Mexico Border. *Antipode*. doi:10.1111/anti.12242.

Slack, Jeremy, Daniel E. Martínez, Alison Elizabeth Lee, and Scott Whiteford. 2016. The geography of border militarization: Violence, death and health in Mexico and the United States. *Journal of Latin American Geography* 15 (1): 7–32.

Slack, Jeremy, Daniel E. Martínez, Scott Whiteford, and Emily Peiffer. 2015. In harm's way: Family separation, immigration enforcement programs and security on the US-Mexico border. *Journal on Migration and Human Security* 3 (2): 109–28.

Spener, David. 2009. *Clandestine crossings: Migrants and coyotes on the Texas-Mexico border*. Ithaca, NY: Cornell University Press.

U.S. Government Accountability Office. 2013. *Border patrol goals and measures not yet in place to inform border security status and resource needs*. Washington, DC: U.S. Government Accountability Office.

Zaitch, Damián. 2002. *Trafficking cocaine: Colombian drug entrepreneurs in the Netherlands*. New York, NY: Springer Science & Business Media.

Zaitch, Damián. 2005. The ambiguity of violence, secrecy, and trust among Colombian drug entrepreneurs. *Journal of Drug Issues* 35 (1): 201–28.

Navigating with Coyotes: Pathways of Central American Migrants in Mexico's Southern Borders

By
YAATSIL GUEVARA GONZÁLEZ

This article presents research from an ethnographic investigation of the role of the men and women who facilitate clandestine border crossings (known colloquially as *coyotes*) in the Mexico-Guatemala northern borderlands. A significant portion of the fieldwork took place at La 72, a renowned migrant shelter in the Mexican border city of Tenosique, in the state of Tabasco. Findings suggest that the daily exchanges between migrants and their crossing facilitators constitute constant social negotiations through which these actors enrich their agency and profit from each other's well-being.

Keywords: human smuggling; transit migration; social navigation; undocumented migration; coyotes; Mexico

The social, political, and commercial exchanges among Central America, Mexico, and the United States are centuries-old and constantly changing. These exchanges have for generations included migratory flows. As a result of the armed conflicts in some Central American countries since the end of the 1970s, the displacement and undocumented migration, toward Mexico and the United States, of people from Central America's Northern Triangle (comprising El Salvador, Guatemala, and Honduras), has generated significant interest in migration scholarship due to its alleged magnitude and visibility. While often described as unprecedented, the current flows reflect long-standing, even if evolving, socioeconomic and

Yaatsil Guevara González is a doctoral researcher in sociology at the Bielefeld Graduate School in history and sociology. She is a fellow in The Americas as Space of Entanglement(s) project at the Center for Inter-American Studies in Bielefeld University. Her research centers on forced migration and refugees in Central America and Mexico.

Correspondence: yaatsil.guevara_gonzalez@uni-bielefeld.de

DOI: 10.1177/0002716217750574

political processes that are taking place among Central American countries and Mexico.

The current exodus of people from Central America is not new, but reinforced immigration and border control mechanisms are (Foster 2007). Ongoing measures to control migration from Central America by Mexico take place at formal and informal crossing points along the Mexico-Guatemala and Mexico-Belize borders, as well as in states across southeast Mexico. Together, checkpoints, inspection sites, detention facilities, and other surveillance controls form a vast containment belt across southern Mexico that seeks to hold the flow of Central American migrants. The efforts have born fruit. Mexico has become the leader in the number of arrests involving Central America's undocumented migrants, as reflected by United States and Mexican deportation statistics. Starting in 2015 Mexican immigration authorities arrested and removed more Central Americans than its American counterpart, U.S. Customs and Border Protection.[1]

Mexico plays a conflicting role in migration in the Central American region. Until the first decade of this century, the majority of the migrants detained during their clandestine attempts to cross the U.S.-Mexico border were Mexican nationals (U.S. Customs and Border Protection 2016). For decades, the Mexican government has insisted on a binational dialogue with the United States about the protection of the human rights of millions of Mexican citizens who reside in the United States undocumented. Yet over the last 10 years, the reports of violence and corruption by Mexican authorities against undocumented Central American migrants in transit have generated an even higher level of concern. Thousands of Central American migrants have been reported dead or missing in their transit through Mexico, and the experiences of extortion, kidnapping, and sexual assault of many others have been well documented by migrant advocacy groups. The violence present on the road, alongside border controls and immigration enforcement, has in turn resulted in changes to the routes that historically had been used by Central American migrants for their northbound journeys, and in their migratory strategies that aim to reduce the inherent risks. In other words, migrants encounter along their journeys "actors who prey on and attempt to extort money from them; and humanitarian organizations that seek to assist and protect migrants" (Basok et al. 2015, 43), alongside "private actors who facilitate migration for a fee." In the Americas, the facilitators of these migrant journeys are collectively known as *coyotes*, and have throughout the region been the most visible if understudied actors in migrant mobility.

Even though there has been growing interest in the role of smugglers as part of clandestine migration dynamics, there is still a lack of clarity and consensus on what to do with the knowledge produced in current smuggling studies. Attempts have encompassed multiple theoretical orientations and methodological approaches (Baird and van Liempt 2016). In this particular project, I follow an organizational and network approach in an attempt to understand the dynamics of migrant-smuggler interactions undertaken en route that facilitate the transit and crossing of Central Americans across the southern Mexican border. The network approach suggests that smuggling depends on unique network characteristics: "it is the relations of individuals and the structure and distribution of those relations which helps explain concrete smuggling operations" (Baird 2013, 12). By focusing on these exchanges as they take place in the context of migrant shelters, my analysis sheds light on the migration process and the links between constricting migratory policies, implemented mostly by transit and receiving countries, and countermeasures experienced at the micro-level in the smuggler-migrant interaction.

With ethnographic data collected during eight months of field research (September–November 2014; January–March 2015; May and November 2016), I examine how, during their journeys and through their interactions, migrants and smugglers navigate "social terrains" (Vigh 2006, 12) that allow them to devise responses to situations and each other based on shared experiences in mobility. In the same fashion that Baird (2013) highlights the importance of an organizational and network approach to study human smuggling operations, Nielsen and Vigh address the importance of the "social environment" of possibilities created by the agents and "its effects on one's planned and actual movements" (Nielsen and Vigh, 2012, 661) when researching terrains in constant social change. In this vein, migrant shelters in Mexico illustrate this important social terrain or environment in which exchanges and interactions between migrants and smugglers take place. There, they plan and strategize the possibilities for transiting Mexico and moving north. Due to the lack of current research about the nature of the interactions occurring in these places, this contribution explores the effect of the migrant shelter as a "social environment" on the planned and actual trajectories followed by Central American migrants on their way into Mexico and into the United States as witnessed in one of the lesser studied migratory regions connecting Central America to Mexico: the Tenosique-Petén corridor.

Researching Smuggling

In this study, I analyze smuggler-migrant everyday interactions through Vigh's concept of *social navigation*. Migrants navigate "within fluctuating social structures" in which they "act not only in relation to each other, or in relation to larger social forces, but in relation to the complex interaction between [them], the terrain and events," reflecting the "encompass[ing] of social flux and instability … influenc[ing] and becom[ing] ingrained in action" (Vigh 2006, 14). Seeking to identify the praxis of instability and movement, witnessed in the migrant-smuggler interaction, I rely on the testimonies of migrants staying at La 72,[2] a migrant shelter in the city of Tenosique, Tabasco, the first Mexican city on the Mexican side of the border from Guatemala, and adjacent to the Guatemalan Department of Petén.

Across Mexico there are dozens of houses and shelters established by civil society to provide basic shelter to migrants in transit. La 72 is in fact part of a chain of migrant shelters known as *casas de migrantes* and run by catholic priests of various orders grouped under what is called the Pastoral Dimension of Human Mobility, in Spanish, *pastoral de mobilidad humana* (Guevara González 2015).

The shelters are often located in or next to a church, or as a standalone building, and offer temporary lodging, food, and emergency medical services for irregular migrants in transit. Some may offer additional services, such as legal assistance, mental health counseling, and communication services (i.e., access to telephones or email).

The empirical data analyzed here come from eight months of ethnographic fieldwork in the region. My observations were primarily conducted at La 72, where I lived as a volunteer. I conducted collaborative ethnography (Lassiter 2005), relying on participant observation, recording informal conversations, and carrying out retrospective interviews (Fetterman 2010). Volunteering at the shelter allowed me to have an active role as a staff member, participating directly in the conversations and interactions of those who relied on the shelter to plan their journeys—access that as a researcher alone, I would have been unlikely to attain. I chose collaborative ethnography methodology since it "pulls together threads of collaboration between the ethnographers and their consultants" (Lassiter 20005, 17). Due to the instability of the environment in which this research was carried out (that is, the unpredictable length of stays of my respondents), I relied on retrospective interviews, which allow the ethnographer to "reconstruct the past, asking informants to recall personal historical information" (Fetterman 2010, 42). These interviews were mostly recorded in informal social environments, allowing my respondents, despite the changing environment, to "shape the past highlights of their values and reveal the configuration of their worldviews" (Fetterman 2010, 42). I supplemented the interviews with informal conversations during day-to-day life at the shelter and the city of Tenosique, where the shelter is located. In total I conducted fifty-three retrospective interviews and had twenty informal conversations with migrants in transit, coyotes, shelter staff, hotel owners, taxi drivers, restaurant attendants, and members of law enforcement agencies operating locally. All interviews and informal talks were recorded with prior authorization of the involved persons, transcribed, and analyzed.

While living at La 72, I interacted directly with migrants every day. My proximity allowed me to witness migrant-smuggler negotiations occurring every day inside and outside the shelter. These interactions take place in a highly fluid terrain—migrants moving in and out of the shelter in their transits—and therefore one of the main challenges while collecting data was being to carry out long-term observations or interviews with the same respondents. Furthermore, respondents (both smugglers and migrants) were often in highly vulnerable positions due to their lack of status within Mexico and the clandestine nature of their journey. There was also a significant institutional dimension: the fact that smugglers were technically not allowed to remain within the shelter, although they made themselves "pass" for migrants to watch over their clients and perhaps generate additional business, which often led to tense interactions between the smugglers and the shelter's staff. Together these dynamics constituted an "uncomfortable fieldwork" environment (Hume and Mulcock 2004, xxiii), where I simultaneously performed the role of a volunteer and researcher inside the shelter. My dual roles often became entangled in the trust-building processes required in research and my ability to carry out my volunteer work.

FIGURE 1
Mexico-Guatemala Border

SOURCE: Arriola Vega (2014). Reprinted with permission of the University of Pennsylvania
Press.

Beyond these methodological considerations, the "social environment" (Vigh
2006, 12), that is, the unfolding topography of the smuggler-migrant interactions
and how they take place during their shared trajectories, must be described. For
that, one must detail the geopolitical landscape of Mexico's southern border and
its key role in South-North migratory flows.

Mexico's *Other* Southern Border: The
Tenosique-Petén Borderlands

Mexico's southern border (see Figure 1) is approximately 1,139 kilometers long,
of which 962 kilometers border with Guatemala and 176 with Belize.[3] The
Suchiate and Usumacinta rivers traverse along half of the border (Kauffer Michel
2010, 32). Simultaneously, 87 percent of the border between Mexico and Belize
is demarcated by the Hondo River (García García and Kauffer Michel 2011,
145). The jungle, rainforests, swamps, and bodies of water extend beyond the
limits of Mexico into Central America, creating a porous and shifting border.[4]

FIGURE 2
The Tenosique-Petén Border

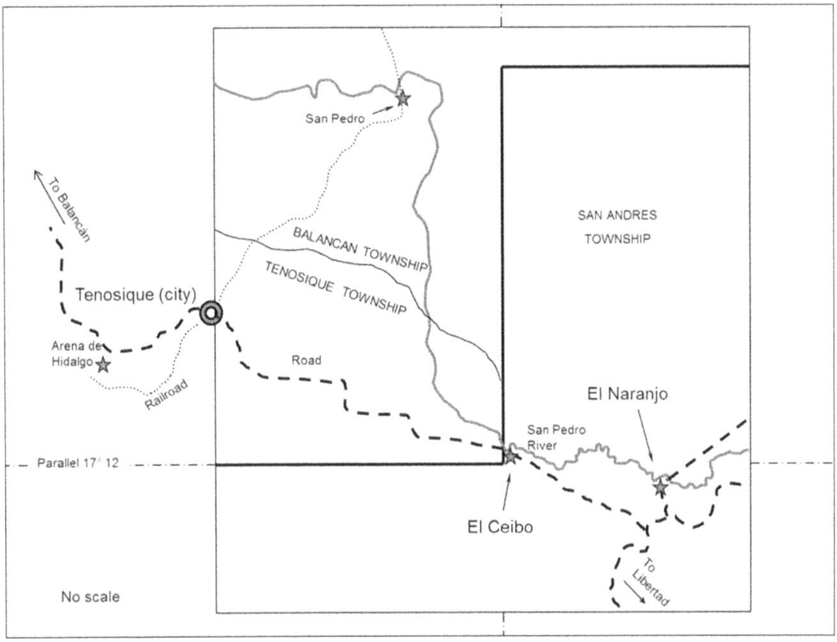

SOURCE: Arriola Vega (2014). Reprinted with permission of the University of Pennsylvania Press.

For decades, Central American migratory flows into Mexico, the United States, and Canada, currently estimated at four hundred thousand per year,[5] have primarily gone through the crossing point of Ciudad Hidalgo–Tecún Uman, which connects the southern Mexican state of Chiapas with Guatemala. This corridor has been historically the most often discussed in analyses of Central American migration. The experiences of migrants crossing into Mexico through the Mexican states of Tabasco, Campeche, and Quintana Roo (about seven hundred kilometers to the north) have remained virtually unexamined. The region where this project was conducted is a section of the border known as the Tenosique-Petén borderlands (see Figure 2). It covers sixty kilometers along the Mexico-Guatemala border, connecting the state of Tabasco in Mexico with Guatemala's Petén.

The Tenosique-Petén section is the second busiest crossing by Central American migrants (Arriola Vega 2012, 184). Although officially there is only one border checkpoint managed by the Mexican authority in charge of immigration in this region, the El Ceibo checkpoint, there are at least five other informal border crossing points in the area (Arriola Vega 2012, 186). Along this stretch of the borderland, the city of Tenosique plays an important role as a transit city for migrants. It is the first city on the Mexican side of the border. It is also here where migrants get atop of the cargo train (known as *La Bestia*) heading toward the U.S. southern border. These factors make Tenosique-Petén fundamental when exploring the effects of the immigration enforcement policies at the local level, and the responses and practices of those who participate in the migration industry.

The geopolitical dimension of the Tenosique-Petén borderlands: Reshaping trajectories in uncertain terrains

Migration scholars identify a series of events as critical in the transformation of undocumented migration patterns into Mexico from Central America. Perhaps the most prominent is the signing of the North American Free Trade Agreement (NAFTA) between Canada, the United States, and Mexico in 1994 (Ángeles Cruz 2010), followed by the reinforcement of the Mexico-U.S. border after the 9/11 attacks (Arriola Vega 2012). The war against drug trafficking in Mexico, which was publicly declared in 2006 by then–Mexican president Fox (Basok et al. 2015), and the international agreements between Mexico and the United States to "seal" the southern Mexican border through economic development programs (Casillas 2007; Sandoval Palacios 2011), also shaped migration flows and routes in response to border militarization and enforcement. Other factors such as crime levels in Guatemala, Honduras, and El Salvador (Castillo 2010); environmental and natural catastrophes in El Salvador and Honduras (Rivas Castillo 2010); and the exploitation of natural resources by mining and bioenergy companies in the entire Central American region (Sandoval Palacios 2001) have also been cited as factors in the outflows of Central American migrants into Mexico seeking to reach the United States. In addition, Mexico's national immigration enforcement and control initiatives backed by the United States' government (namely Plan Sur Program in 2001 and Southern Border Program in 2014) as well as international aid and development programs (Proyecto Mesoamérica in 2001 and the Merida Initiative in 2007) have led to increased restriction of Mexico's southern border (see Figure 3), prompting continued creation and reconfiguration of routes of passage by migrants (see Figure 4). The need to avoid border controls has led those seeking to enter Mexico to venture into more remote mountains and away from main roads and highways, exposing migrants to significant risks ranging from environmental exposure, physical and sexual assaults, abuse at the hands of the authorities, kidnappings, and even death. In fact, multiple organizations have raised concerns over the increased number of reported deaths and disappearances of migrants in transit through Mexico (Amnistía Internacional 2012; CNDH 2011).

While the precariousness of Mexico's migratory landscape has led to research seeking to understand "how geopolitics shape and animate the everyday experiences of clandestine migration journeys" (Mainwaring and Brigden 2016, 244), some social actors have received more attention than others because of the way they are construed and/or represented in the rhetoric of border security. In representing the facilitation and restriction of migrants' journeys, smuggling

FIGURE 3
Migratory and Territorial Controls along the Guatemala-Mexico Border

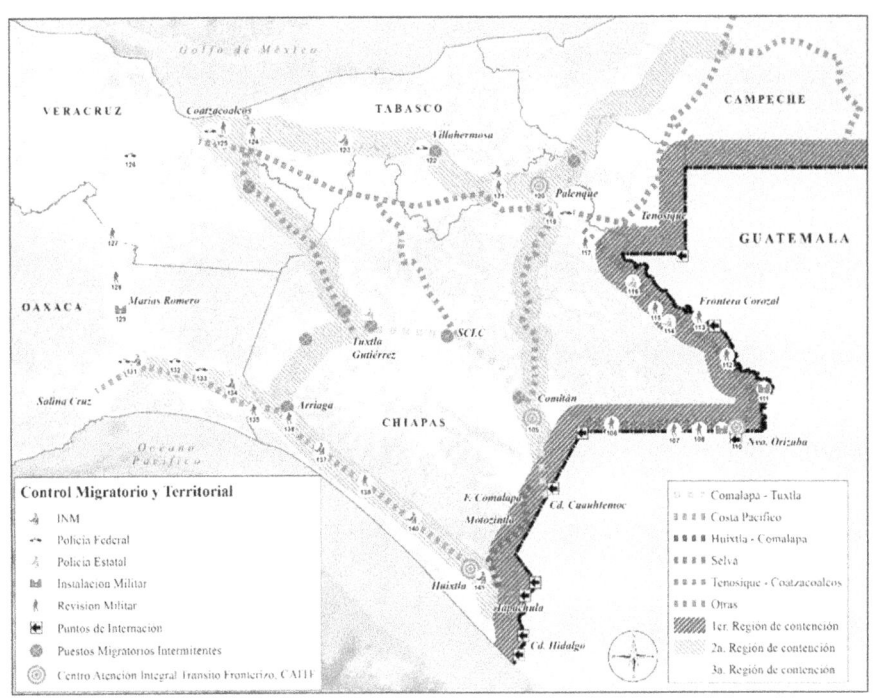

SOURCE: Paz Carrasco, Cerda García, and Ledón Pereyra (2016).

facilitators or coyotes often predominate. While they are often depicted as unscrupulous characters who cheat migrants of their money and victimize them physically and emotionally, growing literature suggests that coyotes are invested in the provision of efficient and safe services because of their desire to continue business and to protect their own safety (Sanchez 2015; Spener 2009; Galemba 2013). As facilitators of mobility, coyotes develop and implement passing strategies to assist their clients in reaching their desired destinations. In the Tenosique-Petén borderlands, they negotiate journeys with migrants, serve as interlocutors with institutions and networks, and are aware of the ever-changing dynamics in the entire southern border, their home.

The Tenosique-Petén migration industry

While *coyote* is used here as a blanket term to designate any individual engaged in the facilitation of migration journeys, there are other ways to facilitate a journey, other types of facilitators, and facilitators with different tasks, and they vary in "cost, complexity, availability, security and probability of success" (Spener 2008, 132). In my fieldwork at La 72 migrants traveled primarily with the help of

FIGURE 4
Transit Cities

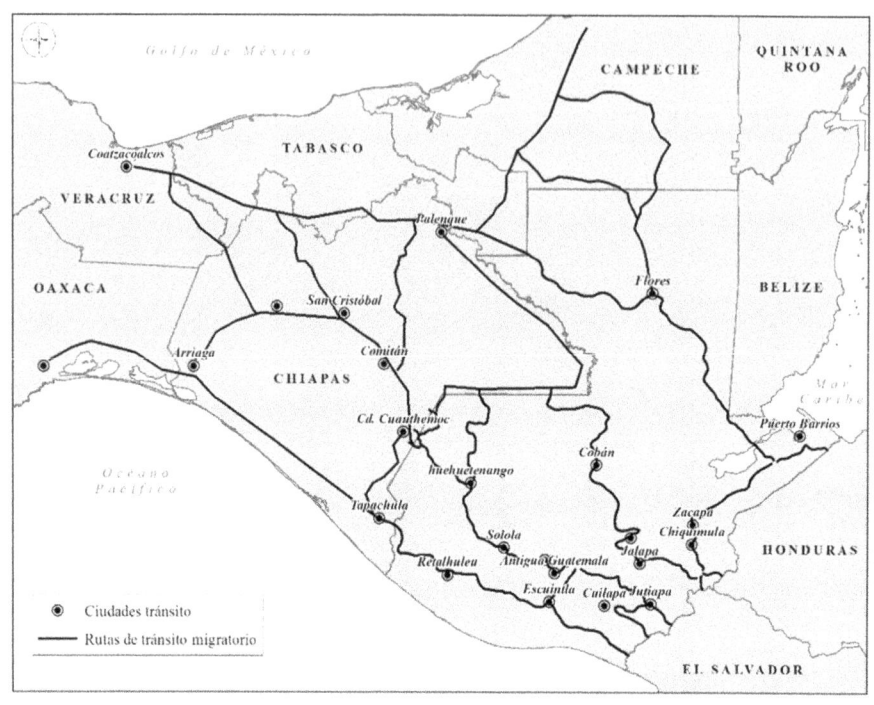

SOURCE: Paz Carrasco, Cerda García, and Ledón Pereyra (2016).

coyotes and guides. Coyotes are known for providing a full-service package, which includes the facilitation of journeys across Mexico and into specific destinations within the United States from the place of origin or residence of the migrant. Few migrants travel in this all-inclusive way, though, because of cost: coyote-led door-to-door journeys are quite expensive. During the period in which this research was carried out, the prices of such all-inclusive packages ranged between 4,000 and 6,000 U.S. dollars. This service involves finding and contracting a reliable (i.e., successful) smuggler with known access to a network of brokers who can in turn ensure a relatively smooth journey for the migrant. These services are usually hired and paid for by friends and/or family members of the migrant who already reside in the United States (Hagan 2008). The high price of this kind of comprehensive service makes it virtually inaccessible to most migrants (Sanchez 2015), who must instead rely on guides who cover specific segments of their journeys or they must forgo all forms of guidance or help.

Most Central American migrants staying at La 72 reported relying on the segmented facilitation, where they relied on a guide (*guia* in Spanish) to lead them through specific portions of their journeys. *Guías* are typically local residents of the Tenosique-Petén corridor with knowledge of the terrain. They also tend to have legal residence permits for one or more countries in the region (in the case of the Tenosique-Petén corridor, most guides interviewed were citizens or residents of Guatemala, Belize, or Mexico), which allowed them to travel with no restrictions across the border. The guides' role is to walk migrants across short distances and help them avoid immigration controls.

Since most migrants rely on the segment-based option, it is important to describe how and where it operates. While guides do in fact play a fundamental role in their facilitation, clandestine journeys rely on a larger logistics structure comprising accommodations, food, and transportation services, alongside brokers such as taxi drivers, hotel owners, and boat operators. In the Tenosique-Petén corridor, the town of Santa Elena, on the Guatemalan side of the border, constitutes an important migration industry hub. As migrants arrive into town, they are approached by taxi drivers who offer their transportation services. Drivers recommend specific hotels or accommodations to their customers, receiving in turn a commission based on the amount of business they bring in. Hotels also serve as brokerage points for those who arrive without a guide. Once at a hotel, migrants in transit can select from a vast range of options, including accommodations, meals, transportation toward the border with Mexico, and assistance crossing the southern border, mainly to Tenosique or Palenque (both cities on the Mexican side of the border) for a fee. For example, Felipe,[6] his wife, Francheska, and their two young children arrived in Santa Elena from Honduras seeking to cross into Mexico. At a hotel, Felipe and his family were offered services, since the owner had agreements with both coyotes and guides. Felipe and his wife explained:

We took a bus directly to Santa Elena, we stayed there for like 2 or 3 days in a hotel, and from there we came here to the place of *El Manco*.[7] He crosses people over there by El Naranjo.

… We got to Santa Elena and I remember that we arrived at the hotel, and asked "How much for a bed?" "Per night? 100 quetzales," said the owner. "Ok," I said, "give me four beds, one bed each." "Ok," the owner said, "the rooms come with a fan." We stayed there that night. The following night we were still there because the owner was helping us set up a ride to get us from [there] to El Naranjo, with a man they call *El Manco*.[8]

Other migrants skip the hotel in Santa Elena with the hope of finding a "good deal" that can fit their budget. That was the case for Jorge and his brother, who avoided the hotel in search of a guide who offered a package to get them across the river. Jorge's experience is another example of the segment-based option that many migrants use:

It only took us three days to get [to Tenosique]. We crossed through El Pedregal, by boat. I would say it is about two hours from here by boat. You just have to get to El Naranjo and there are some boatmen. The same boatmen have rooms for rent for the night. We took the bus right before El Naranjo; we arrived there around 5 or 6 pm. We wanted to take the *marianela*[9] so we started looking for a way to cross. One guy told us it would be 30 quetzales[10] to cross, but another one offered us a better price. The said, "Hey guys, just because you are from Guatemala. You are from here, so it will be very cheap: 10 quetzales for each one of you, including the boat. We arrange everything for you by tomorrow morning, you will have to pay just a little more [to the boatman] and we will transport you all the way to El Pedregal, all the way across the border! Moreover, we will include the truck to get you there and the other truck once you are on the other side, all for the same price!" So I told him it was ok, and we traveled with him.[11]

There is, as these testimonies indicate, a solid infrastructure supporting migrants and their needs. Guides, hotel owners, taxi drivers, and coyotes all operate as brokers, being more than "simply nodes in a network which bridge two yet unconnected nodes by just passing on information" (Faist 2014, 39).

The Migrant Shelter as Smuggling Hub

Another fundamental node in this chain is the one constituted by migrant shelters. Facilitators and migrants often resort to these humanitarian aid institutions to rest, secure medical care, or obtain food. Simultaneously, facilitators act as brokers between migrants and humanitarian aid institutions within migrant shelters, connecting networks to increase the success of their clients and for their business.

Most migrant shelters do not allow coyotes and guides into their facilities; they consider facilitators exploitative and abusive, and likely to cause conflicts. As a result, coyotes often pretend to be migrants in transit themselves to be allowed into the shelter. Once in the shelter, the coyote may reconfigure a migrant's journey, especially in light of immigration enforcement controls, or he or she may even connect clients with other facilitators. El Pelón, a coyote, described the following segment of the route to his clients while at the shelter:

Look, things are difficult right now. So, we will have to do the following. … Some of you are coming with me, and the others, well I am dealing with my *compas* (trusted friends), they are people who have my trust, they are *compas*, they are people of their word. It is getting very hard to cross right now, so we cannot go more than five people at the time. Let me arrange things and see when they can pick up you [points to four others]. You would have to leave [the shelter] and meet [my friends] outside, they cannot pick up you here, but I'll give you the details, you know, you have all my contact details. In a little while I'll tell you how *the move [la movida]* is going to be.[12]

As the quote illustrates, coyotes use their stays at the shelters to secure new clients and to organize new stages or rounds of services. Migrant shelters draw new social horizons, that is, "spaces of possibilities and spheres of orientation that constantly arise in the interaction between agents in motion and the shifting social and political circumstances they seek to move within (Vigh 2006, 30).

Migrant shelters are also places of conflict. They become spaces where migrants can share with others through conversations and gossip their perceptions of specific coyotes. Shelters are in fact difficult spaces for facilitators to navigate, as they provide on one hand the respite they often need and opportunities for future business, but, on the other, the possibility of running into their competitors, also eager to profit from the presence of migrants and their often-scant resources.

Perceptions of specific ethnicities as being more reliable than others come into play in the micro-cosmos of the shelter, where migrants may stop relying on a specific coyote and turn to another perceived as able to provide better services and improved chances of success. Among migrants in my sample, Mexican coyotes and guides were perceived as more reliable than Guatemalan or Honduran facilitators. Mexican coyotes know they can benefit from the bad reputation of their Central American counterparts, and do their best to maintain the tensions around this imaginary, consequently improving their chances of generating business. During a conversation at La 72, Felipe shared:

> Do you remember El Tico [from Costa Rica]? He was bringing people all the way to Villa. But then La China found out and unleashed a war of rumors against him. Some say that she threatened him and that is why he is leaving soon. But she told her clients to tell the staff at the shelter that he was a coyote. I think he is losing his clients, because now they say they came to find out he is not as experienced and that he does not know the route well.[13]

In addition to the tensions that emerge among facilitators in the struggle to retain clients, facilitators face another challenge: the very existence of borders and migration controls. During a negotiation between a migrant and a facilitator in Santa Elena, I witnessed an exchange in which Alonso, a facilitator, positioned himself as the best option for potential clients aspiring to cross into Mexico:

> I charge you US$1,000, but that journey is guaranteed. From [Santa Elena] to Tenosique, all the way through the border checkpoint, but it is guaranteed. You will find no muggings, no immigration controls. We will be heading to El Naranjo with the trucks, across the border, everything. You stay here, you don't go out anymore. I bring you everything you need, food, etc. I will tell you which clothes to put on so you are well prepared. Your friend is going to have to cut his hair and he can't wear that hat he has on. We are going to leave at 3 am.[14]

Alonso's testimony reflects his awareness of the difficulties in migrating resulting from migration control policies within the Mexican territory, the likelihood of violence along the migration journey, and exposure to harsh physical environments. Yet simultaneously, he situates his knowledge of these challenges as an advantage: he can secure the supplies that are needed for the journey, and can even help them change their appearance to improve their chances of a successful and uneventful crossing. It is clear from his sales pitch that Alonso recognizes the "social terrain" as "being at times a non-transparent social topography, at other times fluid and in continual movement and at yet other times volatile and explosive" (Vigh 2006, 12).

Coyotes must acknowledge the challenges likely to occur during migrants' journeys, while providing evidence of how they are effective at counteracting their impact. They recognize that migrants are deeply aware of the risks inherent to the journeys and are seeking facilitators who can provide protection. Offering their services cannot simply involve promises, but rather evidence of how the risks inherent to the journey have been overcome in the past. The conversation between Rubén and "El Manco" attests to these negotiations:

Rubén: So, the amount includes checkpoints? Because at the shelter we heard there are currently four checkpoints from Tenosique to Villa.

El Manco: Everything is included. Checkpoints, la migra,[15] and password for El Norte.[16] You have to give me one half [of the fee] here and the other half when we arrive; the crossing into United States is not included. I can give you some contacts, but I don't cross personally.

Rubén: OK, OK. But I need to go through Mexico City, I don't want to cross through Tamaulipas. Some friends told me that Mexico City is easier and safer.

El Manco: Yes, but the bribes to the *migra*[17] and the federal police have increased on that route, there is more control now because everybody is using that route. If you want to use Mexico City it is OK, but then is not the price I told you yesterday.[18]

The dialogue between El Manco and Rubén attests to the knowledge that migrants have of the dynamics along migration routes, and of the multiple complexities that smugglers face in the provision of their services. The facilitation, particularly along the Mexican landscape, does not merely involve the transportation process; rather, it requires navigating the landscape of authorities that can be bribed along the way and especially along the safest or fastest routes, which are also known and requested by migrants. Access to these areas involves higher costs not only for the migrants who seek to cross them, but also for the facilitators.

Migrants often describe coyotes as intentionally scamming their clients. On one occasion, four migrants shared their concern about a coyote with whom they had been "in conversations" during the last few days. They had given him money in advance, and two days later he disappeared and had not returned to the shelter:

> We were in negotiations already for a few days ago, because well my friend came here with a coyote, but he abandoned him here. So we met another one in here, and we heard from others that he had already crossed several people and he had not failed. He even knows the other coyote that left my friend here, and he told us that that one was a cheater and that's why he usually offers low prices. We thought he was honest because some people in my city know him, and well we gave him an advanced payment, but it's already been four days since then and he has not showed up, and we're all worried because each of us gave him US$400. And well, we already feel kind of mistrust because if he does not appear what are we going to do?[19]

Scams like the one Ángel and his friends experienced are common. Many smugglers do take advantage of the vulnerability of migrants and create elaborate schemes that lead unsuspecting clients to believe in routes or services that do not exist. Scammers take advantage of the inability of migrants to report the crimes committed against them to the authorities.

While some smugglers do profit from the trust of their clients and refuse to abide by the terms of their verbal agreements, smuggling services are on many occasions impacted by enforcement controls, ramped up security, or interruptions to the chain of contacts that allow them to carry out business in the region. Responding to the challenges they encounter, smugglers have adapted. At La 72, some facilitators offered border crossing packages that included multiple crossing attempts. If the migrant was detained by immigration authorities, robbed along the way, or extorted by drug trafficking organizations, becoming unable to complete the journey, he or she could contact the facilitator after to use his or her additional travel "credits." Most facilitators delivered on their promises, and once their clients had crossed the Tenosique-Petén region, they connected them with other facilitators for the remaining segment of their journeys.

That was the case for Beatriz, who left Honduras with her sister and hired a coyote to take them all the way to Mexico's northern border. Both sisters were arrested by Mexican immigration authorities during their journey and were deported back home. As soon as they arrived in Honduras, they contacted the coyote to use their credit for a second attempt. On this occasion, the sisters reached La 72 in the company of the facilitator. Having attempted twice to move his group of migrants from the shelter, the coyote decided that the conditions were not optimal for the journey given ongoing migratory controls. This decision, of course, was made to the dismay of the people he was transporting, including Beatriz. She described her experience:

> I don't know if I should continue or I should go back to Honduras and forget this idea of going to Houston. But I also made an effort to get the money, and also the first time that we traveled [Mexican immigration] got us. You have no idea … I wanted to die, it was my first time going to jail and the immigration officers are nasty! We got deported and tried again. This time [the coyote] told us to wait here in the shelter, and then he said he was going to divide the group. He took just some of us; my sister and I stayed. And then he came back twice [to the shelter] with more people. Eventually he said he was not going to take us anymore because of the [enforcement conditions] but then he said he neither was going to give us our money back. And what can I do? I cannot go to the police and say "I want my money back because I paid thousands of pesos to the coyote."[20]

While most literature on migration attributes the unwillingness of smuggling facilitators to fulfill service agreements or promises to an almost preternatural desire to hurt or take advantage of their clients, or to simply profit financially, many other factors and actors constrain the ability of coyotes to effectively deliver services. In the context of Mexico, informal or unexpected checkpoints set up by the National Immigration Institute or INM (the federal agency in charge of immigration controls); changes in the usual staff members at surveillance or control points; the increased activity of groups involved in robberies, kidnappings, and extortion; and the activities of drug trafficking organizations along migratory routes often impede facilitators from providing the most basic of services. Omoa, a Central American migrant, shared his experience:

> I was almost in Reynosa, I had everything. The coyote already had told me which password I should give, everything. But the problem was the opposite cartel stopped our bus, and well … everything went to hell. They took us and got out of the bus … me and other three, we stayed in a house for 12 days, they beat us, they tortured us. … I did not understand if the coyote fooled me, or if something happened to him because I did not hear from him afterwards. I did not want to give my mom's number because they were going to ask for ransom, but there was a lot of torture. The good thing is that one day after I gave them the phone number, there was a federal police raid and then when they came in some of us were able to run away. Neither cops nor Zetas, I lived.[21]

The risks related to entering into spaces controlled by states or by criminal organizations are also taken into consideration by coyotes, who are also likely targets of violence. While described primarily as perpetrators, it is common for facilitators to be among those being kidnapped, arrested, or extorted in their attempts to smuggle their groups. Some smugglers have reduced their risk by entering into agreements with those who control routes or access to specific segments of the migrant trail. In some cities of northern Mexico, drug trafficking organizations have access to migration routes and impose fees that must be covered up front by smugglers, even if the amount is then passed on to migrants. This tax, referred to in the literature as *piso* (Slack and Campbell 2016; see also Slack and Martinez, this volume), allows migrants and facilitators to travel and operate without fear of violence. Attempting to travel through parts of Mexico that the drug traffickers control without paying *piso* may be counterproductive for smugglers, who can face threats of violence, assaults, and, in some cases, homicide. There are also some reports of coyotes being forced to involuntarily work with criminal groups, or assaulted and even murdered by organized crime members (see O'Leary 2012; Izcara Palacios 2015).

The narratives of abusive and exploitative smugglers must be interpreted with caution, as decisions to move onward or to altogether cancel a journey often take place within the much larger context of border security and immigration controls, in turn embedded in larger dynamics of risk and violence. Smugglers are often faced with having to make decisions for the safety of the group, even against the will of specific clients, who may feel cheated or lied to (Hagan 2008). While some migrants may opt to return home, others will continue on their journeys with the assistance of other facilitators, often despite warnings from the original coyote about security conditions and an increased likelihood for victimization.[22]

It is common to find migrants who have become coyotes themselves because of their multiple failed attempts to cross the border.[23] In this sense, migrants also become agents of knowledge and develop strategies that draw from their own experience and that allow other migrants to achieve the goals that they did not reach.

> It was hard. Living in the street, under bridges, my *padrino* [godfather] was my coyote. He didn't abandon me, I [just] didn't have luck to get in to the U.S., but I can say he did his best. Maybe God wanted me to stay here in Mexico, I am happy; nowadays I can help my fellow citizens. I have [Mexican] residence now, I can go back and forth, while they can't. I learned very important things at a time when I was very naïve, when I tried to cross with my *padrino*.[24]

Previous crossing experiences become important resources of knowledge. For Mariana, who tried unsuccessfully to cross into the United States on at least four occasions, her "failures" were the most important tools to achieve her permanent residence. She fled Guatemala due to gender discrimination because of her sexual orientation and tried to get to the United States. On the first two attempts she relied on smugglers' services, one of whom was her godfather, but after the first two attempts she felt confident enough to embark on the journey alone. While living in La 72, Mariana found out she could apply for refugee status in Mexico.

Her application was initially denied. On her fourth attempt she was approved and was able to secure permanent residence in Mexico. Today she works crossing migrants from south to north Mexico. The networks and ties that she has acquired in the process of her migration allowed her to help others.

Conclusion

Mexico's southern border has for generations been crossed by Central American migrants in their attempts to reach the United States. Current migration controls and border enforcement policies on the part of the Mexican government, alongside geopolitical changes, in the Central American region have led to changes not only in migration flows from Central America, but also in the development of a local industry of migration along the Mexico-Guatemala borderlands. In this article I discussed the case of the Tenosique-Petén corridor, which, located to the north of the most commonly studied border crossing of Ciudad Hidalgo–Tecun Uman, registers a high volume of border crossings and of irregular migration facilitation.

As the constraints posed to human mobility by border control and immigration enforcement along Mexico's southern border have increased, the role of border crossing facilitators has become fundamental in securing safe passages. While smuggling facilitators or coyotes are known for their role in the provision of reliable, fast, and effective mobility services, they are also often described as persona non grata who abandon, betray, and kidnap migrants in transit, the latter of whom are often portrayed as naïve and easy to manipulate. My empirical data indicate that the interactions that emerge among migrants and those behind their journeys are far from what that dichotomy implies. Migrants are not only aware and knowledgeable of the many challenges associated with their journeys; they are active, engaged agents in the identification of smuggling services. Furthermore, the smuggler-migrant dynamic goes beyond a financial transaction. Both parties play the roles of confidant, partner, and employer for each other, becoming invested not merely financially but also in terms of securing each other's well-being.

Migrants as well as smugglers are often forced to interrupt their trajectories by the challenges they encounter—enforcement, robberies, and injury to name a few. Migrant shelters across Mexico are fundamental in the process of remapping a path forward. Shelters do provide a safe and secure space away from agents such as the police and criminal organizations and the risks they pose. However, they are also a place of business, where smuggling facilitators and migrants can interact and strategize. The safety associated with the shelter allows both smugglers and migrants to improve their chances for success, through the identification of better-suited smugglers, new contacts, and advice from other people on the move. But they are also locations where conflict and tension can emerge, as smugglers compete for clients. Both smugglers and migrants must therefore devise practices of negotiation and resistance to benefit from their interactions.

Migrants and smugglers are agents that have responded to the new politics of persecution and restraint of migratory flows. Challenges to mobility have led to the creation of new tendencies and strategies for clandestine border crossing. The once-established transit routes, mostly demarcated by the cargo train railroads, have changed; crossing prices have increased as militarization and enforcement of borders have escalated. And the nature of the interactions between migrants and smugglers has changed as well. While violence against smugglers and migrants are an ordinary occurrence, some migrants have become smuggling facilitators themselves.

Finally, it is important to underline that daily exchanges between migrants and their crossing facilitators constitute social negotiations, through which these actors cultivate and enrich their agency. The analysis of their interactions allows us not only to reformulate the habitual narratives and imaginaries of the smuggler-migrant dynamic within the migratory corridors around irregular migration, but also to understand how border enforcement and immigration control mechanisms affect practices and contestations between social actors involved at the local level in the migration industry. Without romanticizing the complex dynamics between these groups, it is crucial to explore smugglers' role as transit-knowledge brokers as well as intermediaries who mitigate migrants' risks along their journeys. As such, smugglers play a role too important to be considered solely criminal or deviant.

Notes

1. See https://www.wola.org/es/2015/06/mexico-ahora-detiene-mas-migrantes-centroamericanos-que-los-estado-unidos/;https://www.wola.org/analysis/haiti-crossroads-understanding-current-political-impasse/.

2. I opted not to give a pseudonym to the shelter where I carried out my fieldwork as La 72 Hogar-Refugio para personas migrantes is well known in the migration literature as a research hotspot and has been identified by multiple other researchers in the course of their work. The names and nicknames used in the article, however, do not reflect the real names of the respondents.

3. The length of Mexico's southern border varies across authors. Some authors put it at 1,139 kilometers, while others estimate it at 1,149 or even 1,225 kilometers (Kauffer 2010, p. 40).

4. Here I draw from Benedikt Korf's notion of the "permeability or hardness of the border" (Korf and Raeymaekers 2013). He proposes that institutions and power relations around borderlands determine those border's characteristics. I use porous or porosity to clarify that negotiations between the diverse power relations taking place in these borderlands are flexible, unstable, and filterable, but also to emphasize that geographically and geopolitically entangled conditions play a central role in border trade practices.

5. The statistics on the number of undocumented migrants who cross the southern border are unknown. The complexity of mobility dynamics and their resulting conditions further complicate accuracy. Mexico's Instituto Nacional de Migración (National Migration Institute) provides the number of monthly and annual arrests, yet there are gaps in these statistics. For example, a person can be detained several times in a single month or year.

6. All interviewees' names were anonymized.

7. A man missing an arm.

8. Felipe, interview by Yaatsil Guevara González, Tenosique, Tabasco, México, November 2014.

9. A small boat or dingie.

10. Quetzales are the Guatemalan currency.

11. Jorge, interview by Yaatsil Guevara González, Tenosique, Tabasco, México, November 2014.

12. El Pelón, interview by Yaatsil Guevara González, Tenosique, Tabasco, México, November 2015.

13. Felipe, interview by Yaatsil Guevara González, Tenosique, Tabasco, México, November 2014.

14. Alonso, interview by Yaatsil Guevara González, Santa Elena, Guatemala, February 2015.

15. The colloquial term used to designate the authorities in charge of immigration.

16. Mexican northern cities. Routes of undocumented migration in Mexican northern cities are usually controlled by drug trafficking organizations and therefore migrants need a "password" (provided commonly by their facilitator) to avoid kidnapping or extortion.

17. Immigration authorities.

18. Rubén y El Manco, interview by Yaatsil Guevara González, Tenosique, Tabasco, México, February 2015.

19. Ángel, interview by Yaatsil Guevara González, Tenosique, Tabasco, Mexico, March 2015.

20. Beatriz, interview by Yaatsil Guevara González, Tenosique, Tabasco, Mexico, September 2014.

21. Omoa, interview by Yaatsil Guevara González, Tenosique, Tabasco, México, September 2014.

22. There is a correlation between distance and the vulnerability migrants face. The farther one person is from home, the more likely he or she will be to encounter violence, as the ties between the person in transit and the smuggler who was originally hired to provide services and his or her networks become weaker. In other words, the level of safety a smuggler can provide is related to the proximity of his or her home and social capital. See Majidi, this volume.

23. The participation, or rather the migrant to smuggling facilitator continuum, has been identified by Achilli (2016) in the case of Syrian smuggling facilitators; while Mengiste (2017), in his work on Eritrean smugglers, has also recognized the information that is shared among migrants in transit as constituting a form of knowledge, echoing Sanchez and Natividad (2017).

24. Mariana, interview by Yaatsil Guevara González, Tenosique, Tabasco, México, March 2015.

References

Achilli, Luigi. 2016. Irregular migration to EU and human smuggling in the Mediterranean: The nexus between organized crime and irregular migration. In *Mobility and refugee crisis in the Mediterranean*, 98–103. Barcelona: IEMED.

Amnistía Internacional. 2012. *Culpables conocidos, víctimas ignoradas. Tortura y maltrato en México*. Reino Unido: Amnistía Internacional.

Ángeles Cruz, Hugo. 2010. Las migraciones internacionales de la frontera sur en México. In *Los grandes problemas de México. Migraciones internacionales*, eds. de Manuel Ángel Castillo and Gustavo Verduzco Francisco Alba, 438–79. México: El Colegio de México.

Arriola Vega, Luis Alfredo. 2012. Crónica de la migración centroamericana en tránsito por la ruta del Golfo. In *El Estado de la Migración. México antes los recientes desafíos de la migración internacional*, eds. Telésforo Ramírez García and Manuel Ángel Castillo, 179–204. México: Consejo Nacional de Población.

Arriola Vega, Luis Alfredo. 2014. Migration, violence and "security primacy" at the Guatemala- Mexico border. In *Binational human rights, the U.S.-Mexico experience*, eds. William Paul Simmons and Carol Mueller, 112–25. Philadelphia, PA: University of Pennsylvania Press.

Baird, Theodore. 2013. Theoretical approaches to human smuggling. Danish Institute for International Studies Working Paper, Copenhagen.

Baird, Theodore, and Ilse van Liempt. 2016. Scrutinising the double disadvantage: Knowledge production in the messy feld on migrant smuggling. *Journal of Ethnic and Migration Studies* 42 (3): 400–17.

Basok, Tanya, Danièle Bélanger, Martha Luz Rojas Wiesner, and Guillermo Candiz. 2015. *Rethinking transit migration. Precarity, mobility, and self-making in Mexico*. Inglaterra: Palgrave Macmillan.

Casillas, Rodolfo. 2007. *Una vida discreta, fugaz y anónima: Los centroamericanos transmigrantes en México*. México: Comisión Nacional de los Derechos Humanos/Organización Internacional para las Migraciones.

Castillo, Manuel Ángel. 2010. Las políticas y la legislación en material de inmigración y transmigración. In *Los grandes problemas de México. Migraciones internacionales*, eds. Manuel Ángel Castillo y Gustavo Verduzco Francisco Alba, 547–78. México: El Colegio de México.

Comisión Nacional de Derechos Humanos (CNDH). 2011. *Informe Especial sobre Secuestro de Migrantes en México*. México, DF: Comisión Nacional de Derechos Humanos México.

Faist, Thomas. 31 October 2014. Brokerage in cross-border mobility: Social mechanisms and the (re)production of social inequalities. *Social Inclusion*, 38–52.

Fetterman, David M. 2010. *Ethnography: Step-by-step*. Thousand Oaks, CA: Sage Publications.

Foster, Lynn V. 2007. *A brief history of Central America*. 2nd ed. New York, NY: Checkmark Books.

Galemba, Rebecca B. 2013. Illegality and invisibility at margins and borders. *Political and Legal Anthropology Review* 36 (2): 274–85.

García García, Antonio, and Edith F. Kauffer Michel. 2011. Las cuencas compartidas entre México, Guatemala y Belice: Un acercamiento a su delimitación y problemática general. *Frontera Norte*, 131–62.

Guevara González, Yaatsil. 2015. Migración de tránsito y ayuda humanitaria:Apuntes sobre las casas de migrantes en la ruta migratoria del pacífico sur en México. *Forum for Inter-American Research (FIAR)* 8 (1): 63–83.

Hagan, Jacqueline Maria. 2008. *Migration miracle: Faith, hope, and meaning on the undocumented journey*. Cambridge, MA: Harvard University Press.

Hume, Lynne, and Jane Mulcock. 2004. *Anthropologists in the field: Cases in participant observation*. New York, NY: Columbia University Press.

Izcara Palacios, Simón Pedro. 2015. Coyotaje and drugs: Two different businesses. *Bulletin of Latin American Research* 34 (3): 324–39.

Kauffer Michel, Edith F. 2010. Migraciones y agua en la frontera entre México, Guatemala y Belice: Aproximaciones en torno a una relación multiforme. *LiminaR. Estudios sociales y humanísticos* 8:29–45.

Korf, Benedikt, and Timothy Raeymaekers. 2013. *Violence on the margins: States, conflict, and borderlands*. New York, NY: Palgrave Macmillan.

Lassiter, Luke Eric. 2005. *The Chicago guide to collaborative ethnography*. Chicago, IL: University of Chicago Press.

Mainwaring, Ćetta, and Noelle Brigden. 27 April 2016. Beyond the border: Clandestine migration journeys. *Geopolitics*, 243–62.

Marfleet, Philip. 2006. *Refugees in a global era*. New York, NY: Palgrave Macmillan.

Mengiste, Tekalign Ayalew. 2017. Struggle for mobility: Risk, hope and community of knowledge in Eritrean and Ethiopian migration pathways towards Sweden. PhD dissertation, Stockholm.

Nielsen, Jonas Østergaard, and HenrikVigh. 2012. Adaptive lives: Navigating the global food crisis in a changing climate. *Global Environmental Change* 22 (3): 659–69.

O'Leary, Anna Ochoa. 2012. Of coyotes, crossings, and cooperation: Social capital and women's migration at the margins of the state. In *political economy, neoliberalism, and the prehistoric economies of Latin America*, eds. Ty Matejowsky and Donald C. Wood, 133–60. Bradford: Emerald Group Publishing.

Paz Carrasco, Miguel Ángel, Alejandro Cerda García, and Aldo Ledón Pereyra. 2016. *Mirar las fronteras desde el sur. Salud y migración en la frontera México-Centroamérica*. Mexico, DF: Autonomous Metropolitan University. Division of Social Sciences and Humanities.

Rivas Castillo, Jaime. 2010. Centroamericanos en el Soconusco: Reseña de su presencia a través de sus paradojas. *Revista LiminaR. Estudios sociales y humanísticos*, 106–28.

Sanchez, Gabriella E. 2015. *Human smuggling and border crossings*. New York, NY: Routledge.

Sanchez, Gabriella, and Nicholas Natividad. 2017. Reframing migrant smuggling as a form of knowledge: A view from the US-Mexico border. In *Border politics*, eds. Cengiz Gunay and Nina Witjes, 67–83. New York, NY: Springer.

Sandoval Palacios, Juan Manuel. 2001. El Plan Puebla-Panamá como regulador de la migración laboral mesoamericana. In *Mesoamérica. Los Ríos Profundos. Alternativas plebeyas al Plan Puebla Panamá*, ed. Armando Bartra, 215–68. México: Instituto "Maya," A.C., El Atajo Ediciones, Fomento Cultural y Educativo, A.C.

Sandoval Palacios, Juan Manuel. 2011. El Proyecto de Integración y Desarrollo de Mesoamérica (Proyecto Mesoamérica) en el marco de la Alianza para la Seguridad y Prosperidad de América del Norte

(ASPAN), la política de Seguridad Democrática y la Iniciativa Mérida. In *Planes geoestratégicos, desplazamientos y migraciones forzadas en el área del proyecto de desarrollo e integración de Mesoamérica*, eds. Juan Manuel Sandoval Palacios, Raquel Álvarez de Flores, and Sara Yaneth Fernández Moreno, 109–40. Medellín: Universidad de Antioquia.

Slack, Jeremy, and Howard Campbell. 2016. On narco-coyotaje: Illicit regimes and their impacts on the US–Mexico border. *Antipode* 48 (5): 1380–99.

Spener, David. 2008. El Apartheid gobal, el coyotaje y el discurso de la migración clandestina: Distinciones entre violencia personal, estructural y cultural. *Migración y Desarrollo*, 127–56.

Spener, David. 2009. *Clandestine crossings: Migrants and coyotes on the Texas-Mexico border*. Ithaca, NY: Cornell University Press.

U.S. Customs and Border Protection. 31 October 2016. *Stats and summaries*. U.S. Border Patrol Apprehensions From Mexico and Other Than Mexico (FY 2000-FY 2016). Available from https://www.cbp.gov/sites/default/files/assets/documents/2016-Oct/BP%20Total%20Apps%2C%20Mexico%2C%20OTM%20FY2000-FY2016.pdf.

Vigh, Henrik. 2006. *Navigation terrains of war. Youth and soldiering in Guinea-Bissau*. New York, NY: Berghahn Books.

Historicizing Mobility: *Coyoterismo* in the Indigenous Ecuadorian Migration Industry

By
VICTORIA STONE-CADENA
and
SOLEDAD ÁLVAREZ
VELASCO

Based on ethnographic research in the Ecuadorian Highlands, this article puts the mobility, migration, and smuggling practices of Ecuador's indigenous people in historical and contemporary context. The people of Ecuador's Southern Highlands have been on the move for generations, and migration is deeply embedded in the social and cultural landscape. In the rural communities of Cañar, indigenous coyotes are more than facilitators of migration: they are community members operating amid broader structural constraints, which have led to the emergence of specific trends in the facilitation of *irregularized* migration, yet they are expected to adhere to communal principles of reciprocity and trust. We place indigenous migrant narratives of mobility and identity at the center of our analysis of human smuggling, articulating a counternarrative to that of criminalization prevalent in transnational debates of irregularized migration, national security, and border control.

Keywords: human smuggling; *coyoterismo*; migration; Ecuador; Cañar; indigenous people

*I*rregularized migration[1] from Latin America via smuggling networks, while hypervisible in the media, has received scant empirical research attention. The domination of the

Victoria Stone-Cadena is a broadly trained sociocultural anthropologist whose research interrogates gender, race, indigeneity, and ethnic identity in the Americas. She conducted her dissertation research with transnational indigenous migrant families in Southern Highland Ecuador and New York City. Her analyses draw from emerging mobility, migration industry, and indigenous studies, including critical race theory.

Soledad Álvarez Velasco is a PhD candidate in the Department of Geography at King's College London. Her research investigates the nexus between irregularized transit migration and violence and the capitalist state, particularly in the case of the Ecuador-Mexico-U.S. extended migratory corridor, focusing on the production of Ecuador as a zone of transit used by irregular migrants moving toward the United States.

Correspondence: vstone@gradcenter.cuny.edu

DOI: 10.1177/0002716217752333

U.S.-Mexico migratory experience as the prototypical example of Latin America's migration has often hidden other flows that are occurring in the region. In fact, across Latin America, multiple countries have been key players in global migration flows. Ecuador is a case in point.

Ecuador is an important migrant-generating country. Most Ecuadorian migrants live in the United States, while several hundred thousand reside in Europe, primarily in Spain and Italy (Instituto Nacional de Estadísticas y Censos [INEC] 2013; Instituto Nazionale di Statistica [ISTAT] 2012). Since 2000, local and global factors such as border securitization, regional conflicts, natural disasters, a dollarized economy, and Ecuador's open-border framework also turned this South American country into a destination for regional and extracontinental migrants. Refugees, asylum seekers, and economic migrants from countries as diverse as Cuba, Iraq, and Ghana, alongside Ecuadorian returned migrants, come together in Ecuador along their journeys to the North (Álvarez Velasco 2016; Jokisch 2014).

The facilitation of irregularized migration via smuggling, or *coyoterismo*, as the practice is referred to regionally in academic and policy circles, constitutes a prominent element of migrant journeys in Ecuador (Ruíz and Álvarez Velasco 2016). There is, however, scarce scholarship on the topic. The lack of empirical data and historical work on smuggling operations constitutes a concerning gap in migration studies globally. This article reduces that paucity of work by contributing to a deeper understanding of mobility strategies, by illuminating *coyoterismo* in Ecuador.

Within contemporary national and international discourses on migration, migrant brokers or facilitators (known across the Americas as coyotes) are continually cast as entrepreneurial criminals, discursively framed as coldhearted and profit driven, offsetting critical analyses of the role of nation-states in the global, targeted development of migration controls. However, as described by other authors in this volume, not all of those involved in the smuggling market fit the exploitative criminal image often circulated in the media and by organizations vested in countering irregularized migration flows.

Using two waves of ethnographic research in Ecuador's Southern Highlands conducted between June 2007 and August 2009, and November 2015 and November 2016, we contextualize migration and its facilitation via coyotes against the backdrop of the history of mobility and subsistence practices within indigenous communities in Ecuador. This article assesses the role of ethnic identity as a strategic variable in migration activity. By placing indigenous migrant narratives of mobility and identity at the center of the analysis of human

NOTE: This article draws from key findings of two independent, though interconnected, research projects. Victoria Stone-Cadena's dissertation research in anthropology at the CUNY Graduate Center analyzed the impact of migration patterns on indigenous migrant households in Southern Highland Ecuador, with the support of a Fulbright fellowship. Soledad Álvarez Velasco's doctoral dissertation in human geography at King's College London analyzes the production of Ecuador as a global zone of transit of irregularized transnational migration, on a full scholarship from the National Secretariat of Higher Education, Science and Technology (SENESCYT) of Ecuador (2014–2018).

smuggling, we articulate a counternarrative to that of criminalization prevalent in transnational debates on national security, border controls, and irregularized migration.

In the sections that follow, we provide an overview of the critique of migration studies vis-à-vis indigenous mobility, followed by a summary of the Ecuadorian migration context. We then provide a history of mobility practices predating the current indigenous migration patterns, primarily through the testimonies of indigenous and mestizo[2] people from the Ecuadorian Southern Highlands. Further, we outline contemporary and current trends in smuggling practices. We close with a series of conclusions and policy recommendations.

Indigenous Mobilities

Mobility within the context of globalization creates a "new order of instability in the production of modern subjects" (Torres and Carrasco 2008, 13). Indigenous Cañaris from Ecuador's Southern Highlands, often wearing the wide-brimmed white hats associated with agrarian life, are now commonly seen in the driver's seats of new pick-up trucks transporting goods and people through town. New consumption practices and entrepreneurial activities, such as investments in small businesses and vehicles, challenge long-standing forms of economic and social inequalities sustained by middle-class and professional mestizos. Another entrepreneurial activity is migration.

Migration is not new among indigenous communities. Cañaris have been on the move for generations. Regional trade precedes the arrival of the Spaniards (Murra, Wachtel, and Revel 1986). Cañari history has also included short-term migration to urban areas and the coast, as well as between haciendas in the highlands (Baraona 1965; Clark and Becker 2007). For most of the twentieth century, these patterns of circulation were interspersed with periods of stasis, as legislation often bound rural people to labor relationships with landed oligarchs (known in Spanish as *latifundistas*).

Migratory practices in Ecuador have been described as constituting a regional migration industry (Kyle and Goldstein 2011; Ruíz and Álvarez Velasco 2016).Yet scholars have paid less attention to the importance of indigeneity as a form of social capital that indigenous people have mobilized within their social networks and intermediary organizations in the context of irregularized migration (Stone-Cadena 2016). Migration industry scholars have analyzed the institutions involved in migration control, such as legalization (Hernández-León 2013), detention (Hernández-León 2013; Nyberg Sørensen and Gammeltoft-Hansen 2013), and deportation (Berg and Tamagno 2013), alongside the vast social and economic networks of migration facilitators and mobility management. Indeed, historical and regional social networks, economic practices, and informal networks within the region are extremely important in the growth of international migration from the region. Yet our goal here is to demonstrate how identity, as discussed by indigenous migrants and migration merchants, shapes opportunities and strategies in the practice of *coyoterismo*.

A growing body of literature on indigenous migration looks at different aspects of the migration experience: from its significance in the destination countries (Andolina, Laurie, and Radcliffe 2009b), to the migratory networks (Torres and Carrasco 2008), and within the nations and communities of origin (Cadena and Starn 2010), while other authors have examined indigeneity as (re)defined within a transnational context through a broadly comparative approach (Castellanos, Gutiérrez Nájera, and Aldama 2012).

We understand identity, territory, and community as mutually constructed categories and recognize mobility as a fundamental aspect of indigenous livelihoods (Torres and Carrasco 2008). While the nation-state has shaped a discourse about indigeneity, which is both temporally and territorially limited (Bretón, Jove, and Vilalta 2007), some have criticized such state-centric notions of indigeneity and instead sought to deconstruct reified and monolithic conceptualizations of indigenous identity (Andolina, Laurie, and Radcliffe 2009a). Following the path of these scholars, our work seeks to point to *identity* as a conceptual category, and to the moments in which indigenous identity is mobilized in the context of migration facilitation by coyotes.

Through transnational social networks, indigenous people have "encounter[ed] new anchors for identity that aren't fixed in territory or community, but rather formed through new spaces of social cohesion and socioeconomic and political relationships" (Torres and Carrasco 2008, 14). In Ecuador's Southern Highlands, these new concepts of indigenous identity circulate largely through social media and surface in the work of pan-indigenous organizations and local-level community projects to preserve agrarian practices and community life. In constructing counternarratives to migration, the state has emphasized the negative repercussions of migration on families, traditions, and community obligations, all of which are seen as tied or inherent to indigenous rural life. The state has claimed that migration leads to the decline of traditional practices, festivals, and other community activities; yet indigenous leadership and organizations have been at the forefront of mitigating these changes. The transnationalization of festival participation and sponsorship from community members abroad demonstrates that indigenous rural life is changing but not as state-centric narratives may portray. This article shows that the experiences of indigenous coyotes and migration entrepreneurs do not seem to conform to those narratives, either.

Regional Background

Ecuador is the fourth smallest country in Latin America. It has four distinctive geographic regions: the Pacific coastal lowlands, the highlands (Andean cordillera), the Amazonian jungle, and the Galápagos Islands. It is also one of the most bio-diverse countries in the world and encompasses numerous distinct ecological environments. Each region has played a role in the political and economic development of the nation. Crude oil exports compose close to 50 percent of the nation's export earnings, estimated at US$11.4 billion in 2014 (Organization of the Petroleum Exporting Countries [OPEC] 2015). Earnings from oil are followed by remittances from immigrants abroad, estimated at US$2.3 billion in 2015 (Banco Central del Ecuador 2015).

International migration from Ecuador is not new, but the dynamics have changed significantly since its early inception in the late 1960s. Prior to the 1960s, overseas migration was minimal. Scholars identify the demise of the regionally based Panama hat export industry in the mid-1960s in the highland southern provinces of Azuay and Cañar as leading to the pioneering migratory movements to the United States (Kyle 2000; Gallegos and Ramírez 2005). These flows predominantly involved young male merchants who migrated to the United States by relying on the connections they had made through their participation in the hat trade. Most of them migrated without authorization and found employment in restaurants as busboys or dishwashers, while a smaller number worked in factories or construction sites in cities such as New York, Chicago, Los Angeles, Miami, and Minneapolis (Jokisch 2014). By the 1970s, the provinces of Azuay and Cañar, and Ecuador's third-largest city, Cuenca, constituted the core migrant-sending zone in Ecuador. The main sending communities relied on subsistence agriculture and maintained the tradition of women weaving Panama hats for export to New York, and male seasonal migration to the coast.

The global petroleum crisis during the 1980s prompted another spike of Ecuadorian migration as rural laborers struggling to subsist in a weakened economy traveled to the United States. Yet a more dramatic crisis occurred in late 1999 and early 2000s as a result of low oil prices and natural disasters. Migration to Spain, Italy, and, to a lesser extent, Germany and Russia, surpassed migration to the United States during this time. Increased border controls in the United States following the passage of the Illegal Immigration Reform and Immigrant Responsibility Act of 1996 (IIRAIRA), which criminalized illegal entries, increased migration risks and costs to the United States. And so, from 1998 to 2006, between 0.5 and 1 million Ecuadorians migrated overseas, primarily to Spain, where low-skilled work was available and migrants did not have to worry about learning a new language (Jokisch 2014). Spain did not restrict visas for Ecuadorians, which allowed many migrants to obtain work permits.[3]

This second wave of migration was much more geographically and socioeconomically diverse. Migrants came from every province and were more urban and better educated; they also represented various ethnicities. By 2013, it was estimated that between 2 and 3 million out of a total of almost 16 million Ecuadorians lived abroad (INEC 2013). The global recession in 2008 and changes to immigration law in Spain, which imposed visa restrictions on Ecuadorians in 2003, impacted migration flows to Europe.

Currently, border securitization and the extension of immigration controls into Mexico have further shaped the dynamics of irregularized migration from Ecuador. The country has emerged as a "revolving door" (De Genova 2005) for Ecuadorians who seek to return to the United States following their deportation. Increased immigration controls in Mexico have also led to the deportation of Ecuadorians from that country. An estimated fifty Ecuadorians on average have been deported by Mexico every month since 2009. It is also estimated that more than 7,500 Ecuadorians have been deported from the United States between January 2012 and June 2016 (Directorate of Attention and Protection of Ecuadoreans Abroad [DAPE] 2016). Furthermore, while the last decade has seen some improvements in Ecuador's economy and living conditions, most advances are concentrated in urban areas (INEC 2013). Poverty remains high in regions with high concentrations of rural and indigenous populations (Chiriboga 2013). National unemployment is also high, and approximately half of the economically active population works in the informal economy (INEC 2013). Furthermore, the open-border migration policies put into place by former president Correa allowed migrants from countries from regions as distant as West Africa and as close as the Caribbean to enter Ecuador without a visa. This led Ecuador to become an important springboard from which transcontinental migrants could embark on the journeys that would eventually take them north. In the aftermath of several events involving confrontations between migrants in transit and the state forces,[4] the Ecuadorian parliament signed the Law of Human Mobility on January 2017, which sought to regulate the entry of foreigners into the country. The law implements, among practices such as visa restrictions, the detention and removal through deportation of those who fail to enter the country legally (Ruíz and Álvarez Velasco 2016).

The leading destination among migrants leaving Ecuador is the United States. The route, which includes crossing at least seven national borders, is traversed by land or a combination of air and land routes. Most travel from Ecuador to Honduras; from there, they travel by land to the Mexico-U.S. corridor. Another route from Ecuador is to Colombia or Peru to Panama, from which migrants travel into Mexico and on to the United States. Historically, the majority of these migratory flows have involved migration facilitators in the formal and informal markets, ranging from travel agencies to coyotes (Kyle and Siracusa 2005). While Ecuadorian investigative journalism has remained the primary source of information on the facilitation of irregularized migration from or through the country, there is a vacuum of empirically informed scholarly work on the operation of smuggling groups, as knowledge of their contexts and processes remains scant.

Historicizing *Coyoterismo*

To explore the dynamics of irregularized migration and *coyoterismo* in Ecuador, we turned to ethnography as our main data collection strategy. Following Marcus's example of multisited ethnography and "following" people, things, metaphors, stories, relational conflicts (Marcus 1995), our field methods focused on the spatial contexts of social relations to understand the dynamics of *coyoterismo*.

There are several considerations for "following" migrants "en route" or "capturing" the clandestine dynamics of circumventing border control. The waiting times and pauses during migration allowed us to capture the complexity of movement (Urry 2007; Auyero 2012). Apart from finding key ethnographic sites, we identified places and moments of pause along the migration process to build trust, develop deep conversations, and carry out *in situ* observations. The first stage of this study took place between June 2007 and August 2009, and was carried out in the *cantón* (province) of Tambo and the nearby province of Cañar. A total of twenty-seven structured interviews with indigenous families who had at least one migrant family member were conducted, along with participant observations at community meetings and *mingas* (community projects). During the second stage, which took place between November 2015 and November 2016, we conducted multisited ethnography in urban Ecuador, including sites such as Quito (Ecuador's capital city and one of the main receptors of deported migrants) and the southern cities of Gualaceo, Chordeleg, El Descanso, Azogues, and Cuenca in the provinces of Azuay and Cañar, the historical centers of Ecuadorian irregularized migration facilitation. In Azuay and Cañar, we identified entry contacts and then relied on a snowball technique to reach additional respondents. In Quito, we supplemented those initial interviews with additional interviews and observations at the Human Mobility Management Unit of the Provincial Government of Pichincha.[5]

In total, eighty local respondents—including civil servants; border agents; members of local NGOs, social organizations, and international organizations working in migration affairs; local inhabitants; Ecuadorian deported migrants; their family members; and members of smuggling networks (brokers, middlemen, lawyers, transporters, and money lenders or *chulqueros*)—were asked questions regarding the history of *coyoterismo* in the region, its current trends, the identities and community perceptions of coyotes, and the challenges indigenous migrants and families working alongside coyotes face.

Coyotes: "They are part of us"

Here, everybody knows about *coyoterismo*. Everyone has a direct experience, or knows someone who knows something about someone else. Coyotes are part of us. Anybody will tell you a bit. Everybody knows.

In the Ecuadorian southern provinces of Azuay and Cañar, "everybody knows" something about *coyoterismo*, as this statement from Azuay's attorney general indicates. Local authorities, taxi drivers, market vendors, waiters, shopkeepers, priests, teachers, street vendors, lawyers, NGO representatives, and of course, migrants and their families all appear to have had interactions with Ecuadorian irregularized migration.

Most of those who migrated during the first wave of migration following the decline in Panama hat production in the 1960s were male. These men knew or were aware of the migration route, having learned it through their own journeys, and likely perfected it through their contact with Mexican coyotes, later providing the service themselves on behalf of other people, likely as a favor ("The one who knew the route took someone else," stated the former priest of Gualaceo), thus beginning a social process of translocal and transnational clandestine movement.

However, not just anyone could become a coyote. In the early period of migration, only a few mestizo families occupied the lucrative positions of informal moneylenders and coyotes, relying on their connections in the United States through close friends and family members. The middle-class merchant families, who had profited during the straw-hat economy prior to its decline in the mid-1960s, composed the first wave of migrants to the United States and established and developed the initial migration facilitation networks.

The entrepreneurial middlemen in irregularized migration have deep historical roots in Ecuador's southern region. In the early half of the twentieth century, middle-class mestizo men would act as liaisons between indigenous households and landed oligarchs, religious officials, and coastal landowners seeking seasonal laborers, and were often called *enganchadores* (recruiters). In the early 2000s, a similar term was used for young men, riding in luxury pick-up trucks, who would drive through rural towns and villages telling people about the services of coyotes that they represented. Prior to 2008, most migrant brokers in the region were connected to merchant mestizo families who had dominated human smuggling activities for the previous 20 years. In the Southern Highlands of Ecuador, this identity-based, exclusionary economic practice perpetuated social and economic inequalities of the local agro-artisan economies, which were themselves shaped by a long history of indentured agrarian labor on the haciendas.

Migrants from rural locations described how peasants began migrating to the United States in the mid-1980s. They would get dressed in their best clothes before they visited the coyote in Cuenca—in indigenous narratives, this coyote was described as a mestiza woman—who would facilitate their journeys. The presence of a woman in a male-dominated business may be an indicator of the absence of male counterparts, as migrants in the region were primarily men. However, it might also point to the often invisible roles of women in smuggling, which often involve coordinating or putting facilitators and clients in contact (Sánchez 2016).[6] Regardless of their gender, mestizo coyotes controlled the process, exerting an exclusive and privileged financial and social role in the community.

By the 2000s, a critical shift occurred as a result of indigenous migrants' journeys. Indigenous people were able to forge their own social networks and connections and began to exercise the role of coyote themselves. The more established mestizo families had begun to lose the once exclusive connections to the United States because of U.S. migration reform, which criminalized illegal entries. There were also changes in the social dynamics of migrant communities, connected to the impact of globalization on rural areas. The crisis had indeed led to a significant shift in migration trends, which this time impacted all social classes and ethnicities, as the fluctuation of oil prices created significant job instability among the entire Ecuadorian society.

Overall, indigenous people welcomed the shift in the coyote-migrant dynamic. There was an expectation that the relationship between coyotes and migrants by virtue of sharing a common indigenous identity would be fairer, and more likely to take place in Kichwa, the indigenous language. The language barrier for monolingual Kichwa speakers who wanted to migrate was reduced, and would-be migrants were able to understand what the contracts entailed or what to expect from the journey. Indigenous people also believed that the community itself would have greater leverage over the actions of coyotes because of their membership in the community, therefore ensuring the safety and protection of migrants traveling under their watch. A male respondent from a smaller province in Cañar pointed out that there was also an expectation that indigenous coyotes would be more accountable to their communities, as the ties were stronger than with mestizos, especially if the coyote resided in the same village or province in which he recruited clients. Furthermore, the existence of extended family and kinship networks identifiable through indigenous surnames were thought to further reduce the possibility for abuse, threats, or intimidation from coyotes or money-lenders. The testimony of the same respondent attests to the transition:

> [Indigenous] men have been the ones showing up, more or less, they take the jobs from the mestizos. They work with more tranquility, seriousness, and honesty because they are part of the Kichwa community. The mestizos would take advantage of the lack of knowledge in these communities, while [the indigenous coyotes] are bilingual, explain everything in both languages and explain it well to the travelers. They are Cañari. Since 2002, there are Cañari coyotes. There's more trust. Perhaps because of the security. Also people can hold them accountable. Before there wasn't that opportunity.[7]

The changes, however, did not occur smoothly. While ethnic solidarity was expected, the broader transnational and global economic pressures also played a role in shaping the market. The economy of irregularized migration in Ecuador had developed within deeply entrenched social and economic inequalities, and eventually an even larger number of indigenous people joined the migration markets as transnational peasants (Kyle 2000) because of the persistent economic turmoil.

By the mid-2000s, indigenous coyotes had a significant role in the lucrative informal economy of the migration industry, which mestizo elites had long dominated. These changes signaled an important shift in the socioeconomic and ethnic stratification between mestizo elites and indigenous and rural workers. Raul, a 34-year-old indigenous leader from Cañar, states:

> There are no Cañari *chulqueros* (moneylenders), they are all mestizos, because the mestizos wouldn't let them in on the game and they got angry. Possibly that will change in the future. When they—the *chulqueros*—come for their payment, they are abusive. Back in 2001–2002, there were no coyotes here, only in the cities, there was one in Cuenca, a mestizo, and there was a big fight.[8]

Within the indigenous communities, social stratification has also increased between households with migrant members abroad and those without. The monetization of goods and services due to the influx of remittances, among other factors, has also exposed the deep differences and enduring inequalities that persist between indigenous and mestizo Ecuadorians.

Coyotes' perceptions in the community

Indigenous people are cognizant of the broader economic forces at play and the individual decision-making processes of coyotes. A Cañari man expressed jokingly: "We may not like what [coyotes] do but we may need their services one day."

Migration entrepreneurs, coyotes, and moneylenders are tolerated in their communities because they are a part of the social fabric. In interviews conducted during the first wave of this study (2008–2010), coyotes were described as performing a necessary role, and there was broad recognition that in communities like those in southern Ecuador somebody would eventually need their services. By the second wave of our study (2015–2016), local community actors and migrants were already describing coyotes based on their direct or indirect experiences. If the migrant had successfully arrived at their location, coyotes were praised and cast in a favorable light. Conversely, if there had been any failures (such as scams, accidents, disappearances, shipwrecks in the Pacific Ocean, or deaths), coyotes were defined as reckless, violent, or abusive. As Gonzalo, a 24-year-old deported migrant stated, a coyote was "someone to fear, and someone who gave me very bad memories."

Despite failed experiences, local residents and migrants in general asserted that coyotes were trusted facilitators or enablers of migration. Paul, a 21-year-old deported male, said, "Coyotes aid people to move, not only from Ecuador but from poverty. Why should we judge them? Those who should be judged are the ones who impede our free movement." In local urban towns, such as Gualaceo, Chordeleg, or El Descanso, coyotes are perceived as benefactors or *padrinos* (godfathers), as Zoila, a 54-year-old resident of Gualaceo, reflects:

> If you don't have a *padrino*, you cannot baptize the child. Right? It is the same: without a coyote, you won't make it, you cannot risk it, much less if it is your first time, you need him. In some rural communities, [coyotes] even become local *priostes*.[9]

On the other hand, coyotes were also depicted as disconnected from their communities and as likely to exploit migrants and their families. It is important to underline that the perceptions tied to smuggling facilitators or coyotes depended on the respondent's direct or indirect experiences with them, and these experiences were hardly ever easy to conceptualize as solely exploitative or supportive. For example, a law enforcement official we interviewed initially described coyotes as "men who take advantage of migrants" and "men who subject migrants to violent experiences." However, he also described them as "[being] part of us," recognizing the coyotes as members of the community.

So who are the coyotes? Kyle (2000) suggested that an understanding of Ecuadorian *coyoterismo* requires recognizing that a "migrant export model" has operated in the country—one in which migration merchants were central in the configuration of social networks, based on trust but often predatory financing to enable clandestine transits. Alongside coyotes, Kyle (2000, 66–67) identified the moneylender or *chulquero*, who often charges high interests on loans used by migrants to embark on clandestine journeys. Oftentimes the coyote plays the role of a *chulquero*, ensuring a higher return in profits. In other cases, the coyote refers the migrant to a reputable *chulquero*, usually local lawyers or business owners. By doing so, the social network of irregularized migration facilitation is extended to include the mainstream economy through document forgers, travel agents, airline staff, consular officials, and law enforcement to name a few.

In this social network, *chulqueros* are most often seen as a burden for migrants, and not necessarily as a trustworthy figure. To lend families or individuals money for migration journeys, *chulqueros* demand that they sign apocryphal contracts or surrender property titles. These documents, while in many cases illegal, constitute effective intimidation tools. In fact, references to *chulquero's* frauds and abuse of power were more common than those pertaining to coyotes in our sample. As Andrés, a 29-year-old migrant deported from the United States stated:

> The problem is not the coyotes. With certain exceptions, they usually keep their word and they guide people to reach the U.S. Otherwise, *coyoterismo* would have ended. Do you think we will still be trusting an activity that is destined to fail? Of course not. As migrants, we are not dumb. Accidents do happen on the route, but people arrive. Coyotes give us three attempts. *Chulqueros* are the problem: they abuse us and steal our properties, while threatening us.

However, while en route, coyotes in our study did engage in abusive behavior, which often went unpunished. This happens not only because migrants fear reprisal, but because of other social mechanisms put into place to reduce the likelihood of conflict through mediation. As one government prosecutor stated:

> People rarely report coyotes. When they do, usually the *chulquero* or someone else who works with the coyote negotiates with migrants' families and charges are not filed. It is very difficult for us to seek justice in this matter because people protect coyotes and cases come to a standstill. Scams linked to *chulqueros* are much more likely to be reported, though *chulqueros* also negotiate [solutions] in the shadow.

Coyotes may also not be criticized because of their historical role in the local economy. As an official at the Cañar's State Attorney General stated:

> It is very difficult to catch a coyote. Before him there is a lot of other people who won't dare to report him because the business would end. He hides behind them. The *chulqueros* or *enganchadores* (brokers) are caught before a coyote. But once caught, new people are immediately recruited. It has been and still is a super business.

Across communities in the Southern Highlands, the existence of *coyoterismo* ensures the emergence of often lucrative business opportunities, with legal and illegal business transactions becoming blurred, creating an income source that few want to jeopardize.

Contemporary Trends in Ecuadorian *Coyoterismo*

The testimonies of indigenous Ecuadorians are effective in identifying new transitions in and elements of the irregularized migration facilitation experience.

Despite the absence of official data on the number of people who rely on coyotes to embark on their routes or of empirical work on the dynamics of smuggling facilitation, our research identified a series of trends in the testimonies of migrants and their families.

Perhaps the most important of them is that despite the historical processes of migration and immigration enforcement in that country, the community-based, trust-dependent form of facilitation exists to this day. The irregularized migration facilitation processes that are primarily based on trust among coyotes, *chulqueros*, migrants, and their families are still commonplace in Ecuador, alongside other more recent forms of facilitation.

For example, in our research we identified a "relay-race" modality of *coyoterismo*, which has emerged to circumvent at least in part the border controls along the route. It relies on the contacts that coyotes have built over decades of journeys with their counterparts across the continent. While this form of *coyoterismo* only involves local, regional operations, it requires skill and knowledge in building relationship with coyotes from other countries who by virtue of possessing the same social capital, can "push" migrants forward. Hernan, a taxi driver describes how this works:

> Starting in the late 1980s, Ecuadorian coyotes developed direct links with Mexican coyotes. A coyote from Gualaceo would guide a group of migrants all the way into Mexico, or even further north. Now it is different. With so many controls, [coyotes] work as in a relay race: one coyote takes the people from here to Colombia, then another [takes them into another country] and it goes on [until their destination].

Hernan's testimony illustrates how *coyoterismo* has transformed because of the externalization of the U.S.-Mexico border—the implementation of stronger migration controls beyond the U.S.-Mexico border into the south has led others to adopt the tactics of Ecuadorian coyotes. The tightening of visa requirements, not only in the United States but also in Mexico, Guatemala, and Costa Rica, has also complicated transits that in the past could be easily carried out. Mexico has also implemented, in collaboration with and in response to demands from the United States, stricter migration controls in the last two years. Mexico has detained more migrants than the United States in the context of the program "Frontera Sur" or "Southern Border" (Badillo 2017).

As a result, since the end of the 1990s Ecuadorian coyotes have increasingly become part of a broader system of coyotes that operates along the continent. Unlike the 1970s or 1980s when coyotes were capable of transporting their clients from their place of origin to their destination, some Ecuadorian facilitators have opted to execute only a single segment of the journey, for instance from Ecuador to Bolivia or from Ecuador to Colombia (in some isolated cases, they do cover the entire segment, Ecuador-Mexico), in conjunction with other coyotes in the region.

Our field work has not produced evidence of any involvement of transnational organized crime. However, we did find strong connections between Ecuadorian and foreign coyotes along the migration route. Most of the communication among coyotes across borders takes place via cell phones. Coyotes exchange information and coordinate smuggling activities through their phones, and rely on wire transfer services such as Western Union or Money Gram to collect their funds undetected. The Internet and other mobile technologies has further strengthened coyotes' ability to conduct business virtually and remotely, often without even having to meet other smugglers, or even their clients.

Our respondents reported that access to phones has altered the interactions that once characterized the coyote-migrant relationship: services have become impersonal, distant, and the once taken-for-granted level of care has eroded. Andres, a deported migrant explains: "People meet with coyotes less now because we exchange phone numbers and stay in touch via text messages or Whatsapp. We then sort out things such as payment arrangements or departing points solely by phone." A government official supported this claim, alleging: "the upsurge of border control has led to a complex situation: migrants do not know their coyotes. Today, it is *coyoterismo* without a face." Coyotes are, therefore, increasingly becoming anonymous, and their traditional and expected roles as caregivers[10] are diminishing. When migrants or their families ran into trouble during their journey, they often found themselves alone, and they lacked the ability to get help or to report or confront those who they had hired. Respondents stated that the change in the facilitation of irregular migration has played a role in the increased vulnerability of migrants, namely, disappearances, and in the incidence of violence and death along the migration corridor.

Reports of robberies, extortion, discrimination, collective or individual kidnapping, torture, sexual assault, traffic accidents, disappearances, and murders are not uncommon along smuggling routes. Smugglers are not the only perpetrators of these crimes. Border control authorities, police, thieves, members of drug trafficking organizations, gangs, other migrants in transit, and ordinary citizens are all among those behind acts of violence against migrants in transit. These crimes remain largely unreported and are therefore never punished. The depersonalization of smuggling facilitation, as reported by respondents, creates the conditions for these abusive practices to continue.[11]

Another serious consequence of the depersonalization of *coyoterismo* and its increased reliance on mobile technology is the growing number of migrants who engage in self-smuggling, as well as in the provision of amateur services to others. This change appears to stem from the increased number of deportees returned from Mexico and the United States. As border securitization increases risks in crossing and thus smuggling costs, Ecuadorians often lack the funds to hire coyotes. As a result, when these deported migrants embark on their return north, they act as their own coyotes and often assist others in similar situation as a cost-saving measure. These practices are perceived by locals as chaotic, and as placing the migrant and those who decide to travel along at risk. A government official states:

> Deported migrants do not necessarily know the route. Even though some of them have recently been on transit along the route, others left [Ecuador] one or two decades ago. Today there are new rules in this game and [migrants] do not know them. Deportation

has caused more disappearances because [deportees] think they can guide but they cannot.

Deported migrants often do not know the route nor do they have experience negotiating or dealing with more seasoned coyotes. This lack of experience and connections can lead to violent confrontations with more established smugglers. Still, though, there is no shortage of deported migrants who begin a new journey north on their own. Wi-Fi hotspots and GPS-enabled phones give these less-experienced migrants the confidence to begin their journeys once again. And because of cell phones, migrants can remain in constant contact with friends and family members, tapping into the collective knowledge created, shared, and updated by migrants in transit. Facebook, Skype, Google Maps, and Whatsapp give many the confidence to launch their personal smuggling operation without having to pay a coyote or deal with a *chulquero*. Manuel, a deported migrant in the process of planning his journey, stated:

> Why do we need to pay? I know the route, I already went through once, and I have this [showing his Smartphone]: I need a Wi-Fi connection and that's it. I have maps, routes and my contacts that will guide me. You know what? I'm not leaving alone, I'll go with my friends. I'll take them and they pay [me].

The access to such shared migratory knowledge means coyotes' traditional monopoly of smuggling knowledge is being challenged and perhaps may even be rendered unnecessary in the future. The arrival of "amateur" coyotes is changing the dynamics of *coyoterismo* in ways that warrant further research.

Conclusion

Historicizing mobility and placing identity at the center of the analysis of human smuggling provides a nuanced narrative of human smuggling that in most ways contradicts the dominant characterization of smuggling as a criminal activity amid rising securitization of national borders. Within the small villages of Southern Highland Ecuador, mobility for labor and trade is deeply rooted in the cultural norms of indigenous communities. However, globalization and migration regimes have led to the transformation of mobility practices and to the reconfiguration of the players in the informal economy of smuggling. In the testimonials here, indigenous coyotes were considered to be more than facilitators: they were community members who were expected to adhere to communal practices of reciprocity and trust, in contrast to the relationships with mestizo coyotes. However, ethnic solidarity did not necessarily mitigate exploitation within the informal economy.

Migration provides "new anchors" for identity beyond those centered on the nation-state, region, or locality. As indigenous leaders mobilize and organize based on indigenous identity, territory, and community, there is a growing cosmopolitan vision of indigeneity that emerges out of transnational migration and globalization (Cadena 2010; Delugan 2010). In Ecuador, national discourse about rural migration is largely negative despite the dependence on remittances throughout the country. This discourse casts the migrant as reckless and irresponsible, and makes a false correlation between their "abandonment" and the overwhelming burden that it places on state institutions, such as schools and other social service centers. On an international level, scorn is largely reserved for migrant facilitators. However, as we see here, there is much to take into consideration about who coyotes are, what roles they play, and the historical and sociocultural depth around which people organize their personal migration projects.

The reinforcement of border controls in the Americas since the 1990s has had direct repercussions on the social and behavioral processes of *coyoterismo* and irregularized migration. Increases in deportations have turned Ecuador into a revolving door, a temporary place of respite to recommence another journey toward the north, further promoting the demand for *coyoterismo*.

Rather than defining it solely as a criminal or a benign practice, *coyoterismo* in Ecuador is best understood as a practice and an element within the continuum of migrants' decision-making, and in which migrants play clear and active roles. In response to ever-changing migratory policies, *coyoterismo* must, therefore, be understood as a contingent sociohistorical process. Technological advances in communication have brought about profound changes to the modus operandi of smuggling operations. Nowadays smuggling is carried out in tranches controlled by local coyotes, who also operate as brokers for other coyotes on the continent. Migrants, however, are not passive by any means. They share tips, strategies, and routes, and sometimes travel without using coyotes' services.

Restrictive state responses to migration fuel mobility and are consequently responsible for the further proliferation of *coyoterismo*, as is in the case of Ecuador. The inability of the United States' government to develop comprehensive immigration policies—including mechanisms for expedited family reunification—has also encouraged the growth of *coyoterismo* (Álvarez Velasco and Guillot Cuéllar 2012). In the Ecuadorian case, coyotes represent a much more agile and effective way to bring together children and their immigrant parents and to reunite families.

Despite the complexity and long history of smuggling in Ecuador, the media and political discourse continues to treat the phenomenon as a criminal activity deserving tough punishment. This push toward criminalization suggests that the Ecuadorian government has failed to understand the complexity of migrant smuggling. While constructing smuggling as a problem makes it easy to promote and legitimize state interests, the social and cultural processes of *coyoterismo* involve complex and often hidden factors such as the reliance on the informal economy as a way of subsistence, and the poverty and inequity that for decades have encouraged irregularized migration among indigenous people. The Ecuadorian state's views on irregularized migration differ fundamentally from local, indigenous understandings in which coyotes, far from being a "threat," are part of local everyday life—they are "part of us."

Notes

1. The term *irregularized migration* instead of *irregular migration* is used in this article to bring attention to the social, political, and juridical processes that consign some migrants to an "illegal" or "irregular" status. The more commonly used term "irregular" migration suggests the existence of an antagonist and supports a binary discriminatory regime between "desired" and "nondesired" migrants, where regular—and all possible synonyms, such as documented, authorized, legal—is directly linked to the former and irregular to the latter. In an attempt to surpass the binary trap, critical migration scholars argue for denaturalizing the term and focusing on the processes that produce it, appealing for an understanding of the social and political processes that render some people "illegal" or "irregular" (De Genova 2002; Bauder 2014; Dauvergne 2008).

2. The Ecuadorian population is ethnically diverse and can be roughly categorized into four ethnoracial groups: white (of Spanish/European descent), mestizo (of Spanish/European and indigenous descent), Afro-Ecuadorian (of African and European or indigenous descent), and indigenous.

3. Jokisch (2014) indicates that most of the first migrants to Spain were women who posed as tourists and traveled with the help of Ecuadorian travel agencies. These women typically obtained work as domestic workers.

4. The forceful removal of 147 Cuban nationals from El Arbolito Park the night of July 6, 2016, comes to mind.

5. The Human Mobility Management Unit of the Provincial Government of Pichincha is a local public office located in Quito, Ecuador's capital, which provides social, psychological, and legal support, and economic advice to Ecuadorean returned and deported migrants, to worldwide immigrants including migrants in transit, and to asylum seekers and refugees.

6. Smuggling is a highly gendered occupation. Tasks are feminized, with women performing caregiving and cleaning roles, while men guide groups and drive vehicles; they execute tasks that are often deemed as carrying more importance than those performed by women. See Zhang, Chin, and Miller (2007) and Sánchez (2016).

7. Interview with Victoria Stone-Cadena, Cañar, Ecuador, 2008.

8. Ibid.

9. A *prioste* is a person chosen or self-appointed to finance community celebrations, often as a mark of status.

10. See Vogt (2013) on care and intimacy in the smuggler-migrant relationship.

11. Majidi, in this volume, found that the protection smugglers are able to provide to migrants in transit diminishes the farther they get from home, as smugglers' contacts are more likely to be unknown or unrelated to the ones the migrant originally hired.

References

Álvarez Velasco, S. 2016. Crisis migratoria contemporánea? Complejizando el vínculo migración irregularizada, violencia y Estado capitalista a partir de la dinámica de dos corredores migratorios globales. *Ecuador Debate* 97:63–88.

Álvarez Velasco, Soledad, and Sandra Guillot Cuéllar. 2012. *Between violence and invisibility. An analysis of Ecuadorian unaccompanied children and adolescents in the migratory process to the USA.* Quito: SENAMI.

Andolina, Rober, Nina Laurie, and Sarah Radcliffe. 2009a. Development, transnational networks, and indigenous politics. In *Indigenous development in the Andes: Culture, power, and transnationalism*, 23–52. Durham, NC: Duke University Press.

Andolina, Robert, Nina Laurie, and Sarah Radcliffe, eds. 2009b. *Indigenous development in the Andes: Culture, power, and transnationalism*. Durham, NC: Duke University Press.

Auyero, Javier. 2012. *Patients of the state. The politics of waiting in Argentina.* Durham, NC: Duke University Press.

Badillo, Diego. 2017. Suben las deportaciones de centroamericanos desde México. *The Economist*.

Banco Central del Ecuador. 2015. *Evolución de las Remesas.* Nacional Resumen Anual 2015. Quito.

Baraona, Rafael. 1965. Una tipología de haciendas en la sierra ecuatoriana. In *Reformas agrarias en la América Latina*, ed. Ó. Delgado, 688–96. México and Buenos Aires: Fondo de Cultura Económica.

Bauder, Harald. 2014. Why we should use the term "illegalized" refugee or immigrant. *International Journal of Refugee Law* 26 (3): 327–32.

Berg, Ulla, and Carla Tamagno. 2013. Migration brokers and document fixers: The making of migrant subject in urban Peru. In *The migration industry and the commercialization of international migration*, eds. Ninna Nyberg-Sørensen and Thomas Gammeltoft-Hansen, 190–214. New York, NY: Routledge.

Bretón, Victor, F. Garcia, A. Jove, and M. J. Vilalta, eds. 2007. *Ciudadanía y exclusión: Ecuador y España frente al espejo.* Madrid: Catarata.

Cadena, Marisol de la, and Orin Starn. 2010. *Indigeneidades contemporáneas: Cultura, política y globalización.* Lima, Perú: Instituto Francés de Estudios Andinos, Instituto de Estudios Peruanos.

Castellanos, M. Bianet, Lourdes Gutiérrez Nájera, and Arturo J. Aldama, eds. 2012. *Comparative indigeneities of the Americas: Toward a hemispheric approach.* Tucson, AZ: University of Arizona Press.

Chiriboga, Manuel. 2013. *La situación del campo ecuatoriano. Documento de trabajo enpresentación powerpoint presentada en el taller preparatorio para la elaboración del documento final de investigación: Capacidades, limitaciones y desafíos sociales, políticos, económicos y ambientales del Ecuador contemporáneo.* Quito: OSE & PNUD.

Clark, Kim, and Marc Becker, eds. 2007. *Highland Indians and the state in modern Ecuador.* Pittsburgh, PA: University of Pittsburgh Press.

Dauvergne, Catherine. 2008. *Making people illegal: What globalization means for migration and law.* New York, NY: Cambridge University Press.

De Genova, Nicholas. 2002. Migrant "illegality" and deportability in everyday life. *Annual Review of Anthropology* 31:419–47.

De Genova, Nicholas. 2005. *Working the boundaries: Race, space, and "illegality" in Mexican Chicago.* Durham, NC: Duke University Press.

Delugan, Robin Maria. 2010. Indigeneity across borders: Hemispheric migrations and cosmopolitan encounters. *American Ethnologist* 37(1):83–97.

Directorate of Attention and Protection of Ecuadoreans Abroad of the Ministry of Foreign Affairs and Human Mobility of Ecuador (DAPE). 2016. *Estadísticas globales de deportaciones de ecuatorianos desde Estados unidos de américa 2012–2016.* Azuay: DAPE.

Gallegos, Franklin Ramírez, and Jacques Paul Ramírez. 2005. *La estampida migratoria ecuatoriana. Crisis, redes transnacionales y repertorios de acción migratoria.* Quito: CIC.

Hernández-León, Rúben. 2013. Conceptualizing the migration industry. In *The Migration industry and the commercialization of international migration*, eds. Ninna Nyberg Sørensen and Thomas Gammeltoft-Hansen, 24–44. New York, NY: Taylor & Francis Group.

Instituto Nacional de Estadísticas y Censos (INEC). 2013. *Encuesta Nacional de Empleo, Desempleo y Subempleo Urbano y Rural, 2007–2012, and Censo Nacional.* Quito: INEC.

Instituto Nazionale di Statistica (ISTAT). 2012. *Cittadini non comunitari regolarmente presenti in Italia.* Available from: http://demo.istat.it/altridati/noncomunitari/ index_e.html.

Jokisch, Brad. 2014. *Ecuador: From mass emigration to return migration?* Washington, DC: Migration Policy Institute. Available from: http://www.migrationpolicy.org/article/ecuador-mass-emigration-return-migration.

Kyle, David. 2000. *Transnational peasants: Migrations, networks, and ethnicity in Andean Ecuador.* Baltimore, MD: Johns Hopkins University Press.

Kyle, David, and Rachel Goldstein. 2011. *Migration industries: A comparison of the Ecuador-U.S. and Ecuador-Spain cases.* San Domenico di Fiesole: European University Institute.

Kyle, David, and Christina Siracusa. 2005. Seeing the state like a migrant: Why so many non-criminals break immigration laws. In *Illicit flows and criminal things: States, border, and the other side of globalization*, eds. Itty Abrahamn and Willem van Schendel, 153–76. Bloomington, IN: Indiana University Press.

Marcus, George E. 1995. Ethnography in/of the world system: The emergence of multi-sited ethnography. *Annual Review of Anthropology* 24:95–117.

Murra, John V., Nathan Wachtel, and Jacques Revel. 1986. *Anthropological history of Andean polities.* New York, NY: Cambridge University Press.

Nyberg Sørensen, Ninna, and Thomas Gammeltoft-Hansen, eds. 2013. *The migration industry and the commercialization of international migration*. New York, NY: Taylor & Francis Group.

Organization of the Petroleum Exporting Countries (OPEC). 2015. *Annual statistical bulletin*. Vienna: OPEC.

Ruíz, Martha C., and Soledad Álvarez Velasco. 2016. *Entre el enfoque de derechos humanos y las lógicas de seguridad y control: Análisis de las políticas públicas en torno a la trata de personas y el tráfico de migrantes en Ecuador (2004-2016)*. Quito: Save the Children, FLACSO.

Sánchez, Gabriella. 2016. Women's participation in the facilitation of human smuggling: The case of the U.S. Southwest. *Geopolitics* 21 (2): 387–406.

Stone-Cadena, Victoria. 2016. Indigenous Ecuadorian mobility strategies in the clandestine migration journey. *Geopolitics* 21 (2): 345–65.

Torres, Alicia, and Jesus Carrasco. 2008. *Al filo de la identidad: La migración indígena en América Latina*. Quito: FLACSO-Sede Ecuador, UNICEF, AECID.

Urry, John. 2007. *Mobilities*. Cambridge, MA: Polity Press.

Vogt, Wendy. A. 2013. Crossing Mexico: Structural violence and the commodification of undocumented Central American migrants. *American Ethnologist* 40 (4): 764–80.

Zhang, Sheldon X., Ko-Lin Chin, and Jody Miller. 2007. Women's participation in Chinese transnational human smuggling: A gendered market perspective. *Criminology* 45 (3): 699–733.

Migrant Smuggling: Novel Insights and Implications for Migration Control Policies

By
ANNA TRIANDAFYLLIDOU

This article offers a critical review of how migrant smuggling arises out of restrictive migration policies and how it has become increasingly sophisticated and professionalized. Reflecting on the innovative empirical findings presented in the contributions to this volume of *The ANNALS*, I highlight how migration control has hardened borders, disrupted cross-border flows of goods and people, and transformed local economies. Understanding better the relationship between migration control policies and migrant smuggling and the social and moral nature of the agent-customer transactions has important implications for the policies adopted to address irregular migration and migrant smuggling on both sides of the Atlantic.

Keywords: migrant smuggling; *passeurs*; migration control; enforcement; moral economy; migration control policy

Migrant smuggling is commonly represented through images of desperate people crossing inhospitable territories, notably the Arizona Desert from Mexico to the United States, and the Sahara Desert from Niger to Libya or Algeria, and of course the Mediterranean Sea to the Italian or Greek shores. Migrant smugglers are often portrayed in the media as callous criminals who send derelict and overcrowded dinghies across the Mediterranean. Or as unscrupulous coyotes who do not hesitate to abandon their customers-victims in the desert. The common element in these representations is death, abuse, severe deceit, and exploitation. Smugglers are portrayed as the perpetrators of criminal acts for profit. They benefit from the poor and vulnerable

Anna Triandafyllidou is a full professor in the Global Governance Programme (GGP) at the Robert Schuman Centre for Advanced Studies (RSCAS), European University Institute. Within the GGP, she coordinates the research area on cultural pluralism. She is the editor-in-chief of the Journal of Immigrant and Refugee Studies.

Correspondence: anna.triandafyllidou@eui.eu

DOI: 10.1177/0002716217752330

of the world who seek a better life and work opportunities in foreign countries. Their customers, the migrants, are seen as victims of ruthless criminal networks (Kyle and Koslowski 2001; European Commission 2015). This volume of *The ANNALS* goes against this conventional wisdom and dominant media discourse to argue that migrant smuggling is a complex phenomenon; that portraying smugglers as criminals and migrants as their victims oversimplifies a nuanced relationship; and that we need to think harder and dig deeper into realities on the ground, not least through qualitative empirical research and through comparative analysis, to understand the relationship between migrant smuggling and migration control policies.

The aim of this policy article is to review how migrant smuggling arises out of restrictive migration policies and how it has become increasingly sophisticated and professionalized. Reflecting on the innovative empirical findings presented in the contributions to this volume of *The ANNALS*, I highlight how migration control has hardened borders, disrupted cross-border flows of goods and people, and transformed local economies. While the "smuggling business" turnover has dramatically increased, previously custom *passeurs* have turned to professionalized and well-equipped networks. In addition, I seek to illustrate how monetary transactions are embedded in wider systems of social relationships and what several of the authors contributing to this volume (e.g. Achilli, Maher, Majidi, Brachet, Ayalew) conceptualize as moral economies and wider systems of social relationships. While these relationships by no means justify the work of migrant smugglers, they point to the relevance of historical patterns (see for instance Stone-Cadena and Velasco) and to the wider economic and political factors that play a part in migrations (see for instance Majidi, but also Ayalew and Guevara González). Understanding better the relationship between migration control policies and migrant smuggling and the social and moral nature of the agent-customer transactions has important implications for the policies adopted to address irregular migration and migrant smuggling on both sides of the Atlantic.

Irregular Migration and Migrant Smuggling

The causes of irregular migration broadly lie in the intersection among people's search for life prospects, labor market demand, and restrictive immigration controls. This is of course no news in the study of international migration, and yet there is something qualitatively different about migration today by comparison to the early twentieth century and even to the 1970s or 1980s. While globalization has intensified, integrating all countries into a global economy, expanding trade, intensifying communication, and making distant production systems interdependent, one of its naturally ensuing phenomena, notably the movement of people, is increasingly stiffened and restricted. In this sense, we may argue that irregular migration and migrant smuggling are phenomena of the late-twentieth and early-twenty-first centuries. This does not imply that there were no cross-border flows prior to this time or that all such flows were documented. It signals that hard territorial and digital borders[1] have started solidifying mostly since the

1970s and particularly in the last 20 years. This has codified flows as irregular/illegal (see also Düvell 2006) and led to the emergence of social and criminal networks aimed at facilitating cross-border movement where movement is not legally authorized (Massey, Durand, and Pren 2016; Salt and Stein 1997; Triandafyllidou and Maroukis 2012). In other words, we need to reconceptualize *irregular migration* as a structural feature of late-modern society rather than as an exception or social pathology.

Migrant smuggling emerges when and where borders are fixed, relatively impermeable, and protected by a border bureaucracy, which includes border crossing points, border guards, passport controls, entry visas, and stamps on one's passport when entering or leaving a country (Mountz 2010). This bureaucracy involves a range of border actors including not only state authorities and border guards but also nongovernmental organizations, international organizations, and of course migrant smuggling and human trafficking networks. Thus, people who wish to move to a new country without appropriate authorization may organize their trip on their own or with the help of family and friends based at the country of transit or destination but also increasingly rely on specialized networks of facilitators, *passeurs*, coyotes, handlers, or also *scaffisti*. This happens as a direct consequence of the very mechanisms and instruments mobilized to control borders. The higher the hurdles, the more professionalized the assistance unauthorized migrants (and asylum seekers) will need.

As Kyle and Koslowski (2001, 5) argued more than a decade ago, the smuggling of migrants into countries where they are not allowed to enter is not new, what is new is the global spread and development of the phenomenon. Sixteen years later, in 2017, there has been a development of the human smuggling and trafficking networks in the breadth and size of their criminal activities and business turnover—the amount of money involved in these two sectors as fees paid or profit made from these two activities—and a growth in the concern of governments and international organizations in combating these two related phenomena. Indeed the smuggling of migrants in general, as well as into Europe in particular, has been a priority for the United Nations Office on Drugs and Crime (UNODC) and its special antismuggling and antitrafficking training programs. Trafficking in human beings, an issue closely related to human smuggling, has also become a priority[2] for international organizations such as the International Organization for Migration (IOM). Most recently, the EU created a special office within Europol called the European Migrant Smuggling Centre.[3]

The Challenge for Policy

Increasing restrictions on migration or asylum seeking risks perpetuating a vicious circle: the restrictions generate irregular migration, increasing the risks and costs to migrants and their dependence on smuggling networks, the latter of which turn to more sophisticated methods to avoid controls, and hence of course provide reasons for even more restrictions and heightened controls. In addition, irregular migration routes and smuggling activities further blur the distinction between different categories of migrants, as asylum seekers and economically motivated migrants share the same routes, services, and networks (Van Liempt 2007, 14; Koser 2010; Van Hear 2009).

There are four distinct issues that cast light on the dynamics of this vicious circle. First, borders that used to be formal but very permeable are being hardened, disrupting and transforming cross-border exchanges and movements. Second, migrant facilitation activities should be understood as embedded in local economies, often through the involvement of local "travel" agents of various sorts. Third, these loose networks operate through a combination of economic motivation and profit, as well as social meanings of trust and community in a highly insecure environment that needs to be appraised in all its complexity to effectively understand the roots of migrant smuggling. Fourth, the increased restrictions and police violence at the border and in transit lead to the transformation of such loose networks to more professionalized, organized, and, indeed, criminal networks. While open borders may not be viable, the current emphasis on border securitization and externalization of controls to transit countries (neighboring and more distant to the United States and the EU) contributes to the professionalization and criminalization of smuggling networks while it does not stop irregular migration flows because the motivations to migrate, both economic and political, are too strong. There is an urgent need for a more comprehensive approach that mainstreams local economic and community factors in the effort to manage unauthorized migration. I outline some of these aspects next.

Hardening borders

First, borders that used to be formal but permeable are being hardened, disrupting and transforming cross-border exchanges and movements. Brachet (this volume) highlights the dynamics of the cross-Saharan flows of goods, which also include transporting people across Niger to Libya. The city of Agadez was a main transit point, a traditional stop for old caravan routes, that was buzzing as a stopover for trucks that would transport goods back and forth. Prospective irregular migrants would speak directly to these lorry drivers and arrange prices for their transportation. Both the lorry drivers and the migrants would see this as an informal transportation service rather than as an unauthorized border crossing. West Africans seeking employment in Algeria and Libya usually took this migratory route; only a few among them would end up farther north to attempt a crossing into Europe (Pliez 2003). The truck drivers who would today qualify as migrant smugglers were understood, according to Brachet, as traders.

However, the breakdown of the Khaddafi regime in Libya has created lawlessness and chaos, and disrupted the national economy that was the source of employment for West African migrants. Thus, migration has moved farther north through the Mediterranean, to Europe. European countries have responded by improving their sea border controls and by externalizing migration controls to transit countries. Thus, as Brachet so aptly explains, the borders between Niger and Libya and Algeria have been hardened and the governments of those countries pressured to tighten border controls. International organizations opened local offices to manage cross-border movement. Police and border forces were pressured to change tactics, stopping and controlling lorries. Passing became more risky, bribes increased, and the means of transport changed. Cross-border movement shifted from informal to clandestine. Drivers of commercial lorries were no longer willing to run the risk of carrying irregular migrant workers. However, security guards from the gold mines near Agadez were ready to step in to transport migrants. Informal travel agencies closed and migration facilitation became more organized; more expensive; riskier, as it had to cross through desert points rather than formal border crossings; and more violent, as local police and military forces in Niger sought to stop the flows. New laws criminalized facilitation and transportation of migrants.

A similar process has been taking place in Mexico, as Guevara González illustrates in this volume. Pressures on Mexico to control Central American migration through the country toward the United States has led to the tightening of Mexican borders and the criminalization of informal movements. In this case, the border has become an internal boundary. Migration control takes place in public spaces, such as through random checkpoints on highways and in public squares, or bus and train stations, or even on board the trains. The journey has become particularly risky and unsafe (see also Sanchez 2015), which has increased the need for migrants to hire professional smugglers. This need has contributed to the professionalization of smuggler services. Guevara González points to how migrant services are now divided between the local guides who cover short legs of a longer journey, and the coyotes who facilitate irregular migration on to the United States. Guevara González shows how these practices lead to what Collyer (2010, 275) has termed "fragmented journeys." Notably the transit takes more time and more money, and it often involves interruptions due to bad health, running out of money, being arrested and detained, and being sent back and moving forward again.

Disrupting local economies

Tightening the borders does combat migrant smuggling networks, but it does not address the local economic dynamics that support the services of smugglers. As Achilli (this volume) suggests, the EU-Turkey statement and joint action plan, as well as the initial conception of Operation Sophia (aimed at destroying boats and dismantling smuggling networks), temporarily tackled migrant flows out of Turkey, but they did not address either the root causes of or the local economic factors in migration. These included, notably, the large number of small shop owners who were making a living by selling life jackets and related gear, the car owners who helped with transportation of "customers," and the owners of houses and hotels in the areas near the port of Mersin or Izmir where Syrians and others stayed before boarding the boats to Greece. These actors do not qualify as criminals, but they have created the habitus within which migrant smuggling or facilitation takes place. As Achilli, Brachet, and Guevara González illustrate in this volume, smuggling provides for such side-jobs and thus has its own socioeconomic dynamic.

Brachet further emphasizes this point by noting that in the Sahel such services were not always labeled as illegal and are still not considered criminal to this day. Money paid to stay at provisional shelters or to buy food and supplies and even the bribes paid to police and border guards were fed into the local economy, indirectly undermining any motivation to turn to criminal activities, such as that existing today. While the EU and the United States are spending millions to support border controls, open international organization offices, and build capacity in transit countries, they are at the same time taking away valuable sources of cash for local communities. It is unclear whether government funding to build migration control capacity and setting up local IOM or Frontex branches is feeding in any way into the local economies or rather exacerbating local and regional inequality.

Profit and trust: Complex morality

Economic motivations and profit, as well as social meanings of trust and community in a highly insecure environment, need to be taken into account to fully understand migration facilitation. Moving away from a simple understanding of migrant as victim and smuggler as criminal, contributions to this volume highlight the complex system of trust, interdependence, community ties, and profit that is used during the smuggling process. There are several important findings in this volume that help us to understand the complex "morality" of smuggling.

First, initial contact with and choosing the smuggler take place within the community, through the recommendation of other migrants and through relatives and fellow villagers. Second, the smuggler and migrant face hardships together during the crossings. Preparations for a long and perilous journey from Senegal to the Canary Islands (see Maher, this volume), for example, reveal the boat captains' concerns for the safety of their passengers.

Ayalew (this volume) points to the accumulation of knowledge that is necessary for navigating border controls and perilous journeys. Ayalew points to the creation of communities of knowledge that involve Eritreans at home, Eritrean diasporas in neighboring (Ethiopia or the Sudan) and distant (Europe) countries, and pilots (boat captains) who navigate high danger areas and avoid kidnappings or death. Similarly, Achilli (this volume) points to the hardship shared by facilitators and migrants on the road from Turkey to Greece and further north.

Majidi (this volume) also discusses the role of community ties for Afghans and Somalis—two groups that have increasingly sought protection outside their own countries in the last decade. The interplay between moral obligation and economic profit and dependence is very tight. At the end of the day, the intermediary, the *hawala* (Afghanistan) or the *dahabshiil* (Somalia), keeps the money until the journey is successfully completed; this guarantees that the initial trust is honored and the service is provided.

Slack and Martinez's contribution offers an interesting distinction between satisfaction with the service and trust in one's smuggler. While satisfaction with a smuggler is affected by the success of the journey, recommending a smuggler to a close relative has more to do with the quality of the service en route, including safety (particularly of women) and humane treatment, than with success or completion of the journey.

All contributions to this volume point to the sense of moral obligation that these smugglers feel toward their customers and to the transnational systems of trust and knowledge that emerge from this obligation. While the policy implications of these findings may not be apparent at first glance, the findings do point to the complex role of the migrant smuggler that is not reflected in current policies and certainly not in law enforcement and to the need to go beyond a criminal justice framework to work with local origin and transit communities.

Transformation of the smuggling networks

Several studies have elaborated on the distinctive roles of those involved in smuggling networks, distinguishing among local guides and transnational contacts, those who meet people at ports or airports or other arrival places and those higher up in the hierarchy who have contacts with, for instance, corrupt border guards (Antonopoulos and Winterdyk 2006; Içduygu and Toktas 2002; Içduygu 2004; Triandafyllidou and Maroukis 2012). This volume of *The ANNALS* contributes to a more critical and historical view of how migrant smuggling networks were formed and how they built on preexisting local and regional relationships between and within communities. Stone-Cadena (this volume) explains how services facilitating international border crossing are embedded in historical patterns of movement, trade, and exchange across Ecuador. Blanchet argues the same for trans-Saharan crossings.

However, the tightening of borders and the increase of controls disrupt such patterns and lead to the professionalization of smuggling networks. Stone-Cadena and Alvarez-Velasco explain how indigenous *coyoterismo*, based on community relations of interdependence and trust, is now transformed into transnational organized crime networks that operate by phone in which relationships are impersonal and trust is replaced by dependence and fear. They convincingly argue that this change in *coyoterismo* has resulted because of visa restrictions that have stiffened the passage not only to the United States but also through Mexico, Guatemala, and Costa Rica, and because of the role assigned to Mexico by the United States as a buffer zone. Guevara González also shows how these new criminal networks involve both more traditional actors, notably local guides who know the terrain, and professional facilitators, the *coyotes*, who arrange the unauthorized border crossing.

Concluding Remarks: Diverting the Flows

The critical analysis of migrant smuggling that I discuss here and that the articles in this volume elucidate points to the need for a more comprehensive approach to irregular migration and asylum seeking—one that avoids categorical distinctions between victims and perpetrators, migrants and their smugglers. It also points to the disproportional focus afforded in recent years to the criminal activities of smuggling networks and points to how such networks can be the byproducts of the very restrictions that aim to combat them.

Contributions to this volume of *The ANNALS* point to a number of important lessons to be learned by policy-makers:

- **Tightening borders and disrupting local migrant facilitation economies have important implications, albeit in the opposite direction than the one desired.** Instead of discouraging migrants and dismantling smuggling networks, these policies lead to migrants investing more money and facing more risks (and often death) along their journeys, while the networks become professionalized. Trust and community relationships are increasingly replaced by pure profit-seeking and dependence, leading to higher risks and more ruthlessness.

- **Border controls and the fight against migrant smuggling need to take into account wider regional political and economic processes.** For instance, the fall of the Khaddafi regime in Libya and the concomitant dismantling of the Libyan oil economy have deprived both earlier migrants and natives of their local means of subsistence. Further regional economic factors have escaped the radar of European and international policy-makers, such as the closure of gold mines in Djado and Aïr mountains in Niger and the resulting unemployment of young (and armed) local men (see Brachet, this volume).

- **The war in Syria, conflict in Somalia, oppression in Eritrea, insecurity in Afghanistan, inhospitable treatment of Afghans in Iran, poverty and lack of hope in Central America, all lead to strong motivations for moving.** Such motivations cannot be offset by tightening borders and criminalizing smugglers. There is an urgent need to work with origin and transit countries to accomplish the following: (1) Develop bilateral schemes for temporary or long-term employment that would ease migration pressures by providing realistic labor migration options for both highly and low-skilled migrants (see also Triandafyllidou [2017] on a sectorial approach to labor migration management). Such examples have worked, for instance, in the Mediterranean region between Morocco and Spain for employment in the agricultural sector (Gonzalez 2013) and also between Slovakia and Austria in the care sector (Humer and Hrzenjak 2015). (2) Develop information campaigns through local associations in the countries of origin and transit about the dangers of irregular migration and migrant smuggling and the difficult conditions that migrants face not only en route but also upon arrival (lack of rights, lack of employment, very poor living conditions, risk of arrest and expulsion, and so on). (3) Develop international schemes of responsibility sharing for asylum seekers. The emergency quotas for the relocation of asylum seekers among European Union Member States is a partly successful experiment on how to deal with massive arrivals of people seeking international protection (European Commission 2017). Perhaps more can be learned from the UN scheme for the Vietnamese boat people in the late 1970s and more recently the refugees worldwide (Chetty 2001).

- Last, there is a need for a **wider understanding of the monetary value of border control.** The EU and the United States spend millions in fencing and gatekeeping (Triandafyllidou and Ambrosini 2011), not only employing border guards but also buying expensive border control equipment such as infrared cameras, thermic sensors, or radars. In addition, they invest a lot of money to build capacity in transit countries in Central America as well as in North Africa and the Sahel. Such money does not trickle down to the local or national economies. It is often international experts who are employed in these offices who will not spend their money locally (see also Brachet 2016). The funds resulting from the EU-Turkey agreement do not address the grievances of cross border communities either in southeast or in southwest Turkey that had profited from the smuggling business. The investment of Mexican and Moroccan authorities in their border control capacity does not help to address the root causes of West African or Central American transit flows. Increased enforcement risks only exacerbating the violence of police forces and ruthlessness of smugglers while the flows are at best diverted to other routes.

Notes

1. The term *digital borders* refers to the increased securitization of passports and visas through the insertion of holograms and electronic chips that make them hard to counterfeit.

2. For the UNODC, see http://www.unodc.org/unodc/en/human-trafficking/smuggling-of-migrants.html?ref=menuside; and for IOM, see: http://www.iom.int/jahia/Jahia/pid/748.

3. See https://www.europol.europa.eu/about-europol/european-migrant-smuggling-centre-emsc.

References

Antonopoulos, George A., and John Winterdyk. 2006. The smuggling of migrants in Greece: An examination of its social organization. *European Journal of Criminology* 3:439–61.

Brachet, Julian. 2016. Policing the desert. The IOM and Libya beyond war and peace. *Antipodes* 48 (2): 272–92.

Chetty, Lakshmana. 2001. *Resolution of the problem of boat people: The case for a global initiative.* ISIL Year Book of International Humanitarian and Refugee Law. Available at http://www.worldlii.org/int/journals/ISILYBIHRL/2001/8.html.

Collyer, Michael 2010. Stranded migrants and the fragmented journey. *Journal of Refugee Studies* 23 (3): 273–93.

Düvell, Franck, ed. 2006. *Illegal immigration in Europe: Beyond control?* Houndmills: Palgrave/Macmillan.

European Commission. 2015. *Communication from the Commission to the European Parliament, The Council, The European Economic and Social Committee and the Committee of the Regions.* Brussels:

European Commission. Available from https://ec.europa.eu/anti-trafficking/sites/antitrafficking/files/eu_action_plan_against_migrant_smuggling_en.pdf.

European Commission. 2017. *Report from the Commission to the European Parliament, The European Council and The Council.* Fourteenth Report on Relocation and Resettlement. Brussels: European Commission. Available from https://ec.europa.eu/home-affairs/sites/homeaffairs/files/what-we-do/policies/european-agenda-migration/20170726_fourteenth_report_on_relocation_and_resettlement_en.pdf.

Gonzalez, Enriquez C. 2013. Circularity in a restrictive framework: Mobility between Morocco and Spain. In *Circular migration between Europe and its neighbourhood*, ed. Anna Triandafyllidou, 114–41. Oxford: Oxford University Press.

Humer, Ziva, and Majda Hrzenjak. 2015. When the state steps in: An experiment of subsidised hiring of domestic workers in Slovenia. In *Employers, agencies and immigration*, eds. Anna Triandafyllidou and Sabrina Marchetti, 169–89. Aldershot: Ashgate.

Içduygu, Ahmed. 2004. Transborder crime between Turkey and Greece: Smuggling of migrants and its regional consequences. *Southeast European and Black Sea Studies* 4 (2): 294–314.

Içduygu, Ahmed, and Sule Toktas. 2002. How do smuggling and trafficking operate via irregular border crossings in the Middle East? Evidence from fieldwork in Turkey. *International Migration* 40 (6): 25–54.

Koser, Khalid. 2010. Dimensions and dynamics of irregular migration. *Population, Space and Place* 16 (3): 181–93.

Kyle, David, and Rey Koslowski, eds. 2001. *Global human smuggling: Comparative perspectives.* Baltimore, MD: The Johns Hopkins University Press.

Massey, Douglas S., Jorge Durand, and Karen A. Pren. 2016. Why border enforcement backfired. *American Journal of Sociology* 121 (5): 1557–1600.

Mountz, Alison. 2010. *Seeking asylum: Human smuggling and bureaucracy at the border.* Minneapolis, MN: University of Minnesota Press.

Pliez, Olivier. 2003. *Villes du Sahara. Urbanisation et urbanite dans le Fezzan libyen.* Paris: CNRS.

Salt, John, and Jeremy Stein. 1997. Migration as a business: The case of trafficking. *International Migration* 35 (4): 467–94.

Sanchez, Gabriella. 2015. *Human smuggling and border crossings.* New York, NY: Routledge.

Triandafyllidou, Anna. 2017. A sectorial approach to labour migration: Agriculture and domestic work. IOM Migration Research Leaders Syndicate. Geneva: IOM.

Triandafyllidou, Anna, and Maurizio Ambrosini. 2011. Irregular immigration control in Italy and Greece: Strong fencing and weak gate-keeping serving the labour market. *European Journal of Migration and Law* 13:251–73.

Triandafyllidou, Anna, and Thanos Maroukis. 2012. *Migrant smuggling: Irregular migration from Asia and Africa to Europe.* London: Palgrave.

Van Hear, Nicholas. 2009. *Managing mobility for human development: The growing salience of mixed migration.* With Rogers Brubaker and Thais Besa. United Nations Development Programme, Human Development Reports 2009/20. New York, NY: United Nations.

Van Liempt, Ilze 2007. *Navigating borders: Inside perspectives on the process of human smuggling into the Netherlands.* Amsterdam: Amsterdam University Press.

Special Editors' Note

We are keenly aware that many of the conclusions raised by our contributors are controversial and in some instances may oppose the predominant notions of migrant smuggling promulgated by government agencies and international organizations. We are not naïve about the abuses at times inflicted upon transnational migrants at the hands of their smugglers. Yet the research presented here supports the view that using smuggling facilitators as scapegoats of tragedies that can arise from migration enforcement and control measures exempts states from their role in creating the conditions that lead to the emergence of smuggling as a practice. Our collective findings show the urgent need for analyses that unpack the complexity of the interactions that occur in smuggling and the multiple facets of its actors' roles. From the onset of this project, our goals have been to use empirical data to challenge the dichotomous narrative in dominant discourses of smuggling that frame the smuggler as evildoer and migrant as victim, and to start a conversation among the very government agencies and international organizations that play pivotal roles in the arena of global migration. While assembling this volume, we have received nonjudgmental acceptance from the United Nation Office on Drugs and Crime through its Human Trafficking and Smuggling of Migrants Section (HTMSS), which provided venues and sponsored several gatherings for our authors to discuss their work. As the key international organization in charge of promoting cooperation among the United Nations' Member States in their efforts to combat transnational migrant smuggling, we extended an invitation to HTMSS to close out this volume with their reflections on and reactions to our points of view. It is important to remark that the following epilogue does not necessarily reflect the perspectives of the UN or its Member States.

S.X. Zhang, G.E. Sanchez, and L. Achilli

DOI: 10.1177/0002716218759615

Policy Perspective

By
MORGANE NICOT
and
BIANCA KOPP

In major meetings held in international fora, including at the United Nations (UN), ways to best respond to the challenges posed to states by irregular migration and its underlying causes (armed conflict, human rights violations, natural disasters, poverty, and uneven economic development, among others) have been discussed at length. While perspectives differ on how to address these challenges, as rightly pointed out by many of the authors contributing to this volume on the smuggling of migrants, there is consensus that at the core of any action taken must be the protection of migrants' human rights.

This principle is embodied in the UN Protocol against the Smuggling of Migrants by Land, Sea, and Air.[1] The protocol's purpose is fourfold: (1) it provides a framework that encompasses law enforcement's actions to combat the smuggling of migrants as a form of transnational organized crime, (2) it promotes cooperation among states, and (3) it promotes the implementation of equally important prevention and (4) protection mechanisms.

Those negotiating the adoption of the protocol did not reach agreement concerning the

Morgane Nicot, a crime prevention and criminal justice officer in the Human Trafficking and Migrant Smuggling Section of the United Nations Office on Drugs and Crime (UNODC) since 2009, coordinates the Global Programme against the Smuggling of Migrants.

Bianca Kopp, a program officer in the Human Trafficking and Migrant Smuggling Section of UNODC, has been working for the United Nations since 2010, including for the UN Counter-Terrorism Implementation Task Force, the UN Democracy Fund, and UNODC.

NOTE: The views expressed herein are those of the authors and do not necessarily reflect the views of the United Nations.

Correspondence: morgane.nicot@un.org

DOI: 10.1177/0002716218755345

noncriminalization of irregular border crossings. It was left up to the states to make decisions in this regard. Seeking to put an end to smugglers' activities, destination countries along the migration routes have kick-started the international efforts envisioned in the protocol, often by reinforcing border controls. Many states did so on the basis of laws that criminalize the facilitation of illegal entry, whether done with the aim of making a profit or not on these entries (the protocol only calls for the criminalization of profitable forms of facilitation).[2]

This range of decisions created a landscape in which the states' responses to migrant smuggling have not exclusively targeted organized smugglers involved in the movement of people as a form of business. Instead, it has often included the criminalization of any form of assistance to people on the move, including, in some instances, humanitarian assistance provided to asylum seekers when no other options are available to escape war and persecution. This situation in particular has raised a pressing question: Is the protocol being used as a framework to target organized crime, or as a tool to fight irregular migration? The question also sheds light on the scant attention paid to developing a comprehensive approach that would reduce social and economic pressures in origin, transit, and destination countries as an effective tool to prevent and combat the smuggling of migrants, as called for by the protocol.[3]

Today, after a decade of law-enforcement-focused responses against migrant smuggling along migration routes, and while facing complex migratory crises worldwide and the deaths of thousands of people, more voices than ever are calling for a balanced approach to address migrant smuggling. The recent migration crisis in Europe has also shown that the challenges irregular migration poses to states as well as to individuals cannot be dealt with unless multiple stakeholders—from government, international organizations, civil society, and academia—reach out to each other to inform policymaking and assess the related consequences of these policies. The international community acknowledged this when adopting the New York Declaration for Refugees and Migrants in 2016, which specifically calls for the adoption of a multistakeholder approach that includes academia.[4] While there are constant calls in intergovernmental fora for research and knowledge-based policymaking, more efforts to inform the development of safe, orderly, and regular migration in response to migration-related issues are still needed. The UN Office on Drugs and Crime (UNODC) has a long tradition of bringing together experts, including those within academia, to discuss pressing topics and inform policymaking. This volume echoes the debates held in several recent events of which UNODC has been a part[5] and in which criticisms have been made on the ways that states have responded to smuggling so far, amid calls to give the stage to those using the services of smugglers and those in the communities providing smuggling services.

The empirical data researchers have made available to us, alongside perspectives on the historical and social dimensions behind smuggling, serve as a litmus test to the positions of enforcing agencies, states, and international organizations. It is the UN's role to bring these perspectives to its member states and support the latter in the development of comprehensive responses to smuggling. This will include taking a serious stance on providing actual legal channels for migration, including family reunification, and effective access to international protection for those persecuted or fleeing conflict and state violence.

While recognizing, as stated by most authors in this volume, that the majority of smuggling ventures constitute underground exchanges of service against payment in the absence of licit options to migration, the aggravated forms of smuggling that put migrants' and refugees' lives and safety at risk and subject them to inhuman and degrading treatment cannot be left unaddressed. In 2017, for the first time, the UN Special Rapporteur of the Human Rights Council on Extrajudicial, Summary or Arbitrary Executions released her report on Unlawful Death of Refugees and Migrants in which she examined migrant and refugee casualties caused by both state and nonstate actors, including smugglers and traffickers.[6] Whether these deaths are direct consequences of states' policies and enforcement measures, as claimed by some authors in this volume, or caused by the acts of ruthless profit-maximizers (e.g., as those engaged in migrant kidnapping and torture for extortion), tackling these most severe, abusive, and deadly forms of smuggling should be the primary objective of initiatives.

To safeguard the relevance of the Smuggling of Migrants Protocol, 17 years after its adoption, it is essential to monitor the impact of the measures adopted, and reassess on a regular basis whether these measures have actually upheld the rights of smuggled migrants, contributed to greater cooperation between states, effectively prevented the recourse to smuggling services, and brought to justice abusive high-level smugglers affiliated with transnational organized crime. A reinforced collaboration of UNODC and its member states with academia would directly contribute to these objectives and support the crafting of evidence-based policies grounded in empirical research. This would also be essential to tailor action-oriented prevention measures and ensure that the protection of the rights of migrants and refugees remains at the core of any response, reinstating the full purpose of the protocol.

Notes

1. Protocol against the Smuggling of Migrants by Land, Sea, and Air supplementing the United Nations Convention against Transnational Organized Crime Convention, General Assembly Resolution 55/25 of 15 November 2000. The protocol provided the first global definition of the term *smuggling of migrants* and, as of December 13, 2017, has 146 state parties. See http://www.unodc.org/unodc/en/organized-crime/intro/UNTOC.html#Fulltext.

2. *The Concept of "Financial or Other Material Benefit in the Smuggling of Migrants Protocol,"* UNODC Issue Paper (2017), available from: https://www.unodc.org/documents/human-trafficking/Migrant-Smuggling/Issue-Papers/UNODC_Issue_Paper_The_Profit_Element_in_the_Smuggling_of_Migrants_Protocol.pdf.

3. Ibid., Preamble.

4. New York Declaration on Refugees and Migrants (2016), available from: http://refugeesmigrants.un.org/declaration (specific reference to academia is made in para. 69).

5. For example, *When Smuggling Goes Wrong: From a Crime against State to a Crime against Persons,* European University Institute and UNODC (26–27 October 2017, Florence, Italy).

6. *Unlawful Death of Refugees and Migrants: Report of the Special Rapporteur of the Human Rights Council on Extrajudicial, Summary or Arbitrary Executions,* United Nations A/72/335 (15 August 2017), available from https://reliefweb.int/sites/reliefweb.int/files/resources/N1725806.pdf.

⑤SAGE track

Authors!
Submit your article online with SAGE Track

SAGE Track is a web-based peer review and submission system powered by ScholarOne® Manuscripts

The entire process, from article submission to acceptance for publication is now handled online by the SAGE Track web site. 300 of our journals are now on SAGE Track, which has a graphical interface that will guide you through a simple and speedy submission with step-by-step prompts.

SAGE Track makes it easy to:

- Submit your articles online

- Submit revisions and resubmissions through automatic linking

- Track the progress of your article online

- Publish your research faster

THE IMPACT OF THE SOCIAL SCIENCES: How Academics and their Research Make a Difference

Simon Bastow, Patrick Dunleavy, and Jane Tinkler, *all from London School of Economics*

Foreword by Kenneth Prewitt, *Columbia University*

In the modern globalized world, some estimates suggest that around 40 million people now work in jobs that 'translate' or mediate advances in social science research for use in business, government and public agencies, health care systems, and civil society organizations. Many large corporations and organizations across these sectors in the United States are increasingly prioritizing access to social science knowledge. Yet, the impact of university social science continues to be fiercely disputed. This key study demonstrates the essential role of university social science in the 'human-dominated' and 'human-influenced' systems now central to our civilization. It focuses empirically on Britain, the second most influential country for social science research after the US. Using in-depth research, the authors show how the growth of a services economy, and the success of previous scientific interventions, mean that key areas of advance for corporations, public policy-makers, and citizens alike now depend on our ability to understand our complex societies and economies. This is a landmark study in the evidence-based analysis of social science impact.

PAPERBACK ISBN: 978-1-4462-8262-5 • FEBRUARY 2014 • 326 PAGES

LEARN MORE AT SAGEPUB.COM!

⑤SAGE research**methods**

The essential online tool for researchers from the world's leading methods publisher

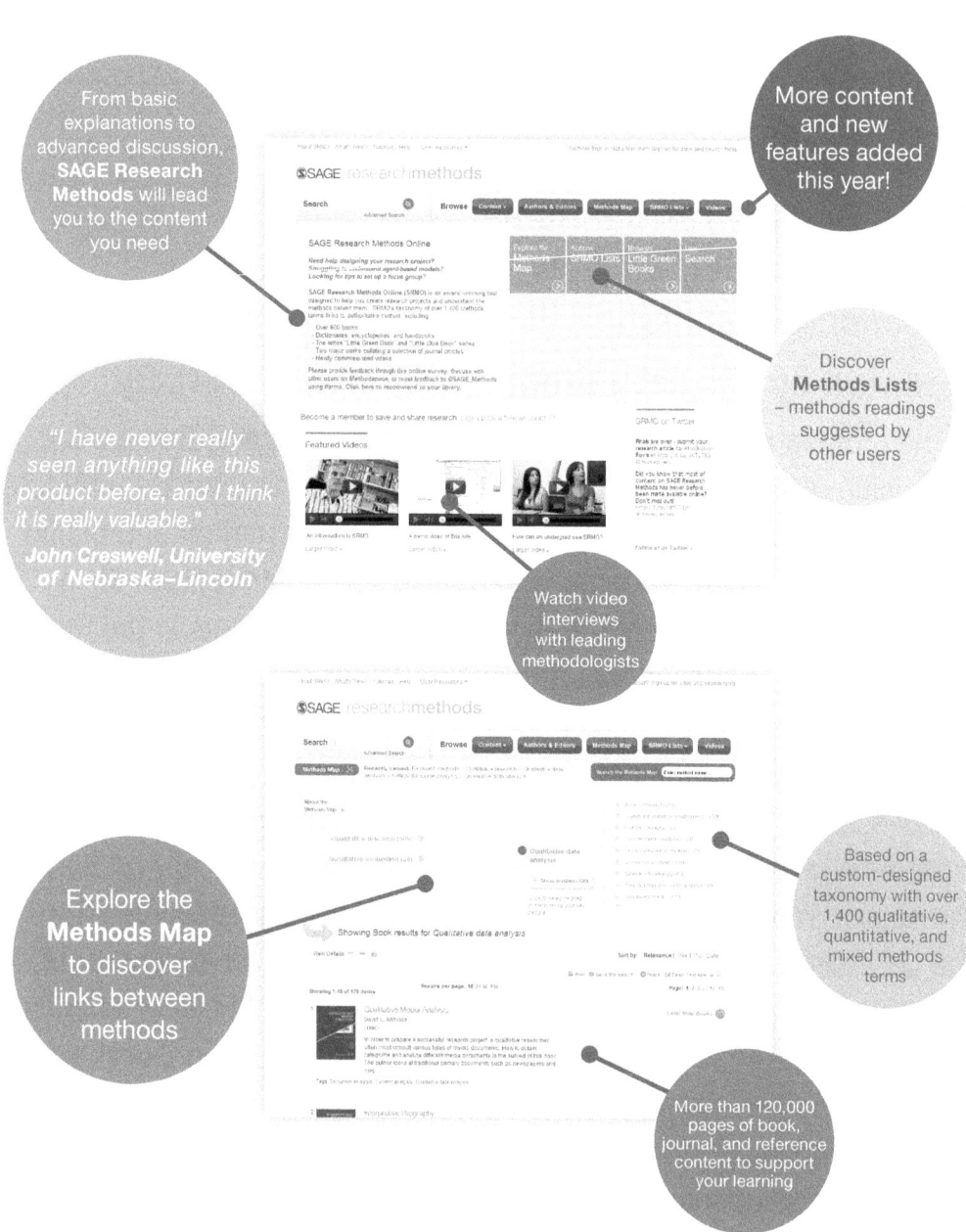

From basic explanations to advanced discussion, **SAGE Research Methods** will lead you to the content you need

More content and new features added this year!

"I have never really seen anything like this product before, and I think it is really valuable."
John Creswell, University of Nebraska–Lincoln

Discover **Methods Lists** – methods readings suggested by other users

Watch video interviews with leading methodologists

Explore the **Methods Map** to discover links between methods

Based on a custom-designed taxonomy with over 1,400 qualitative, quantitative, and mixed methods terms

More than 120,000 pages of book, journal, and reference content to support your learning

find out more at
www.sageresearchmethods.com

In compliance with GPSR, should you have any concerns about the safety of this product, please advise: International Associates Auditing & Certification Limited The Black Church, St Mary's Place, Dublin 7, D07 P4AX Ireland EUAR@ie.ia-net.com

www.ingramcontent.com/pod-product-compliance
Ingram Content Group UK Ltd.
Pitfield, Milton Keynes, MK11 3LW, UK
UKHW022220170526
471099UK00001B/110